Edward Backhouse, Frances Anne Budge

Annals of the Early Friends

A Series of Biographical Sketches

Edward Backhouse, Frances Anne Budge

Annals of the Early Friends
A Series of Biographical Sketches

ISBN/EAN: 9783337029050

Printed in Europe, USA, Canada, Australia, Japan

Cover: Foto ©Thomas Meinert / pixelio.de

More available books at **www.hansebooks.com**

ANNALS

OF THE

EARLY FRIENDS:

A

Series of Biographical Sketches.

BY

FRANCES ANNE BUDGE.

[*Reprinted from the* FRIENDS' QUARTERLY EXAMINER.]

WITH PREFACE BY EDWARD BACKHOUSE.

"WE ARE NOTHING, CHRIST IS ALL."—GEORGE FOX.

SECOND EDITION.

London:
SAMUEL HARRIS & CO., 5, BISHOPSGATE WITHOUT.
1886.

CONTENTS.

	PAGE
WILLIAM CATON	1
JOHN AUDLAND AND HIS FRIENDS	29
EDWARD BURROUGH	55
ELIZABETH STIRREDGE	75
WILLIAM DEWSBURY; AND HIS WORDS OF COUNSEL AND CONSOLATION	97
JOHN CROOK	111
STEPHEN CRISP AND HIS SERMONS	129
JOHN BANKS	147
HUMPHRY SMITH AND HIS WORKS	169
MARY FISHER AND HER FRIENDS	197
THE MARTYRS OF BOSTON AND THEIR FRIENDS	221
PASSAGES IN THE LIFE OF JOHN GRATTON	253
JAMES DICKENSON AND HIS FRIENDS	267
WILLIAM EDMUNDSON	303
WILLIAM ELLIS AND HIS FRIENDS	335
RICHARD CLARIDGE AND HIS FRIENDS	367
THOMAS STORY	393
GILBERT LATEY AND HIS FRIENDS	423
GEORGE WHITEHEAD	451

PREFACE.

The Memoirs and Sketches of the lives of Friends of the Seventeenth Century, which have, from time to time, appeared in the pages of the *Friends' Quarterly Examiner* are, in this volume, presented as a whole, in the hope of thus obtaining for them a more extended circulation. They contain an account of the religious principles of the Early Friends, as well as narratives of the sufferings they underwent in maintaining the testimonies committed to them by the Lord Jesus Christ; and it is hoped that their example may influence *us*, their successors, with boldness to maintain the Truth as it is in Jesus, and keep unfurled before the Churches the same holy banner that He has given to *us* also, "to be displayed because of the Truth."

As a contribution towards the modern literature of the Society of Friends, these memoirs are designed to revive the memory of those who were valiants in their day; and to inform such as may not be conversant with the history of Friends two centuries ago; for they remind us of the costly price our forefathers paid—in blood, in loss of liberty, and of this world's treasure—to procure for *us* the religious freedom we enjoy.*

---

* For more complete details of the foundation and progress of the Society of Friends we would refer to William Sewel's History, which is doubtless to be found in most of the libraries attached to our meeting-houses; to George Fox's Journal; Besse's "Sufferings of Friends," &c.

Many are little aware of the faith, patience, and intrepidity, with which the Friends of the first generation not only endured insults and injuries, but persevered in their Christian course triumphing over every difficulty, notwithstanding the virulence with which the opponents of vital religion persecuted them, in many cases even unto death. From the year 1662 to 1697 (inclusive)—namely in the reigns of Charles II., James II., and William and Mary—John Field informs us that thirteen thousand five hundred and sixty-two Friends suffered imprisonment in England; while if we add the persecutions of the Commonwealth, under Oliver and Richard Cromwell, and of New England and those of Ireland and Scotland, from 1650 to 1697, we find the aggregate of these sufferers for conscience' sake numbers more than twenty-three thousands: and that the total of those who died in gaol, or were executed, is three hundred and eighty-eight.

The volumes published by Joseph Besse containing the account of the "Sufferings of Friends," show the terrible trials they underwent in those days; when, locked out of their meeting-houses, or their meeting-houses having been destroyed and razed to the ground, Friends held their assemblies for worship in the streets, or upon the ruins, notwithstanding the furious attacks of the soldiery, who *broke* their swords and muskets upon their heads, sometimes leaving fifty on the street most shamefully wounded and streaming with blood. Four were hanged in New England by the bigoted professors of religion there: one was squeezed for hours in a torture-hole in the rock in Chester Gaol, called "Little Ease," in consequence of which he died; while let it not be forgotten that many honourable and educated women (among them Elizabeth Horton, the first Quaker minister of her sex), were stripped naked to the waist, by order of Governor Endicott and the Council of Massachusetts, and mercilessly flogged through three towns in succession. Endicott and his fellows raged against the life of religion manifested by the Friends; though they only came into their jurisdiction to preach the Gospel, and specially to demand the repeal of their unrighteous laws, which made it penal for a Friend to enter the Colony. For this four Friends suffered death; for the Governor and Court of Assistants at Boston, who *professed* to have left Old England for the sake of liberty to worship according to their consciences, "knew not what spirit they were of."

Thus our forefathers bought the Truth; and, having bought it, sold it not: for amid all their afflictions, they held that nothing in the whole world could compare with the glorious inheritance they had obtained. That inheritance was a heavenly one; even the kingdom of heaven, into which they had entered; and they valued its holiness and rest beyond the price of rubies or gold, or the treasures of this world, or liberty, or life itself.

Well might they prefer the heavenly country of which they had even upon earth become citizens to anything the world could offer. William Dewsbury testifies to *his own* experience, and says, "My garments are washed and made white in the blood of the Lamb, who hath led me through the gates . . . into the New Jerusalem . . . where my soul now feeds upon the Tree of Life . . . that stands in the Paradise of God." Again and again the Early Friends record their faith in the cleansing blood of the Lord Jesus, and their own blessed experience of its power; testifying that Christ had become their personal Saviour from the power of sin, and that eternal life was theirs. "Yea," says Francis Howgill, "I am entered into the true rest, and lie down with the lambs in the fold of God, where all the sons [of God] do shout for joy, and all His saints keep holyday."

Their exalted views as to the perfection of Christianity (bringing full salvation to every one that will receive it) caused them to express themselves in glowing language worthy of the theme they dwelt upon; but not more so than the glory of the Gospel of Christ manifested to His saints deserves. George Fox in his Journal says, "Now was I come up in spirit through the flaming sword, into the Paradise of God; all things were [become] new . . . being renewed into the image of God by Christ Jesus."

Ann Dewsbury, too, near her close, could say, "I have no guilt upon my spirit. In the covenant of light and life, sealed with the blood of Jesus, I am at eternal peace with the Lord." Stephen Hubbersty—encouraging Friends at a time when they were undergoing deep suffering from the violence of persecution—says, "It is the enjoyment of the sweet presence of God will encourage you to stand; . . . for we are come, blessed be God! to the primitive Spirit, the Spirit of Christ which was in the primitive worshippers. . . . The Lord arm you with patience and boldness; and let all these things drive you nearer and nearer to your Beloved. The Lord sanctify you to Himself, that you may be like the Holy Apostles, who, when charged to speak no more in Christ's name, would not obey, but chose rather to obey God. Let this be *your* choice: and ages and generations to come will bless God for you. . . . . The Wonderful Counsellor preserve you single-hearted, and keep you over all storms: a calm will come again; and the joy of the Lord, which is as the joy of harvest, fill your souls with joy and peace in believing."

John Audland desires that Friends "may be grounded, rooted, builded, established; and in the everlasting covenant of life, find peace; where you may rest in the City of God, whose walls are salvation, and whose gates, praise." Ambrose Rigge, also, after ten years' incarceration in Horsham Gaol, could say, " I have been made both able and willing to bear all, for the testimony of Jesus, and the word of God; not counting my life dear unto me, that I might finish my testimony with joy; being counted worthy not only to believe, but also to suffer for that ancient doctrine, faith, and practice, for which the ancient Christians suffered the loss of their liberties, and, many of them, of their lives."

Their expositions of Scripture truth, and their application of the types and figures to their own experience, as well as to that of the Church, are also extremely interesting. They frequently quote from the Book of Revelation (as well as from all parts of the Old and New Testaments); but, as regards the Apocalypse, George Fox observes, that too many religious people view it as a sealed book; whereas it contains very precious truths, and vividly sets forth many things which it is most important for us to appreciate. He tells us respecting the New Jerusalem, "I saw the beauty and glory of it, the length, the breadth, and the height thereof, all in complete proportion. I saw that all who are within . . . the grace and truth and power of God, which are the walls of the City, *are within the City*, . . and have right to eat of the Tree of Life, which yields her fruit every month, and whose leaves are for the healing of the nations." This cannot be gainsaid; because the New Jerusalem, we are told by the Apostle in describing his vision of it, is "the Bride, the Lamb's wife;" that is to say, is the Church of the Redeemed; which Church is *one*, whether on earth or in heaven. Thus George Fox held that all converted persons who attend to and dwell within the limitations of the grace and truth of God, and live in the power of the Holy Ghost, *are in the Church*, and belong to the family and household of God while here below.

Would that we (who are the successors of the Early Friends) might understand from living experience, as they did, the blessedness of being at rest in the kingdom of heaven: and, like them, know for ourselves that Paradise is regained. Our first parents were driven out of Eden (after they had sinned) lest they should put forth their hands, " and take also of the Tree of Life, and eat, and live for ever." We also, if born again, are entered into the Paradise of God: and like the Early Friends may eat of the glorious Tree of Life; for the Tree of Life is Christ.

They entered into rest: we too may enjoy the rest of the everlasting Sabbath, of which the Jewish Sabbath was but a symbol. This is the true rest; and whether on earth or in heaven it is one. The saints on earth, and the saints in heaven, are at rest in Christ; and drink of the River of the Water of Life; which glorious

River is the one Holy Spirit, into which all the redeemed of the Lord drink.

We think there is a blessed future for the Society of Friends: if only our souls were possessed of a holy ambition to do the will of God on earth, as it is done in heaven: and to work in the Lord's vineyard. That was the ambition which possessed the whole soul of the Early Friends. Edward Burrough was "a son of thunder and consolation," who (to his friend, Francis Howgill's knowledge), " scarcely spent one week to himself in ten years;" while Ames and Caton, and a host of others, would gladly have spread the "Gospel net" over all. Such was the zeal which clothed their spirits, that they were men "who married as though they married not, and possessed as though they possessed not." They stood in dominion over the world, the flesh, and the Devil. The language of William Dewsbury is, "I can never forget the day of His [the Lord's] power, and blessed appearance, when He first sent me to preach His everlasting Gospel. . . . for this I can say, I never since played the coward, but joyfully entered prisons as palaces, telling mine enemies to hold me there as long as they could: and in the Prison House I sang praises to my God, and esteemed the bolts and locks put upon me as jewels! . . . And this I have further to signify, that my departure draweth nigh: blessed be my God, I am prepared, I have nothing to do but to die, and put off this mortal tabernacle, this flesh that hath so many infirmities; but the life that dwells in it transcends above all; out of the reach of death, hell, and the grave; and immortality, eternal life, is my crown for ever and ever. Therefore you that are left behind, fear not, nor be discouraged, but go on in the name and power of the Lord, and bear a faithful and living testimony for Him in your day; and the Lord will prosper His work in your hand, and cause His Truth to flourish and spread abroad, for it shall have the victory. No weapon formed against it shall prosper; the Lord hath determined it shall possess the gates of its enemies, and the glory and the light thereof shall shine, more and more, until the perfect day."

Would that *we*, the successors of these "Valiants for the Truth," may do our parts towards the fulfilment of William Dewsbury's prophecy!

EDWARD BACKHOUSE.

Sunderland.

WILLIAM CATON.

"FAITH is the one condition on which the Divine power can enter into man and work through him. It is the susceptibility of the unseen; man's will yielded up to, and moulded by, the will of God. . . . 'Because of your unbelief' was, for all time, the Master's explanation and reproof of impotence and failure in His Church."

"THE SCHOOL OF PRAYER," BY ANDREW MURRAY.

Annals of the Early Friends.

WILLIAM CATON.

"I know that no visible created thing can satisfy that which longeth to be refreshed with the living streams which issue out from the fountain which watereth and refresheth the whole city of God. . . . A living fountain hath the Lord set open for Judah and Jerusalem; and all that are bathed and washed in it come to enter into the holy city."—W. CATON.

It was on a winter day, early in 1652, that unexpectedly, and for the first time, George Fox arrived at Swarthmoor Hall, near Ulverston, the beautifully situated residence of Judge Fell, who was then absent on his circuit. This visit proved a very eventful one to not a few of the members of that large household.

William Caton was then in his sixteenth year, and had for some time resided at the Hall, sharing the educational advantages of the Judge's only son, who was taught by a clergyman, a relative of the Catons; he soon became a favourite of the whole family, so that difference in social position was lost sight of. He shared George Fell's chamber, and was his companion in field-sports and fishing, as well as in study. From early childhood he had at times been the subject of serious impressions, and had been very carefully brought up by his parents. The sudden change in his style of living had by no means the unfavourable effect which might have been feared, for he says that his heart was softened while thus living in "much pleasure, ease, and fulness, . . . forasmuch as Providence had cast me into such a noble family, where there were such sweet children, with whose company I was more than a little affected. In those days there remained an integrity in my heart towards God, and often did I call upon His name."

In order to be alone whilst engaged in prayer he would of a morning linger in the bedroom until his companion had gone downstairs. He was much exposed to temptation during a few months spent by George Fell and himself at a country school; but, he writes, "The Lord was wonderfully gracious to me, and many times, when I have deserved nothing but stripes from Him, hath He broken and overcome my heart with His Divine love." At times his soul ardently longed for communion with God, and he found that he could not satisfy its cravings by taking notes of sermons or writing paraphrases of them, though such efforts were commended by the family at the Hall.

Much did he marvel at the unfashionable dress and simple manners of their guest from Fenny Drayton, "Yet something in me," he writes, "did love him and own his testimony. And I began to find the truth of what he spoke in myself; for his doctrine tended very much to the bringing of us to the light, with which Christ Jesus had enlightened us withal, which shined in our hearts and convinced us of sin and evil; and into love with that and obedience to that he sought to bring us, that thereby, through the Son, we might be brought into unity and covenant with the Lord."

Deep, also, and lasting, was the effect of George Fox's ministry on the hearts of the mistress of Swarthmoor Hall (a descendant of the martyr, Anne Askew), her young daughters and their governess, as well as on the steward, Thomas Salthouse, the housekeeper, and most of the servants; and when Judge Fell was crossing the sands of Leven, on his homeward journey, he was told that his family were all bewitched. His son, too, we find, was "somewhat touched with the same power," which helped to smooth the path of William Caton, who was experiencing in his own soul the power of the truths which they had heard, though he confesses that they often "extinguished the good" in themselves; "but," he adds, "such was the love of God to me in those days, that I was as surely pursued with judgment as I was overtaken with folly." At times he would retire to some solitary spot that he might seek for spiritual refreshment by drawing near to God.

After awhile his mental conflicts unfitted him for hard study, and Margaret Fell (the Judge's wife), with Christian sympathy and womanly penetration, divined the cause of his inability to write themes and make Latin verses; she therefore suggested that he should leave school and occupy himself in teaching her daughters and acting as her secretary. Her strengthening and soothing influence must have been very helpful to him, for he describes this period as a happy time: he found congenial employment in writing for her of " precious and wholesome things pertaining to the Truth: whereby," he continues, " I came to have good opportunities to be conversant with Friends, in whom the life of righteousness began to bud and spring forth, and who grew in love and unity, with which my soul was exceedingly affected; and I desired very much to be one with them in it." Meanwhile the good work which his Saviour had begun in his soul was carried on more rapidly perhaps than he was himself aware of.

"When I was about seventeen years of age," he writes, "the power of the Lord God did work mightily and effectually in me to the cleansing, purging, and sanctifying of me. . . . And then I began to be broken, melted, and overcome with the love of God which sprang in my heart, and the Divine and precious promises that were confirmed to my soul. Oh! the preciousness and excellency of that day! Oh! the glory and the blessedness of that day! how or wherewith shall I demonstrate it, that *they that are yet unborn might understand it,* and give glory unto the Lord Jehovah?"

This most merciful visitation was shared by many others of the household, and very closely were their hearts drawn together; whilst such was their desire to worship unitedly Him who had done such great things for them that they frequently met for this purpose in the latter part of the evening, when other members of the family had retired to rest. Great was William Caton's disappointment when, in consequence of George Fell's wish to keep early hours—or, it may be, to avoid late meetings—he had to accompany him to his chamber, whilst his heart remained with the little company below; for, he says, the refreshment and benefit of these seasons was indescribable. "If," he adds, " we had suffered loss in the day-time when we had been abroad about our business or the like, then we came in a great measure thus to be restored again, through the love, power, and mercy of our God, which abounded very much unto us."

The young heir of Swarthmoor Hall had become indifferent to such matters, and William Caton was not sorry when, in consequence of his being sent to another school, they were separated. It was true that this might stand in the way of Caton's worldly preferment, but we cannot wonder that this seemed of little moment to one who could say, "I was often overcome with the love of my Father, which did exceedingly break and ravish my heart, and so I know it was with others of that family; and of the overflowings thereof did we communicate one to another to the comforting and refreshing one of another; and truly willing were we to sympathise and bear one with another, and in true and tender love to watch one over another. And oh! the love, mercy, and power of God, which abounded to us, through us, and among us, who shall declare it?" Many Friends at a distance, hearing how remarkably the Lord's power was manifested in this family, visited Swarthmoor Hall, so that occasionally visitors from five or six counties would stay at the house at one time. This gave especial satisfaction to William Caton, who, in consequence of frequently writing for Margaret Fell, had much intercourse with them. George Fox he regarded as a tender-hearted father, who, not content with "having begotten him through the Gospel," endeavoured to lead him onwards in the path of the just; whilst his "entirely beloved friend, Margaret Fell," cared for him as if he had been her own child.

These peaceful days at Swarthmoor were but the preparation for his life labours; freely had he received of the grace of God, and freely was he to share it with others. George Fox says, "He was one like unto Timothy, who was an example in innocence, simplicity, and purity in his life and conversation, after he was converted; for *that* did preach, as well as his doctrine, in the churches of Christ." William Caton himself thus describes his call to the ministry: "Seeing the darkness and ignorance so great in which people were involved, my spirit was stirred within me, and my earthen vessel came to be filled with love to their souls, and with zeal for God and His Truth. And about that time I began to know the motion of His power and the command of His Spirit; by which I came to be moved to go to the places of public worship." Although, at that period, it was not a rare event for laymen to address a congregation at the conclusion of the usual service, it can be no matter of surprise that a youth of seventeen should shrink from thus publicly testifying against the sins of preachers as well as of hearers. But he had given his heart to his Redeemer, and henceforth there was but one way for him to walk in—narrow it might be, and yet an indescribably blessed one. "Wherefore when I saw it must be so," he says, "I put on courage in the name of the Lord; and having faith in Him which stood in His power I gave up to His will." Then he realised the fulfilment of Christ's promise that He would be with him: harassing doubts and the fear of man were alike taken from him, and power was given him—stripling though he was—to speak as "one having authority." Some were willing to hear him; others, "as brute beasts," fell upon him; but the Lord preserved him from evil, and filled his heart with peace.

In market places, too, he often preached, seldom knowing what he should say until he reached the spot, yet never lacking words wherewith to clothe his Master's message. "His word," he writes, "did often powerfully pass through me, and never did I go about any service for the Lord in which I was faithful but I always had my reward with me." Blows and beatings, stocks and stonings, he gave little heed to, for he found in the enjoyment of God's love that which made more than full amends for all; and whenever he was most deeply tried, the tenderness of the Lord's love was most clearly manifested. He alludes also to the great help afforded him from the consciousness of the warm attachment of his fellow-believers.

In the intervals of his ministerial service he industriously employed himself at Swarthmoor, still finding true spiritual refreshment with the household there, as they "spake often one to another and the Lord hearkened and heard." But soon he found that notwithstanding "the glorious days there," the time was at hand when he must bid his friends farewell, and go forth at his Saviour's bidding to work in more distant vineyards. Judge Fell was very unwilling for him to leave his house, but his wife, with truer affection, overcame her first feelings of regret, and freely gave him up. And yet, although they knew that they could still be near one another in spirit, it was amidst the freely-flowing tears, as well as the fervent prayers of the family, that the parting took place, on a winter day, when he was about eighteen.

He travelled chiefly on foot and—bearing this in

mind—his diligence in his holy calling was wonderful. When twelve months had elapsed he had visited, in addition to many English counties, some parts of Scotland, Calais, Rotterdam and other Dutch cities. In London he found several ministering brethren from the north, and, together, they laboured night and day. "The word of the Lord grew mightily," he says, "and many were added to the faith." Here he met with John Stubbs, who soon became one of his dearest friends. In the previous year Stubbs had left the army in consequence of the effect produced on his mind by the preaching of George Fox; a holier warfare lay before him in many parts of Europe, in Egypt and America: he was well skilled in the classics, and a remarkable Oriental scholar. Like William Caton he greatly loved and esteemed Margaret Fell. In one of his letters to her he says, "How often in my distress hath the Lord raised one up to minister in season to me, both by word and by writing. . . . Truly He hath made thee, even thee, as His angel and messenger these two times to publish peace unto me."

Whilst William Caton and John Stubbs were holding meetings in Kent, they were brought before the magistrates at Dover, who decided that a penalty should be inflicted on any one who gave them lodging: they were therefore turned out from the apartments which they had occupied at the inn. In this time of need they were befriended by a shoemaker, named Luke Howard, who having been told on the previous Sunday that a Quaker was preaching in the churchyard, at once went there, and found a sermon even in William Caton's countenance and demeanour; he protected him from abuse and insult, and carefully noticed the house which he entered, in order that he might visit him when the darkness of the winter evening should screen him from observation. But he soon grew bolder, for when the innkeeper no longer dared to entertain the young preachers, Luke Howard said to them, " Go home to my house, for I care not for the rulers nor mayor either;" and he refused to give them up when asked to do so by the constables.

Two meetings were held in his house, of which the latter was regarded by him as the turning-point of his life. When his guests left the town he walked two or three miles with them, and gave them the names of some places on the coast, and also of some persons who might render them assistance: so much did he feel at parting with them that, even after returning to Dover, he found it difficult to keep back his tears. Deep inward trials were for a time his portion, but the Saviour to whom he had fled for refuge suffered not his faith to fail, and when almost ready to despair these words came as a heavenly message to his soul,—" I will cleave the rocks and mountains that the redeemed of the Lord may come to Zion." Casting all his care upon Christ, henceforth hope was the anchor of his soul though tempest after tempest might befall him. Thus, when describing his sixteen months' confinement in Dover Castle for attendance of meetings, he writes: "I had perfect peace, joy, and content in it all; and the Lord made it good unto me both within and without." *

---

* Luke Howard gives the following beautiful description of the consolation afforded him one night during this, or another imprison-

Before leaving Dover John Stubbs and William Caton had remarked in a letter to Francis Howgill and Edward Burrough, "A fire is kindled among them which cannot be easily quenched." Nor were they mistaken in this belief, for Dover was one of the first places in Kent where, in accordance with their advice, a meeting was established by those who were convinced of the truths which they preached. During some years this meeting was held in silence, unless visited by a travelling minister; but Luke Howard, at whose house the Friends at first assembled, says that the Lord was their Teacher, and manifested His power and presence in their midst.

Whilst at Lydd, William Caton and his companion were kindly entertained at the house of Samuel Fisher, a very eminent Baptist minister, to whom they had been directed by Luke Howard. In his earlier life he had been a clergyman, but had resigned his living from conscientious motives. At first he did not fully acknowledge the influence which the ministry of his guests had on him; but when, after visiting some neighbouring places, they had returned to Lydd, and another Baptist

---

ment:—"On the Third-day of the Eighth Month, 1661, in the night-watch, upon my bed of straw and chaff, in the common gaol of Dover Castle, as I lay in a comfortable sleep and rest, the hand of my God fell upon me, and His sweet and comforting presence awakened me, and so continued with me unto the morning-watch; in which time the living presence of my God was with me and the comfortable presence of His Holy Spirit accompanied me; so that my soul was filled with His living presence as with a mighty river, which did overflow the banks, so that nothing appeared but joy and gladness, and the streams of His everlasting virtue ran through me exceeding swift. . . This is my God; I have waited for Him, and His appearance to me is as the morning without clouds, and His beauty hath taken my heart, and His comeliness hath ravished my soul, and with His exceeding riches hath He adorned my inward man, and His everlasting strength is my salvation, even the Son of His love."

minister publicly preached against them and their doctrine, Samuel Fisher arose and said, "Dear brother, you are very near and dear to me, but the Truth is nearer and dearer: *this* is the everlasting Truth and Gospel!" To the preacher's exclamation, "Our brother Fisher is also bewitched," he made no reply; in the course of that year he joined the Society of Friends. For ten years he diligently laboured as a minister at home and abroad, and also as an author, often suffering severe persecution for the cause which was dearer to him than life. He died in the White Lion gaol, in Southwark, after a long imprisonment.

So grateful were some of the open-hearted Kentish people to William Caton and John Stubbs, who had been enabled to labour very powerfully amongst them that they urged them to receive gold, which was declined, with the reply that it was not theirs but them, they sought. But at Maidstone a different reception awaited them; they were sent to the House of Correction, deprived of their Bible, money, etc., then stripped, and, with their necks and arms placed in stocks, barbarously whipped until bystanders wept at the sight. After irons and large clogs of wood had been laid on them, they were ordered to work, and because they did not were kept without food for some days. The women who lived in the house showed their pity by privately offering them refreshment, which they did not think it well to accept. Before they were set at liberty a few things were restored to them; but they were dismissed from the town in contrary directions, each accompanied by constables, to whom (so states an old MS. of Friends of East Kent) "their heavenly images and sober lives and words preached so much that they finally suffered them to travel alone whither they pleased."

Neither knew where the other had gone, and great was their pleasure at meeting in London; but soon they felt bound to return to Maidstone and, though fearing the consequences of so bold a measure, their faith did not fail, and they were preserved from further persecution. On re-visiting other towns in Kent they were cheered by the belief that their patient suffering had tended to confirm the faith of those to whom their ministry had been an effectual message. From Dover William Caton crossed to Calais, where he had what he styles "a very gallant opportunity" at a mansion with some of the chief inhabitants, a Scotch nobleman acting as his interpreter. Soon afterwards he accompanied John Stubbs to Holland. They meant to sail from Yarmouth, whither they had walked from Dover, often travelling many miles a day—no hardship perhaps but for the fact that, in order to avoid expense, they sadly stinted themselves in food. Yet William Caton says that their reward was with them in all places and conditions.

After a delay of three weeks they went on board a vessel, but, to their great disappointment, the captain refused to take them. As it seemed unlikely that they would obtain a passage from that port, they thought it best to go northward. William Caton longed to visit his beloved friends at Swarthmoor, and a suitable opportunity for doing so occurred, to his extreme refreshment of body and soul. Before sailing some meetings were held in Durham, which were of great service.

On returning from Holland, where very rough treatment was encountered, he again spent a short time at Swarthmoor Hall; he writes, "A very precious time we had together, whereby my very life was much revived; and therefore did my soul magnify the Lord, with the rest of His lambs and babes in that place." Soon he started for Scotland with John Stubbs; many were their sufferings within and without, but the Lord sustained them through all, and their exceeding affection for each other was a continual source of comfort. In the following winter, in company with another Friend, William Caton visited Lancashire, Cheshire, etc., and says that time would fail him to relate "the extraordinary good service" which they had. He also attended a large General Meeting in Leicestershire, which was a very blessed time; George Fox, whom he had much wished to meet again, was present. A little later, whilst on his way to Scotland, he visited Ambleside, in which place courage and power were given him to address a congregation in a chapel, though the people first attacked him as if they had been wild beasts. At Edinburgh and Leith many large meetings were held, sometimes in the streets, and much power in the ministry was granted to William Caton and the Friend who was with him.

About this time we find the former ill from the effect of "sore travel" from place to place. On their return to Cumberland they held meetings, which William Caton describes as being very large and precious, and he adds, "Friends were strengthened and confirmed in the precious truth which in those days did flourish and prosper very much; and the Lord's power and presence was with us, through which we were carried on in His work and service, in which our souls delighted to be exercised. There being such an effectual door open abroad in the country I was constrained, through the love of God which dwelt richly in my heart, to labour so much the more diligently, for I knew it was good working whilst it was day; and indeed a glorious and precious time we had, to make known unto the people the way of salvation, and what the Lord had done for our souls; many believed and were converted, and brought to serve and worship the Lord in spirit and in truth."

Many of these meetings were held around Swarthmoor; soon afterwards he bade farewell to his friends there, and bent his steps southward. He was greatly cheered by his intercourse with Friends at Bristol, and with the "large and gallant meetings" held in that city and neighbourhood, and says that he was enabled to "communicate to them of the overflowing of the life and power dwelling" in him. Then we find him travelling westward, usually alone and on foot, to visit George Fox and other Friends in Launceston gaol. Their intercourse was "in the fulness of endeared love," and though William Caton's chief aim might be to carry comfort to the prisoners, his own cup was filled to the brim.

When at Totnes he was brought before the mayor, who threatened him with a whipping; but the other magistrates thought more moderate measures might suffice. When they examined him a clergyman was present, and an excellent opportunity was afforded Caton to uphold the truth as it is in Jesus, for in that very hour, he says, the Lord was much with him. After spending the night in prison he was sent on with a pass from place to place; an arrangement which had by no means the intended effect, for it soon became known, in one town after another, that William Caton was no pauper, but a Quaker, and as people came out of their houses to see him, he addressed them freely on the truths dear to his soul.

After attending a General Meeting in Wiltshire, and some other services, he re-visited Kent. He was but twenty years of age, yet his Saviour's grace and power were so manifestly granted him that he shared in the wonder felt by others at the abundance given for the multitudes who came to hear him. When he turned his thoughts to his own weakness he was ready to faint; but when he placed his confidence in Christ alone, he became strong. Often he did not know what he should say when he entered a meeting, and yet so much was given him to communicate that he would speak for two, three, or, occasionally, four hours. "Not unto me, not unto me, be the praise," he writes, "but unto the Lord alone. I can truly say that which I received from Him I delivered unto His people. . . . An exceeding glorious day I had of it, and did much rejoice in the Lord, notwithstanding my great travails and sufferings; neither were they much to me, with all the perils and dangers I went through, both by sea and land, in comparison of the power and presence of the Almighty."

In the summer of the same year he again sailed for Holland, this time alone—though he longed for a companion—and in poor health from the effect of exposure to heat and cold during his almost incessant journeys. He met with scoffing and abuse from some fellow-voyagers, who were, nevertheless, ready to give heed to his words when he addressed them in their dismay, during a dangerous storm, which had filled them with terror. Deep trials were his portion during this visit, which were increased when he became aware of the evils wrought by the extreme views promulgated by some who had joined the Society. At Middleburgh, William Caton and his interpreter were imprisoned for some days, and then conveyed in a waggon to the coast. They were accompanied by several soldiers to protect them from the violence of the citizens; but, as William Caton says, the Lord was their chief keeper. Great were their sufferings during the following fortnight, whilst prisoners on board a man-of-war, in which they were carried to England. Though the weather was very cold and stormy, they were obliged to lie on the bare planks, and were not even allowed the covering of a piece of sail-cloth. But God had not forgotten to be gracious. Whilst undergoing this treatment, William Caton's health and strength were, in a great measure, restored, though for a time he suffered severe pain in the feet, the result of keeping on shoes and stockings during so long a period of exposure to the cold.

Soon afterwards he paid an extremely satisfactory visit to Sussex. At one place where a meeting was held, a rude crowd marched up to the house with a drum, seeming ready in their violence to pull down the building on the heads of those assembled. William Caton went out to them and asked what they wanted. "Quakers!" was the reply. "I am one," he said, and then power was given him to address them in such a manner as to make them withdraw in shame and fear.

He met with a somewhat similar deliverance during his next visit to the Netherlands, where he spent more than a year engaged in ministerial service and authorship. On his return he was comforted by the blessed meetings held in London, where many were added to the Church; and he speaks of how God bestowed exceeding power and wisdom from above on His servants and handmaids, who, in Christ's name preached the Word of Life, not in meetings only, but in churches, markets, streets, and highways, indeed wherever their Saviour led, and whenever He constrained them. They gave themselves *wholly* to God, and marvellous was the result.

"I made it my sole work to be found doing the work of God, unto which He had called me," writes William Caton, after describing meetings held in the north of England, where, as in many other parts of the country, the labours of Friends were producing extraordinary effect. Now and then he enjoyed extreme refreshment by intercourse with the family at Swarthmoor, " whom," he says, " he found in the same love, life, and power in which he left them." The very remembrance of these days was sweet to him in after years, and the more so from the continued consciousness of the love of Christ, by whose realised presence those seasons had been hallowed. It was this, also, which had often made his weary journeyings and arduous labours a source of delight.

Early in 1659 he attended a meeting of ministers from various parts of the kingdom, held at the Bull and Mouth Meeting-house in London, which he writes of as being "very large and exceedingly precious." In the latter part of the day a meeting was held at Horselydown, where a great concourse seemed much impressed with the truths they heard. William Caton says:— "Great was our rejoicing and comfort which we had in the work and service of the Lord, in which we were abundantly refreshed together. And in that great assembly did our souls, even with one accord, praise and magnify the God of our salvation." A visit to Holland in the same year, with its perilous return voyage, was soon followed by one to Scotland. He set out on the latter expedition from Swarthmoor, and after his friends and himself had, as they thought, fully taken leave of each other, they felt that they could not yet part, and several hours were spent in waiting on the Lord, and in pouring out their souls in prayer. Whilst in Scotland he endeavoured to obtain an interview with General Monk, but, being unable to do so, he wrote an address to him and his army.

A meeting which he attended at Warrington the following winter was broken up by some rough soldiers, who violently forced the worshippers out of the town; but they re-assembled on the road-side, and had, we find, a "sweet and precious meeting." Before long the soldiers again interrupted them, and whilst William Caton was preaching, seized him, and to the great distress of his friends, beat him with their muskets and spears; then, having given vent to their fury, they allowed him to return to the meeting, where, he says, "The Lord's power and presence did exceedingly appear amongst us; for, as our suffering at that time was greater than ordinary, even so was our refreshment in the Lord." About this time he records the death of his "dear mother" whilst he was paying her a visit.

When in London, in 1660, he alludes in a letter to full and peaceful meetings on the previous Sunday; and, after stating that the common topic of conversation was the expected coming of the King, he adds, "But blessed be the Lord for ever, in whose power we can testify that *our King is come who reigns in power and great glory.*" Nor can we wonder at these words from one who drew the strength and joy of his life from the knowledge that his citizenship was in heaven; who might have said in the words of another, "When I die I shall change my place but not my company!" *
Redeemed by the precious blood of Christ, to Him William Caton freely dedicated his life, and the Lord, who loveth a cheerful giver, suffered not his faith to fail —to whatever extent it might be tried, "I have often observed," he says, "that, by how much the more I felt the weight of the service of the meeting before I went into it, by so much the more was my service in it, and my reward accordingly. Blessed and magnified be the Lord for ever."

Before sailing for Holland, in the latter part of the year, he writes from Dover to George Fox. After mentioning the death of a Friend, of Staplehurst— probably a minister—who would be greatly missed in that neighbourhood, he adds, "I believe *there will now be more necessity for Friends visiting them pretty often* than there was before; I desire that thou wouldst be mindful of them . . . . Dearly beloved of my soul," he

---

* " Have you a glimpse of Christ now that you are dying?" was the question asked of an old Scottish saint, who, raising himself, made the emphatic reply, " I'll hae none o' your glimpses now that I am dying, since that I have had a full look at Christ these forty years gane!"

writes, "let thy prayers be for me that I may be kept in the power, life, and wisdom of our God, to His praise and to the comfort and consolation of the brethren, with whom I can rest in the Lord, even in the heat of the day; glory be to the Lord for ever." And, during the voyage, we find that he was "exceedingly filled with the Lord's love, and with the power of His might." One of his fellow-passengers, a Roman Catholic, notwithstanding William Caton's habitually courteous manners, openly avowed his hatred of him and his religion: but before they parted there was a complete change in his behaviour. Well did George Fox say, "Love, patience, and wisdom will wear out all which is not of God."

In a letter of sympathy written from Amsterdam to English Friends, William Caton remarks that he believes those amongst them who were not yet cast into prison were in no greater danger from persecution than were their brethren resident in that city, where it was said that fifty men had conspired to break up their meeting, and pull down the meeting-house. It was about this time that he published a volume with the lengthy title, "An Abridgment or Compendious Commemoration of the Remarkablest Chronologies which are contained in that celebrated Ecclesiastical History of Eusebius." In 1661 William Caton visited Germany with William Ames; at Heidelberg they had interviews with the Prince, and laid before him the sufferings of the Friends in his dominions on account of their conscientious objection to the payment of tithes: he gave them a courteous reception, and made them dine with him. When next at Heidelberg William Caton had the unexpected pleasure of meeting with his friend John Stubbs who, with another Friend, was on the homeward route from Egypt. When the Prince heard they were at William Caton's lodgings, he sent his secretary to ask them to come to the Castle to see him, where, in the presence of his nobles, he conversed very freely with them about their mission, and, after what William Caton calls "a very gallant opportunity," he took an affectionate leave of them.

The enjoyment of William Caton in the society of his brethren was soon shadowed by tidings from Amsterdam of the death of a beloved friend of his, Niesie Dirrix, a faithful labourer for her Lord in her native land; his sorrow was great until he was comforted by the conviction that her mantle would fall on her sister Anneken and some others. On his return to Holland, some months later, he made proposals of marriage to Anneken Dirrix. Warm and enthusiastic as his disposition was, he took extreme care to act rightly in this matter: he wished her first to consider whether she "felt something in it as from the Lord," and asked for no reply until she had deliberately weighed three things:—First the difference in their outward circumstances and how little he had to offer her; secondly, the liberty—more to him than the treasures of Egypt—which he should still need to travel in the service of the Lord: and, thirdly, the possibility that their union might be disapproved of by magistrates, by her relatives or others, and might thus bring trouble upon her. Her reply was to the following effect:—As to the first, it was not means that she looked to but virtue. As to the second, when the Lord needed him for any service she should not be the woman that would hinder him. As to the last, if they "were perfectly clear of the thing before the Lord, she hoped to bear what people without should say, for that would be one of the least crosses!" Still they did not think it right for a time to bind themselves by promise. William Caton thus describes his own feelings during an interview which they had after several months had elapsed:—" Waiting awhile exceeding steadfastly in the light of the Lord, the life began to arise, and the Word of the Lord testified unto me thus, saying, 'She is the gift of the Lord to thee.' Then was my heart also broken, and in the fulness of love and unity in the everlasting covenant did I receive her as the Lord's gift unto me."

About three months after his marriage he embarked for England. Whilst in London he received much spiritual refreshment from a visit to Edward Burrough [of whom there is a sketch in this volume], then a prisoner in Newgate, where he died a week or two later. Their separation was not a long one: each was early called to the ministry; each accomplished the labour of a long lifetime in ten or a dozen years. Like their Divine Master "clad with zeal as a cloak," "*through faith* they wrought righteousness, obtained promises, . . . out of weakness were made strong, waxed valiant in fight, turned to flight the armies of the aliens." On his next visit to England—for his home was now in Holland—William Caton was accompanied by his wife, who greatly longed to become acquainted with the Friends there, of whom she had no doubt often heard; and with a similar desire some other Dutch members of the Society sailed with them.

The London Friends rejoiced, William Caton says, "to see people of another nation, and of a strange language, brought into the same living truth in which they were established, and to bear the same image which they bore,—and to be comprehended in the same Love." At a General Meeting at Kingston he acted as interpreter for one of his Dutch sisters. His wife and the other Friends from Holland returned some time before his mission was accomplished, but in the autumn of 1663 he also set sail. When about ten leagues off Yarmouth, William Caton, who felt sure that a storm was at hand, unavailingly urged the captain to put back. That night a tempest overtook them, and at its height the helm became useless, and, as the vessel was very leaky, she was in extreme peril; the sailors, wet to the skin and utterly wearied by toiling at the pumps and with the sails, were almost ready to despair. William Caton, who had been aiding them in their arduous work, now wrestled in prayer for their deliverance if in accordance with God's will; "though, as for my own part," he says, whilst with deep gratitude recording their remarkable preservation, "I found myself exceeding freely given up to bequeath my soul into His bosom of everlasting love, and my body to be buried in that great deep."

But soon storms of a different character had to be encountered. Whilst waiting at Yarmouth for a change in the wind he attended the meeting there, and, in company with seven other Friends, also strangers, was carried before the magistrates of the town. Because they declined to take the Oath of Allegiance they were committed to the common gaol, where they were confined for more than six months; when it was tendered to William Caton he said that he had never uttered an oath but once, in his boyhood, and having then incurred the displeasure of the Almighty he dared not swear again. So fully had the magistrates anticipated this steadfast adherence of the Friends to their conscientious convictions, that they made out their mittimus before putting them to the test.

In a letter, written a few days later, William Caton alludes to the cruelty of their oppressors, which sometimes made it no easy matter to obtain their bread and water; but says that the only wonder was that he had not earlier found himself in bonds, "unto which," he adds, "I have long been freely given up in the will of God where my soul is in peace with the Lord." And again he writes of how "one day in prison, with the Lord, was better than a thousand elsewhere without the enjoyment of His presence, in whose love his soul solaced itself night and day." Some friends of the prisoners, thinking to beguile the long hours of their confinement, wished to give them a spinning-wheel, but were not allowed to do so.

It was in the early part of 1664 that the Friends were liberated, after meeting with kind consideration from the judge who presided over the sessions, and from a justice of the peace. Five of William Caton's fellow-sufferers belonged to a vessel which had come to Yarmouth for herrings, and as, during this period, she was seized by the Turks, their English captivity was the means of saving them from Asiatic slavery.

In the following winter William Caton wrote an epistle from Rotterdam to his friends in England. After referring to his powerlessness to express the fervency of his love, and of his prayerful longings for them, he adds, "Yet herein can I satisfy myself, in that we come to read and feel one another in that which is immortal." He says that, although his heart is often saddened by the many hindrances to the extension of the Redeemer's kingdom in Holland, he is supported by the "wonted goodness and tender mercy of the Most High, *still perfectly continued to him.*" William Caton died in the latter part of the following year, at the age of nine-and-twenty. His wife did not long survive him.

It has been remarked that "No truth or goodness realised by man ever dies, or can die;" and surely such a life, though lived two centuries ago, has not ceased to convey a lesson. As we look around us we find no warrant for believing that the world no longer needs to be reminded of that Cross to which every helpless soul may cling, and of such truths as Christ's Headship of His Church, the Spirituality of the Gospel dispensation, and the reality of the teaching and guidance of the Holy Spirit.

The fields are white unto harvest still; still the Lord of the harvest has need of labourers; of labourers who, with the knowledge that they are bought with a price, and that "voluntary obedience is liberty"—wholly yield themselves to Him to be trained for, and guided in, any service which He sees meet to assign to them, be it of what kind it may, for "all service is not work, and all work is not service;" consecrating to Him, as occasion may arise, every talent whether natural or acquired—

"Ever by a mighty hope
Pressing on and bearing up."

"Do not," it has been said, "let Satan have all the benefit of ambition in his kingdom." *Excelsior* is no unworthy device for the banner of Christian warriors who are learning that they "are nothing, Christ is all." *
"Behold, the Lord's hand is not shortened that it cannot save; neither His ear heavy that it cannot hear." He can "restore judges as at the first, and counsellors as at the beginning." May no unbelief on our part hinder the performance of "mighty works" on His.

---

* "So long," writes the author of *The Patience of Hope*, "as we are resting on anything within ourselves—be it even in a work of grace—there remains, at least to honest hearts, a ground for continual restlessness and continual disappointment. To know that we have nothing, are nothing, out of Christ, is to know the truth which makes us free."

JOHN AUDLAND AND HIS FRIENDS.

"No harp was ever strung capable of yielding such music as the soul of man attuned to righteous obedience."—MUNGER.

JOHN AUDLAND AND HIS FRIENDS.

"In the Church of God there is no irrevocable golden age in the past. . . . . In God's battles leaders cannot fail."—*Author of "The Schönberg-Cotta Family."*

WHEN John Audland was about twenty-two years of age he was a very popular minister amongst the Independents. Sewel describes him as "a young man of a comely countenance, and very lovely qualities, very religious, and having a good understanding." One Sunday morning, in 1652, he preach at Firbank Chapel, in Westmoreland. Before noon George Fox arrived at this place; it was soon rumoured that he would preach there that day, and whilst some people went away for a time to dine, a large number remained.

George Fox, having quenched his thirst at a stream, seated himself on the summit of a rock near the chapel, and from this elevation he, in the afternoon, addressed the vast multitude gathered around him. In this congregation were several preachers, including John Audland, who had brought his wife, a young lady of good family, with him. Probably as their thirsty souls drank in the words which fell with heavenly power from the stranger's lips, they were hardly conscious that he continued speaking for about three hours, directing all to the Spirit of God in themselves. Glorious was the heritage he pourtrayed as the *present* portion of believers in Christ; that they "might know their bodies to be prepared, sanctified, and made fit temples for God and

Christ to dwell in." He strove to turn the thoughts of his hearers away from all figures and shadows to Christ the Substance; " Christ was come," he said, " who ended both the temple and its worship, and the priests and their tithes; and all now should hearken unto Him."

Effectual as was George Fox's message to many that day, it was more so to none than John and Anne Audland, and it was to their house that he adjourned when the meeting was over. Both were " chosen vessels unto the Lord to declare His name," and the life-long ministry of each began in the following year. Deep was John Audland's distress when his eyes were opened to see that his high profession of religion was valueless. " It is a Saviour that I long for," was now his cry,—" it is He that my soul pants after, Oh, that I may be gathered into his life, and overshadowed with His glory, sanctified throughout by His word, and raised up by His eternal power?"

The answer to his continued prayers was not long delayed; the Lord, in accordance with His promise, fulfilled his desire, heard his cry and saved him.

> " Oh, how wonderful His ways!
> All in love begin and end;
> Whom His mercy means to raise;
> First His justice bids descend."

Thus baptised into Christ John Audland was, ere long, qualified to preach the word with extraordinary power. The remuneration which he had previously received for his services as an eloquent Independent minister he now returned to the parish of Colton.

Anne Audland was the daughter of a gentleman of the name of Newby, who also became a Friend about this time; she had been well educated, and during a seven years' residence with an aunt in London had often associated with Puritans. Before her marriage, when at her home at Kendal, she chose the most serious people of that town for her friends, uniting with some who often met together to wait on God in silence, or for religious conference and fervent prayer. Perhaps on the day of George Fox's memorable visit to Firbank she was already "not far from the kingdom."

Two years later we find her, at the age of twenty-seven, preaching at Auckland, in Durham, on a market-day, in consequence of which she was confined for some hours in the town gaol, through the window of which she continued to address a not unmoved audience, one of whom, a gentleman named Langstaff, who was much respected in the neighbourhood, was so impressed by her ministry that he accompanied her to prison, and afterwards took her to his house; here, however, she declined remaining when she observed his wife's annoyance at the arrival of a Quaker guest, and went out into the fields to seek for some sheltered spot where she might spend the night. But Antony Pearson, a justice of the peace, who had lately become a Friend, had been told by George Fox, who was staying at his house, of Anne Audland's arrival in the town, and came with a horse and pillion to escort her to his residence.

During the following winter, whilst travelling with Mabel Camm (the wife of John Camm), she was committed to prison by the Mayor of Banbury, who had induced two witnesses to swear that she had spoken blasphemy: but after some days, two residents in the town gave bond for her appearance at the assizes, and thus an opportunity for holding a series of meetings was afforded her.

A remarkable blessing rested on these labours; several hundreds, including the two "bondsmen," were effectually led to Christ; many were added to the Society, and not only was a large meeting formed in Banbury, but several others were established in the neighbourhood. These things of course kindled the wrath of her enemies, who threatened that she should be burned. Her husband and other Friends were present at the trial, when the indictment drawn up against her was that she had said God did not live, because, when speaking of a clergyman at Banbury, she had remarked that "True words may be a lie in the mouth of some who speak them," quoting Jer. v. 2. When the judge had questioned her he soon discovered the falseness of the evidence adduced, nor did he fail to observe the innocent fearlessness of her deportment. Some gentlemen on the bench, being afraid that the case would fall to the ground, followed the jury and induced them to bring in a verdict of "Guilty of misdemeanour." It is satisfactory to find that these gentlemen were told by one of their coadjutors that he would not sit with them until they had more regard for justice, and other officers in the Court strongly manifested their censure.

On her refusal to give bond for "good behaviour," she was sent to prison again, although the judge was heard to say that she ought to be discharged. For seven or eight months she was confined in a filthy dungeon, by the side of which was a sewer which received much of the drainage of the town; she had a companion in Jane Waugh, who was also a minister, and had been imprisoned for no other offence than that of visiting Anne Audland. Here, unprotected from cold, and damp, and noxious gases, with frogs and toads crawling around them—kept by the peace of God—they abode, we are told, as in a palace, for they could say:—

> "Thy presence makes my paradise,
> And where Thou art, is Heaven."

After her release Anne Audland and her husband had the joy of meeting each other at Bristol, and after some religious service they returned to their home in Westmoreland. Frequent journeys for the advancement of Christ's cause were undertaken by both, unitedly and separately, to most parts of the kingdom. During John Audland's absence on one of these missions she thus writes:—

"DEAR HUSBAND,—Thou art dearer to me than ever: my love flows out to thee, even the same love that I am loved withal of my Father... O, how I am refreshed to hear from thee of thy faithfulness and boldness in the work of the Lord. O! dear heart, I cannot utter the joy I have concerning thee; thy presence I have continually in spirit, therewith am I filled with joy? all glory and honour be to our God for ever. ... Surely the Lord hath found thee faithful in little and therefore He hath committed much unto thee; go on in the name and power of our Lord Jesus Christ, whence all strength cometh, to whom be all glory and honour for ever. O! dear heart, go on conquering and to conquer, knowing this that thy crown is sure. So, dear heart, now is the time of the Lord's work, and few are willing to go forth into it. The whole world lieth in wickedness doing their own work; but blessed be the Lord for ever, who hath called us from doing our own work into His great work. ... I am full of love towards thee, never such love as this; the mighty power of the Lord go along with thee, and keep thee faithful and valiant, and bold in His pure counsel, to stand single out of all the world. . . . A joyful word it was to me, to hear that thou wast moved to go to Bristol. O! my own heart, my own life, in that which now stands, act and obey, that thou mayst stand upon thy alone guard: so, dear heart, let thy prayers be for me that I may be kept pure, out of all temptations, singly to dwell in the life. So farewell! — ANNE AUDLAND."

A series of meetings were held in 1654 by John Audland and his friend John Camm, near Bristol, in a field called Earl's Mead, and were very largely attended. In a letter to George Fox, Camm says, "We have here, in Bristol, most commonly 3,000 to 4,000 at a meeting. The priests and magistrates of the city begin to rage, but the soldiers (of the Commonwealth) keep them down; for the Governor of the Castle is not against us, and the Captain of the Royal Fort is absolutely convinced, and his wife loves us dearly. And many captains and great ones of the city are convinced, and do believe in us, and that we are of God; and all within ten miles of the city round about the people is very much desirous after Truth. . . . Yea at any point we come we can have 400 or 500, or even 1,000. . . . . And *we hit some every day we shoot,* for ' our bow abides in strength.' " Edward Burrough and Francis Howgill were their fellow-labourers for a short time. These meetings were continued during three or four months, and Charles Marshall describes this period as "the glorious morning of the day of visitation of the love of God, in particular to the city of Bristol." He was then about seventeen, and an earnest seeker after God; having been unable, as he says, to "find the living among the dead professions," he had spent much time alone in fields and woods, where " strong, great, and many," were his cries unto the Lord.

Charles Marshall, before the arrival of John Audland, had been in the habit of meeting with a few others on one day of the week which they kept in fasting and prayer; they assembled early in the morning, and sometimes sat down in silence, but if any felt it right to engage in prayer vocally they did so, and even children occasionally uttered brief petitions. To one of these meetings John Audland and John Camm came. "They spake," writes Charles Marshall, "the powerful word of life in the dread of His name who lives for ever, and we were seized on and smitten even to the heart; and that day, and the visitation of it overtook us, which we had longed and waited for, and from darkness to the marvellous light of the Lord were we turned."

On a Sunday morning Charles Marshall went with the ministers about a mile and-a-half into the country, to a little spring of water, by the side of which he had spent many solitary hours; here they sat down for a considerable time, and then Charles Marshall observed that the minds of his companions were greatly exercised, and soon John Audland said, "Let us be going into the city." When they reached Broadmead Street they found several people who were inquiring for the strangers; Audland asked if any of them had an interest in a field, in which they might assemble, and an old man answered that he had one pretty near. Thither the company repaired, increasing in number whilst passing through the streets. John Audland is described by Charles Marshall as " of a sweet and amiable countenance, and cheerful spirit, one of the wise in heart, filled with the excellent, bright, glorious power of the Lord God."

After John Camm had spoken tenderly and fervently, John Audland arose, and to Charles Marshall it seemed that his face shone as, with a voice of thunder, he uttered the message of his Lord. "I proclaim spiritual war," he began, "with the inhabitants of the earth who are in the fall and separation from God." And the word of the Lord had free course and was glorified: so intense was the emotion of some present that they fell on the ground, whilst others cried out as the preacher laid bare their inward states; many were effectually turned from darkness to light. "Indeed it was a notable day," writes Charles Marshall, "worthy to be left on record, that our children may read and tell to their children, and theirs to another generation, that the worthy, noble acts of the arm of God's salvation may be remembered."

After this day the meetings became larger and larger, so that it was necessary to hold them in the open air, even in frost and snow, and the ministers laboured unweariedly to lead their hearers "to look from dead ways and worships unto Christ Jesus, the Fountain of Life;" and many of these sought eagerly night and day to obtain salvation through Him, giving up their hearts wholly to His government, and walking in the way of self-denial—for we read that "This visitation of God's holy and blessed day was signal and inexpressible." Some, in their eagerness to obtain an opportunity for private conversation with the ministers, called on them before they arose in the morning, so that their labours began at six a.m., and did not end until eleven or even one o'clock at night. They were, indeed, so sought after that "every day was like one long meeting." Soon persecution arose, causing a tumult in the city; the houses of Friends were broken into by the mob, under the pretence of preventing conspiracy, and they were themselves often treated with brutal violence, whilst the law afforded them no protection, and the clergy stimulated the rage of the rioters.

One day, as John Camm and John Audland were crossing a bridge on their way to a village where a meeting had been appointed, they found themselves surrounded by a rabble, by some of whom they were beaten and kicked, whilst others shouted, "Knock them down, kill them, hang them!"—so that they narrowly escaped with their lives.

Charles Marshall was one of those who found in John Audland "a dear friend and father in Christ Jesus," and he afterwards became a very powerful preacher, the deep conflicts through which he had himself passed, the better enabling him to draw out his soul to the hungry, and satisfy the afflicted soul. William Penn writes that "he was one that waited for the feeling of God's living and heavenly power to carry him forth in his ministerial exercises," by which, we find, many were turned to righteousness, and some induced to covet earnestly the best gifts. George Whitehead—who says that he "truly loved him for love's sake"—remarks, that "his sincere love and regard to Christ's ministers and messengers appeared to be a good and necessary preparation for him to be a witness and partaker of the same ministry." His faith was strong; and, unhindered by the heat of persecution, he visited the various meetings throughout the land, his labours being attended by an abundant blessing. When, in 1670, at the age of thirty-two, God called him to the ministry, and laid this work before him, he said in his soul, "How shall I visit Thy people in these times, when the rod of the wicked is upon their backs?" Then this reply seemed to be given him, "Go, *I* will prosper thy way; and this present exercise, which is over my people, shall be as a morning cloud, and I will be to them as the tender dew through the land of thy nativity."

Although during the next two years Charles Marshall visited every county in England, no hand was laid on him, nor did he know of any one who lost five pounds on account of attending his meetings. When describing subsequent labours, he says that he believed thousands received the word of life; and in some places, which had never before been visited by a Friend, meetings were established. "Oh," he writes, "the tenderness which mine eye has seen in many places through the land: the watering showers that descended on the Lord's plantation is beyond description." But long-continued painful labours were also allotted to him in consequence of the spirit of dissension which prevailed in some counties where John Story, John Wilkinson, and their party had obtained a footing. Yet he tells us that God was with him in this day of deep exercise, making his bow strong, and daily replenishing his quiver with arrows, even though his soul was, as it were baptised for the dead.

In one of his pamphlets, "The Way of Life Revealed," etc., he writes:—

"The travail in spirit of the messengers and servants of the Most High in ages past, was the same as now it is, viz., To turn people from darkness unto light, and from the power of Satan to the power of the living God; thereby in nowise invalidating Christ Jesus, His manifestation in that bodily appearance, neither His sufferings, death, resurrection, nor ascension; but brings all people guided thereby unto that which will open the eyes of their understanding, whereby they all come unto such a condition and spiritual understanding, as to see and know their benefit by the appearance of the Saviour of the world; for this we testify, all are perfected by that One Offering that are sanctified."

And again he says:—

"As there is a faithful abiding in inward watchfulness, and continual obedience to this heavenly light, there will be a growing from strength to strength over sin and the nature thereof, until thou seest all the rule and authority of the enemy to be subdued under the feet of the Lord's anointed, and the government in the soul upon His shoulders, whose right it is to rule over all. And here salvation, redemption, and restoration, is effectually enjoyed through faith, and the effectual working of the Almighty power and arm of God, unto whom be the glory of His own work for ever? And so here will be a growing and increasing, until there is a coming into that precious state and image in which man was before he fell."

By profession Charles Marshall was a physician; he was remarkable for his kindness and generosity to the poor, and when on his death-bed he urged this duty on others. In the year 1682, he was prosecuted by a clergyman for the non-payment of tithes, in consequence of which he was committed by the Barons of the Exchequer to the Fleet Prison. After he had been confined there for two years, the clergyman's conscience was so much troubled that he came in person to release him. Charles Marshall then settled with his family near London, where, during many years, he diligently worked for his Lord. He died in 1698, at the age of sixty-one." *

Another of the converts of Audland and Camm during this extraordinary visit to Bristol was a lady named *Barbara Blaugdon*, who had been seriously inclined from childhood; she became a minister, and suffered much from persecution: once, when coming out from a private house at Bristol, where a meeting had been held, a man in the street stabbed her very severely, though no vital part was reached. After her release from a six weeks' imprisonment at Marlborough, she had some conversation with the gentleman who had committed her, in consequence of which he never again persecuted Friends, but behaved with much kindness to them, even giving them his aid when able to do so. He once called at Barbara Blaugdon's house at Bristol, and confessed to her that he was convinced of the truth of the views which she held, although he said that he could not himself walk in the way of self-denial.

During a visit to Devon, where she was thrice imprisoned, she called at the residence of the Earl of Bath—where she had formerly often been received as a visitor—with the intention of speaking to his family on the vanity of the pursuits in which she had once joined them. When she inquired for the Countess, a servant, who recognised her, asked her to go to the

---

* Charles Marshall's wife was the daughter of Mary Prince, who was another seal to the ministry of John Camm and John Audland, when at Bristol, in 1654. Two years later she visited New England as a minister, and, in 1660, travelled extensively on the European Continent with Mary Fisher. She was three times committed to prison in her native city of Bristol, during the severe persecution there in 1663 and 1664.

back-door through which he said his lady would soon go into the garden. But when she reached the back premises a very fierce mastiff was unchained, in order that he might attack her; but before he reached her his ferocity seemed to be altogether subdued, for he suddenly turned and went away whining. Soon the Countess came to her, and after listening to her counsel, thanked her for it.

When Barbara Blaugdon was at Great Torrington she was sent for by the mayor, who was not inclined to treat her with harshness; but a clergyman, who was very anxious that she should be whipped as a vagabond, succeeded in persuading him to send her to Exeter Prison, where she was confined for some time, not being brought to trial when the assizes were held. One day the sheriff came and took her to another apartment, where a beadle, who had accompanied him, whipped her until the blood ran down her back; meanwhile such joy was granted her at being counted worthy to suffer for Christ as to cause her to sing His praise. "Do ye sing? I will make you cry, by-and-by!" exclaimed the beadle, whilst increasing the severity of the strokes; but so graciously and wonderfully was she upheld, that she afterwards said that even had she been whipped to death, in the state she then was, she should not have been terrified nor dismayed.

The sheriff, finding how unavailing their cruelty was, at length bade the beadle cease striking her. He had thought that he had only a woman to deal with in her weakness, but found that he was fighting against God. On the following day she was liberated. The Mayor of Bideford, before whom she was brought, was much impressed by some serious conversation which she had with him, and was so eager to resume it, that, when she left the town, he followed her on horseback, and rode three or four miles with her; before parting she knelt down and prayed for him. Apparently her influence was blessed to him; once, after leaving the county, she wrote him a letter, which he received not long before his death.

In the winter of the following year, 1655, Barbara Blaugdon crossed to Ireland. The vessel in which she sailed was in great peril from a tremendous storm, which the superstitious sailors attributed to the presence of a Friend, and conspired to throw her overboard. When she became aware of their design, she successfully appealed to the captain for protection, saying that, if he permitted such a deed, her blood would be required at his hands. The tempest continued, and as the chaplain was too much terrified to hold the usual service, Barbara Blaugdon went on deck, feeling that it was her duty to address the crew and pray for them. They were very grave and quiet, and afterwards remarked that they were " more beholden " to her than to their chaplain.

On landing at Dublin she went to the house of the Viceroy, but was told that it would be useless to seek for an interview with him, as only on the previous day he had banished Edward Burrough and Francis Howgill from the island; but after a while she was shown into a drawing-room, and a gentleman came to her from the Deputy's chamber, before whom those who accompanied him stood uncovered. Notwithstanding this artifice she was convinced that he was not the Deputy but a clergyman; and, when asked by those present why she did not speak to their lord, replied, "When I see your lord, then I shall give my message to him." Ere long the Viceroy made his appearance, and after he had seated himself on a couch she addressed him, bidding him beware lest he should be fighting against God by opposing His cause and persecuting the innocent; at the same time expressing her belief that he was not so much in fault as were those who instigated him to this conduct. He was evidently impressed by her solemn words; and when she spoke of how the teachers of the people caused them to err, he said to the clergyman, "There's for you, Mr. Harrison!" and afterwards asked him what reply he could make her. "It is all very true and very good," he said, "and I have nothing to say against it if she speaks as she means." Barbara Blaugdon answered that the Spirit of God was true and spoke as He meant, but men of corrupt minds perverted the Scriptures by putting their own construction on them and deceiving those they taught; but the Scriptures were of no private interpretation, being written by holy men of God as they were inspired by the Holy Ghost. She was told that the Viceroy was so much impressed that after she left him he declined joining in bowls or any similar pastime.

From Dublin she went to Cork, where some of her relatives and acquaintances dwelt; frequent were her imprisonments, though whenever she preached there were some who willingly received her message, whilst many of her former friends trembled at her words of warning. Once, when she was addressing the people in a market-place, a butcher swore he would cleave her head; but whilst lifting his cleaver to do so a woman seized his arms, and presently some soldiers came to the rescue. On her next voyage to Ireland the ship foundered near Dungarvan, and she had a most narrow escape of her life, but was providentially saved by the bravery of the captain and one of the sailors.

In Dublin she suffered much in a filthy prison, having given great offence by a religious exhortation to the judges in a court of justice. After a while she was arraigned at the bar, and when requested to plead Guilty or Not Guilty, answered that there was no guilt upon anyone's conscience for what was done in obedience to God. But as this was not considered a satisfactory answer she was sent back to prison. Here she was visited by some of her friends, Sir William King, Colonel Fare, and Lady Brown, who afterwards went to the judge to try to obtain her release; they laughed when he told them, in allusion to Barbara Blaugdon, that he was afraid of his life—saying they had known her from childhood, and were so strenuous in their efforts for her liberation that they at last secured it.

After she was set free she spoke very solemnly to the judge, who died the same night. A short time previously he had condemned six persons to death on a charge of murder, five of whom were apparently innocent; for the only witness against them, when accused by Barbara Blaugdon, who shared the same prison, confessed, while trembling exceedingly, that his evidence was altogether false; and he once made the same admission to the judge, to whom Barbara Blaugdon wrote, begging him to take care that he did not condemn the guiltless, also telling him that the day of his death was at hand, and reminding him that he would have to render an account of his actions. But he took no notice of this remonstrance. At Limerick, also, Barbara Blaugdon found imprisonment awaiting her; on her homeward voyage she was robbed of all she had by the crew of a privateer, but reached England in safety at last.

The latest allusion made to her by the historian Sewel is in reference to her being amongst the one hundred and fifteen Friends who were imprisoned at Bristol in 1682, whilst, in the face of threats and persecution, the meetings in that city were kept up by the children with wonderful faith and courage. During John Audland and John Cramm's remarkable visit there (twenty-eight years earlier), we find that George Bishop and Josiah Coale were also amongst those who "received their testimony."

In 1664, *George Bishop* published the following brief address which was delivered to Charles II. and his Parliament:—

"To the King and both Houses of Parliament; thus saith the Lord:

"Meddle not with my people because of their conscience to Me, and banish them not out of the nation because of their conscience; for if you do I will send my plagues upon you, and you shall know that I am the Lord.

"Written, in obedience to the Lord, by his servant,
"GEORGE BISHOP.

"Bristol, 25th of Ninth Month, 1664.

It will be remembered that the Great Plague visited London in the following year. Whilst the pestilence was at its height the Friends were less frequently banished than before; from his prison in Bristol George Bishop sent them a letter exhorting them to stand fast in the Lord, and assuring them that if they were exiled God would protect them whilst they were faithful to Him,—that "none should root them out, but that they should be planted and built up." At an earlier date he wrote a book giving an account of the cruel persecution of the Friends in New England, in which he quoted Major-General Denison's words to those who ventured to remonstrate with him,—"This year ye will go to complain to the Parliament, and the next year they will send to see how it is; and the third year the Government will be changed!" When this passage was read to the King he was much struck by it, and calling some of his courtiers to hear it he exclaimed, "So! these are some of my good subjects of New England, but I will put a stop to them!" And when, after William Ledra's execution at Boston, Edward Burrough besought him to put an end to such proceedings by sending a mandamus thither, he yielded to his request.

Josiah Coale was about twenty-one when the powerful ministry of Audland and Camm proved an effectual message to his soul. "I saw," he says, "that my heart was polluted, and that there was no habitation for God, which caused me to mourn in desolation, and to wander in solitary places, until I was ready to faint; and I said in my heart, Never man's sorrow was like my sorrow. . . . If Thou, O God," was now his cry, "wilt help me thoroughly, then will I teach transgressors Thy ways, and sinners shall be converted unto Thee." This was no vain vow; it became his "life and joy" to declare the Gospel, and, with lips touched as with a live coal, he laboured valiantly for his Lord, at home and abroad; on one occasion travelling with two other

Friends from Virginia to New England through vast wildernesses and dense forests which had been thought impenetrable to all but the Indians, who treated the white strangers most kindly, although they had previously been greatly exasperated by Europeans. Yet their lives were often endangered by the neighbourhood of beasts of prey and serpents, by the marshes which intercepted their path, and the effects of hunger and cold.

Amongst some of the aboriginal tribes of Massachusetts, especially, Joshua Coale discovered true yearnings after God. "Through the goodness of the Lord," he writes, "we found these Indians more sober and Christian-like towards us than the Christians so-called." After his release from Sandwich gaol, the youthful minister laboured amongst the Algonquins, whose king said to him, "The Englishmen do not love the Quakers, but the Quakers are honest men, and do no harm; and this is no Englishman's sea or land, and Quakers shall come here and welcome."

Two or three years later, when imprisoned in London, he writes:—"Though great suffering and afflictions attended, as yet my heart praised be the Lord is not troubled, neither has fear seized me, because I see the intent of the Lord in it. . . . For the sake of the residue of the seed which is yet ungathered is my life freely sacrificed into the hand of the Lord. . . . So let your prayer unto God be for me that I may be kept unto the end, and finish my course with joy, and in all things bring glory and honour to the name of the Lord." He died at the age of thirty-five, cheerfully laying down his life, we are told, "With perfect understanding, and in an extraordinary enjoyment of the Lord's life, majesty, and presence." Amongst the many hundreds who attended his funeral was Sewel, the historian, who, young as he then was, greatly loved and revered Josiah Coale, and highly appreciated his kindness; always availing himself of opportunities to attend meetings where it was said that he would be present.

In 1656, two years after they had held the memorable succession of meetings at Bristol, John Camm, and John Audland revisited that city. They were devoted friends, and had in the meantime often travelled together, whilst much blessing rested on their labours for their Lord.* In consequence of the delicacy of John Camm's health his son Thomas often accompanied him. The strain on the voice and chest in large meetings, especially when held out of doors, were greater than John Camm's consumptive constitution could withstand, and he did not long survive his second visit to Bristol. As his strength slowly ebbed away he told his friends that his "inward man revived and mounted upward towards its habitation in the heavens."

On the day of his death, at the age of fifty-two, after addressing his family, he seemed to be in a sweet sleep, from which they thought he would never awake. But, hearing their loud lamentations, he said, "Dear hearts ye have wronged me, for I was at sweet rest; ye should not so passionately sorrow for my departure; this house of earth and clay must go to its place; and this soul and spirit is to be gathered up to the Lord to live

---

* *Elizabeth Stirredge*, of whom there is a sketch in this volume, was another on whose mind an indelible impression was made by the ministry of John Audland.

with Him for ever, where we shall meet with everlasting joy." Then, once more taking leave, he lay down and soon expired. His birthplace was Camsgill, Westmoreland, the ancestral seat of his family. From childhood he had been seriously inclined, and, like Audland, had eagerly received the truths taught by George Fox, when he visited their native county in 1652. At that time, we learn from his son, "the world seemed to smile upon him, and the riches and glory of it had exceeding increased and were then likely to increase more." But he willingly counted all things loss for the excellency of the knowledge of Christ Jesus his Lord. He was a powerful minister, and was one of the Friends who visited London in 1654, and published the doctrines of our Society there.

John Audland keenly felt his death, though he found comfort in the companionship of Thomas Camm, who was often his associate in Gospel service. John Audland died at the age of thirty-four, his life being doubtless shortened by the hardships and persecution which he had endured; for, in addition to close imprisonments, we find allusions to "great perils, sore beatings, and cruel mockings—both of the rabble and also of the bitter-spirited professors." He was very patient during his illness, and often said, "Ah! those great meetings in the orchard at Bristol, I may not forget! I would so gladly have spread my net over all, and have gathered all, that I forgot myself, never considering the weakness of my body.* But it's well. My reward is with me, and I am

---

* In a letter written by Francis Howgill to Edward Burrough, when in London in 1656, he says:—"From Bristol we have received letters from our dear brethren John Audland and John Camm; the

content to give up and be with the Lord; for that my soul values above all things."

Notwithstanding his weakness, marvellous power was granted him to make the friends who visited him in some measure sharers of his joy and overwhelming sense of the love of God, with whose praise his heart was filled. As his strength failed he asked to be raised up in order to kneel, and then fervently besought the Lord that His whole heritage might be preserved in the Truth, out of the evil of the world. Though tenderly sympathising with his beloved wife he said to her, "My will is in true subjection to the will of the Lord, whether life or death; and therefore give me up freely to His disposing." And she, we read, "how dear soever he was to her, did so." Ten days after his death she became the mother of a little boy.

In reference to her loss she writes:—"The Eternal God revealed His Son Christ in us, and gave us faith to believe in Him, the eternal Word of Life, by which our souls came to be quickened and made alive. . . . Our hearts were knit together in the unspeakable love of Truth, which was our life, joy, and delight, and made our days together exceeding comfortable. The dolour

---

mighty power of the Lord is that way: this is a precious city and a gallant people; their net is like to break with fishes, they have caught so much there, and all the coast thereabout. Mighty is His work and power in this His day! Shout for joy all ye holy ones! for the Lord rides on in power to get Himself a name." Another letter, with a similar signature, contains a reference to the same Friends:—" Our hearts were broken in separating one from another, for our lives are bound up in one, and we partake of one another's sufferings and of one another's joy." Like John Audland, Francis Howgill had been an eager recipient of George Fox's message at Firbank Chapel, and had found that the seed then sown in his soul was destined to bring forth a hundredfold.

of my heart my tongue or pen is not able to declare; yet in this I contented myself that it was the will of the Lord." Anne Audland afterwards became the wife of Thomas Camm, and for forty years, "in the utmost harmony and nearness of affection," they mutually served their Lord and suffered for His sake. Once he was imprisoned at Appleby for six years, and again at Kendal for three. But trials seemed only to fan the flame of devotion in the heart of his wife, who was greatly gifted as a minister: she spent much time alone in fervent prayer, and in reading the Scriptures and religious books. Humble and retiring herself, she was always ready to encourage the weakest of the flock. During a very severe illness she spoke of how she had enjoyed unspeakable peace *here*, as well as the full assurance of everlasting joy.

In the autumn of 1705, when in her seventy-ninth year, in a farewell sermon at a Monthly Meeting at Kendal, she implored her friends to be diligent in the service of God. The following day she was attacked by the illness which ended her life. After begging her husband to give her up freely, she added, " I have loved thee with my soul and God has blessed us, and will bless thee and be with thee, and make up all thy losses. . . . I am full of assurance of eternal salvation and a crown of glory, through my dear Lord and Saviour Jesus Christ."

She spoke of how much she had desired to send a farewell epistle to Friends at Bristol and Banbury, "tenderly to advise professors of Truth to keep under the power of the Cross of Christ, by which they will be more and more crucified to the world, and baptised into Christ, and put Him on, the new and heavenly man, in whom they will become new creatures and be enabled to serve God in spirit." As she grew worse, her husband suggested sending for one or two of her relatives, but she answered, "Be not careful in the matter; the Lord my God is near me and I have thy company, and it is enough. . . . The Lord gave us to each other; let us bless His name, if He now take us from each other in the outward, *that is all*, for our joining in spirit remains for ever."

One of the earnest messages she left was for her "prodigal son," asking his stepfather still to labour and pray for his return. Some of her last words were, "My hope is only in Thee, my dear Lord."

When, more than fifty years earlier, George Fox was enabled to sow the good seed of faith at Firbank Chapel did he forsee the marvellous results which would directly or indirectly arise therefrom!

Though the rough blasts of persecution in that age caused Quakerism to take deeper root, can there be any need that it should droop and wither in the sunshine of *this?*

> "New to the world at every hour,
> New runners find new races,"

yet are the conditions of discipleship the same as ever they were. From one source, and one alone, must vitality ever spring, and Jesus Christ is the same, yesterday, to-day, and for ever; a Saviour who can inspire the heart with "a love so deep as to make obedience a *delight.*"

EDWARD BURROUGH.

"CONSECRATING the whole manhood, and not merely a few faculties thereof, to God."—CHARLES KINGSLEY.

EDWARD BURROUGH.

"There is no created force in the universe greater than a feeble human soul that in simple faith yields up itself wholly to its Saviour as the mere instrument of His mighty power."

"I HAVE loved Thee from my cradle—from my youth unto this day; and have served Thee faithfully in my generation," were the words of that devoted follower of his crucified Lord, Edward Burrough, when at the age of twenty-eight he laid down his life in Newgate, a victim to the frightfully pestilential air of the gaol, where in one room nearly one hundred Friends were confined with a large number of felons. A fuller record of his inner life, pourtraying more plainly the hidden source of the wonderful outward one, would have been of deep interest, but he seems to have written comparatively little of himself in any way. Edward Burrough's ministry began at the age of eighteen, and, young as he was, it is evident that he had in all reality learnt *by heart* the lessons which it was his Lord's design that he should be instrumental, in no common measure, in impressing on others. The messenger whose own soul dwells in the subject of his message cannot but speak with force of the things which, with the eye and ear of faith, he has seen and heard.

Edward Burrough was born at Underbarrow, in Westmoreland, in 1634; his parents, who were members of the Church of England, gave him a good education. He writes concerning his early life:—

"When I grew up towards twelve years of age something stirred in me, and showed me that there was a higher religion than that I was exercised in. . . . I got to be a Presbyterian, and followed the highest of the priests and professors of that form, and grew in favour with them. Then I left some little of my vanity and lightness, and pride grew up in me. When I was about seventeen it pleased God to show Himself a little to me, and something struck me with terror. . . . . . . At this time I was much separated from the vain ways of the world and from worldly people. The preaching of those whom I had formerly much delighted in was withered and decayed. Yet it pleased the Lord to show Himself in love to me, and I had sweet refreshment coming in from Him to my soul, and had joy and peace in abundance, and openings of the living truth in me which the world knew not of. The mystery of the Scriptures was something opened, and I saw many glorious things which lie hid under the letter. . . . I was brought out of the land of darkness, and could say I was in the light. But not knowing the cross of Christ I ran forth in my wisdom comprehending the mysteries of God. . . . Pride grew more than ever, and my delight was much in discoursing where I gave holy things unto dogs, and cast pearls before swine. . . . The earthly spirit ruled. I had left the Lord my Maker, who had so graciously made Himself manifest to me. I could tell of experiences, but they were dead to me, and something within began to question how it was with me; for I saw myself to be ignorant more than formerly, and I saw that I knew nothing."

He greatly longed for the peace which had once been his portion, for he found that it was in vain to try to comfort himself, as he would fain have done, with the doctrine—very prevalent amongst the Calvinistic Puritans—"Whom God loves once, He loves for ever." He saw the shallowness of much of the religion professed by those around him, and felt that something of a very different nature would be needed to satisfy the cravings of his soul. It was at this crisis, and when he was about eighteen years old, that George Fox came to Underbarrow, and the young student confessed that this faithful servant of the Lord "spoke the language which he knew not, notwithstanding all his high talking;" yet, unwilling to "endure the sound doctrine, he at first turned away his ears from the truth," endeavouring to refute it by skilful arguments. But these half-unconscious efforts to fight against God were unavailing. He soon saw the agreement of George Fox's teaching with the Scriptures, and the Holy Spirit showed him the state of his own heart; this sight was followed by a time of weeping, mourning, and misery. "One vial of wrath after another," he writes, "was poured out, and then I separated from all the glory of the world and betook myself to the company of a poor, despised, and condemned people called Quakers. . . . But praised, praised be the Lord for evermore, who made me partaker of His love, in whom my soul hath full satisfaction, joy, and content." In Christ he had peace, and therefore could be of good cheer whilst in the world he had tribulation.

His parents were so incensed at his joining the Friends that they forbade his remaining in the family, and even refused his request to work for them as a servant. Unchristian and cruel as this conduct was at best, one must not forget that to them Quakerism seemed a dangerous heresy, and they knew that its upholders were in that day despised and condemned not only by members of the Church of England but by Dissenters also. Almost at once Edward Burrough felt that he was called of God to the ministry of the Gospel. Writing of his friends and himself he says:—

"We tried all sorts of teachers, as many do at this day, and remain not gathered to the Lord. Such we were that sought the Lord and desired the knowledge of His ways more than anything beside. For one I may speak, who from a child, even a few years old, set his face to seek and find the Saviour. After our long seeking the Lord appeared to us, and revealed His glory in us, and gave us of His Spirit. . . . We found this light to be a sufficient teacher to lead us to Christ, from whom it came; and it gave us to receive Christ, and to witness Him to dwell in us. . . . We harkened to the voice of the Lord, and felt His word in our hearts to burn up and to beat down all that was contrary to God. Whilst waiting upon the Lord in silence, which we often did for many hours together, with our hearts towards Him, . . . we often received the pouring down of His Spirit upon us, and our hearts were made glad, and our tongues loosened. Things unutterable were made manifest, and the glory of the Father was revealed. Then we began to sing praises to the Lord God Almighty, and to the Lamb who had redeemed us to God."

What was this but a realisation of the prophet's words "Bring ye all the tithes into the storehouse that there may be meat in mine house, and prove me now herewith, said the Lord of hosts, if I will not open you the windows of heaven and pour you out a blessing that there shall not be room enough to receive it"?

In company with others who had, like himself, been deeply reached by the ministry of George Fox, and had willingly given up the world for Christ, Edward Borrough visited the Northern counties of England and some parts of Scotland. In that "day of good tidings" how could they hold their peace, though their onward path led them through perils and prisons, and brought "beatings and bruisings" upon them? It was not possible that such labour should be in vain in the Lord; and there were many who showed the reality of the change wrought in their hearts, by willingness to join a people who met with persecution on every side. Places of public worship, markets, and streets, alike witnessed the ministerial work of Edward Burrough, who was enabled very strikingly to discern the spiritual state of those to whom his words were directed. Whilst in prison he prepared a paper called "A Warning from the Lord," at the end of which he thus addressed his suffering brethren: "Be glad and rejoice in the Lord, for you hath He chosen to shine as lights in the world, and to be a burdensome stone to the nations."

In the spring of 1654, Edward Burrough came to London. One of the first Friends who had visited this city was Gervaise Benson, a justice of the peace, who in the previous year told George Fox, in a letter, that he had been brought there by the love of God, and was kept there waiting on the Lord, to do whatever He might require of him. A little before this time some works written by Friends had been published in the Metropolis, printed, we learn, "For Giles Calvert, and sold at his shop at the Black Spread Eagle, at the West end of Paul's." Many persons who had heard of the rise and growth of the Society of Friends in the North of England wished to know more about them, and to such Gervaise Benson's attention was turned. Soon afterwards, Isabel Buttery came from the North to distribute in London a paper by George Fox, on "The Kingdom of Heaven." Whilst engaged in this work one Sunday evening in St. Paul's Churchyard, she was brought before the Lord Mayor, and committed by him to Bridewell for the offence of Sabbath-breaking! There she and a maid-servant who had been with her were lodged in the common gaol, where only those of the lowest character were usually confined. At this period the first meetings of Friends were held in London, in the houses of two brothers named Dring, and were oftentimes of silent waiting on the Lord, though occasionally a little was said by Isabel Buttery.

It was with Francis Howgill (who was about sixteen years older than himself) that Edward Burrough entered London. So greatly was his ministry blessed that many hundreds were effectually brought to the knowledge of the Lord. Having experienced much of Christ's teaching in his own soul, he was made skilful in speaking the word in season to others. Thomas Ellwood describes him as "bold in his Master's quarrels, yet open and free to every thirsty lamb;" and he has been styled a Son of Thunder, yet withal a Son of Consolation. His eloquence and his powerful voice, like all else, were consecrated to his Saviour's cause, and from Francis Howgill we learn that, "Ofttimes buffetted, and sometimes knocked down, loaded with lies, bearing an exceeding weight of service, he made the work of the Lord his whole business," not spending even one week for himself during the ten years which lay between his conversion and his early death.

The "subtle spirit of the Londoners" was at first disheartening to these preachers from the Northern dales; but it could prove no insurmountable obstacle, for they came "in the name of the Lord of Hosts," who so gave the increase, that ere long they could say, "Hundreds are convinced and thousands wait to see the issue; very many societies we have visited are now able to stand." One incident is so characteristic of the age and of this young champion of the Cross, that even in this short sketch we cannot pass it by.

At London, Sewell tells us, it was usual in the summer evenings for many young men, on leaving work, to meet in the fields to show their strength in wrestling, to a crowd of eager onlookers; passing near the ring at Moorfields, Edward Burrough, then about twenty years of age, stood still and saw how a strong and skilful youth, who had already thrown three combatants, vainly challenged others, none of whom would venture to enter the lists. At this crisis Edward Burrough stepped forward, whilst with bated breath the bystanders watched the issue, not knowing that "it was quite another fight he aimed at."

Little was the successful wrestler prepared for such an adversary as now opposed him, and he quailed under the steadfast gaze and crushing words of one whose strength had been sharply tested in the conflict with spiritual wickedness. Presently his powerful voice, a fitting medium for the overwhelming words of his message from on high, was heard driving home to the hearts of the wondering and spell-bound multitude the reality of the " good fight of faith," as "he reasoned of righteousness, temperance, and judgment to come." Seemingly the seed was sown in stony ground, yet none cared to continue the sports, and the crowd separated; some to confess afterwards that this season had been the turning-point in their lives.

Whilst Edward Burrough and Francis Howgill were still in London they were thus addressed in a letter from George Fox:—"Stir abroad whilst the door is open, and the light shineth. The Lord give you an understanding in all things, and His arm go along with you that ye may be to His glory. Dear Francis and Edward, in the life of God wait, that ye may with it be led, . . . that as good *plow-men* and good thresher-men ye may be able to bring out the wheat."

How well Edward Burrough heeded this counsel we may learn from the Autobiography of William Crouch, who, although six years his senior, says that the spiritual relation in which he stood to him was that of a child to a father. "He was a man—though but young—of undaunted courage." William Crouch writes, "The Lord set him above the fear of his enemies, and I have beheld him filled with power by the Spirit of the Lord. For instance, at the *Bull and Mouth*, when the room, which was very large, hath been filled with people many of whom have been in uproars, contending one with another, some exclaiming against the Quakers, accusing and charging them with heresy, blasphemy, sedition, and what not; that they were deceivers and deluded the people; that they denied the Holy Scriptures, and the resurrection: others endeavouring to vindicate them, and speaking of them more favourably. In the midst of all which noise and contention, this servant of the Lord hath stood upon a bench, with a Bible in his hand, for he generally carried one about him, speaking to the people with great authority. . . . And so suitable to the present debate among them, that the whole multitude was overcome thereby, and became exceeding calm and attentive, and departed peaceably and with seeming satisfaction."

Two distinct kinds of meetings were then held in London. In one of these the Friends gathered quietly together in the name of Christ the great Head of the Church, to worship the Father in Spirit and in truth, that the strength which was ofttimes severely strained might be renewed, that their sinking souls might mount up as on eagles' wings, and that, with hearts enlarged by the more conscious indwelling of the Comforter, they might run and not be weary, and walk — though through much tribulation — and not faint. In this time of our outward ease have we, their successors, less need than they for putting on the inward armour?

The other class of meetings were "for all sorts and all sects," and were often very large; the service resting, as George Fox suggested, "on three, or four, or six Friends who were grown up and strong in the Truth." With such workmen,—the secret language of whose souls was, "We have no might, neither know we what to do, but our eyes are upon *Thee;*" willing to wait, whilst willing also at their Master's bidding to go forward in faith; "steadfast, unmovable, always abounding in the work of the Lord," because in Him their life was hid,—it was no marvel that many should be added to the Church.* "When we see such multitudes," writes Francis Howgill, "we are often put to a stand where one might get bread to satisfy so many; but the wisdom and power of God has been with us." Very many eagerly drank in the words of these earnest Gospel ministers, who spoke in demonstration of the

---

* Twenty-five years later there were 10,000 Friends in London alone.

Spirit and of power; for their doctrine was no new thing, but the uplifting of Christ as the Light of the World, as being made unto man "wisdom and righteousness, sanctification and redemption;" as bearing "our sins in His own body on the tree, *that we, being dead to sins, should live unto righteousness.*"

In the summer of 1654 Edward Burrough and Francis Howgill went to Bristol, where persecution was already threatened. A meeting held in the Castle was attended by several hundreds. When it was over they went for rest to the country house of a captain in the army, whither they were followed by so many anxious to converse with them that the house was filled. Meetings were held daily in and around the city, which were largely attended, and on which the Divine blessing manifestly rested. The following Sunday morning they were in the city in the dwelling of a military officer; but his house proving quite too small to hold all who came, they went in the afternoon to the Fort, where about 2,000 persons assembled, including many of the chief people of the place. The company was a very quiet one; but when leaving the spot Edward Burrough and Francis Howgill were so pressed by the awakened crowd as to be glad to turn aside into a private room. The following day they were summoned before the mayor, aldermen, justices of the peace, and clergy. Many officers and other gentlemen, whose hearts had been touched by their ministry, accompanied them, but were not allowed to be present during their examination. When asked why they came to the city, they answered, "By the command of the Lord, to whose name we have to bear witness, and to declare the Gospel committed unto us." On being ordered to quit the town, they said, "We are freeborn Englishmen, and have served the commonwealth in faithfulness, being free in the presence of God from the transgression of any law. To your command we cannot be obedient; but if by violence you put us out of the city, and have power to do it, we cannot resist."

For a while longer they laboured in Bristol, and apparently without further interference. During this time some Baptists, from a town in Wiltshire, who had challenged them to a public dispute, were obliged to lay down arms, and were cowardly enough on their return home to report that the Friends denied Christ and the Scriptures. When, therefore, the two Friends visited this town, its inhabitants, in their indignation, had but a rough reception for them, though granting them leave for a meeting in the market-place to clear themselves. With a deep sense of their own helplessness, they drew near the large assembly, silently seeking for strength from Him whose promise is, "Call upon me in the day of trouble; I will deliver thee, and thou shalt glorify me." Then for two hours they spoke with irresistible authority. That evening the mayor called on them, confessing that they had spoken the truth, and that if he did not witness to it his conscience would witness against him; and a justice of the peace asked them to his house, and was, we learn, with his wife, "convinced of the Truth." This meeting was the means of opening a door for them in the county.

After a few weeks of earnest work in London, Edward Burrough and his friend again visited the country. A very large meeting was held in the Isle of Ely, to which Colonel Russell (whose son married a daughter of Oliver

Cromwell) sent two ministers, who reported to him that the Quakers were " far before " them. This led the Colonel to invite them to his house, where, in a religious family gathering, some hearts seemed to be touched, and the Colonel's wife shed many tears.

In the spring of 1655, Edward Burrough believed that he was called to preach the Gospel in Ireland. On the day of receiving this summons from on high, whilst committing himself wholly into the hands of God, a promise was granted him that his life should be preserved. Unknown to him, Francis Howgill was guided to the same field of labour, and with a conviction that Edward Burrough would be his companion in it. From Dublin, the latter — who, notwithstanding his incessant active avocations, was a great writer — addressed a general epistle to his brethren, whom he styles " The camp of the Lord in England."

Of himself, in a letter to Margaret Fell, he remarks: "As in suffering with Christ I do abound, so my joy by Him and consolation in Him are increased also. . . . We have not spared to wound on the right hand and on the left; and 'Victory, Victory,' hath been our word of watch." Of this visit he elsewhere writes: "Truly great service for the Lord we had; . . . there is a precious work begun and seed sown, which shall never die."

At the end of the year the two friends were placed by force on board a vessel bound for Chester. After travelling in the northern counties, Edward Burrough went to London, where he was soon joined by Francis Howgill, and, holding about twenty meetings a week, it is not to be wondered at that he was " almost spent;"

especially as much mental suffering was endured by himself and his companion in contending with the evil around them. In the following year, sometimes with a prison for his study, he still freely used his pen: it is interesting to read his unequivocal reply to Bunyan's charge that the Friends said that "salvation was not fully and completely wrought out for sinners by that man Christ Jesus." He answers: "This accusation is clearly false, and wickedly cast upon us; for there is not salvation in any other, nor is it wrought by any other, but by Jesus Christ. It is fully and completely brought forth by Him unto everyone who believes and receives the testimony of it in themselves." His simple definition of faith is as follows: "Faith is an act of God in the Creature. . . . It gives the Creature to believe God in all that He hath promised."

In an epistle of encouragement to "Such as are found worthy to suffer," this passage is found: "Be ye more watchful, and faithful, and valiant for the Truth upon the earth unto the end; that you may . . . receive the fulfilling of the promise of God, and may witness God within you, the Emanuel, the Saviour, God with us. *All that know this need not go forth to the right hand nor to the left, but salvation is come unto us.* He takes away sin, and saves from it and from condemnation. . . . Believe not that spirit which draws back into the world, into its lusts and liberty and fashions, which pass away. That Spirit forgets God." He repeatedly wrote addresses of remonstrance to Oliver Cromwell, and in 1659 published a very remarkable prediction of the persecutions that awaited the persecutors of the Friends, and which was fully verified when, in the following year, Charles

II. was made king. In it he says that whilst in Warwickshire he was one day meditating on the woful wrongs of his people, when a cry went through him, "The Lord will be avenged! The Lord will be avenged upon His enemies! He will avenge the cause of His people;" accompanied with the command, "Write unto the rulers, and yet once more warn them."

Soon after this Edward Burrough went with Samuel Fisher to Dunkirk (which was then possessed by the English), their object being to visit Jesuits, Friars, and Priests. After conversation with the Capuchin Friars, Edward Burrough sent them some queries in Latin: "Is it an outward abstinence," he asks, "by the force of locks, and doors, and bolts, or self-separated and secret places, that subdues the world's nature in men and women? Is it by such means that Christ gives victory over sin and overcomes it in His people? Or is it not by the power of God in the heart only?" Many meetings were held here, and opportunities were found for satisfactory service in the army, leading Edward Burrough to remark that he "must commend the spirit of our Englishmen for moderation more than the men of any other nation."

Later in the year he published a long document, styled, "A message to the present Rulers of England," containing the following prophetic words: "Your estates shall not be spared from the spoiler, nor your necks from the axe; your enemies shall charge treason upon you, and if you seek to stop the Lord's work you shall not cumber the earth very long." When in 1661, a committee was appointed by the House of Commons to prepare and bring in a bill to prevent any injury to the Government from Quakers, etc., refusing to take oaths, and unlawfully convening together, Edward Burrough, George Whitehead, and Richard Hubberthorne obtained an interview with its members. Characteristically, the last thing said to them by Edward Burrough was that should this measure be passed, " so far from yielding conformity thereunto, he should, through the strength of Christ, meet among the people of God to worship Him; and not only so, but should make it his business to exhort all God's people everywhere to meet together for the worship of God, notwithstanding the law and all its penalties; and that he desired this might be reported to the House"! Well might Francis Howgill say that " he was of a manly spirit in the things of God."

A little later he had an audience with the king on account of the persecuted Friends in New England, one of whom had already been put to death; telling the monarch that a vein of innocent blood had been opened in his dominions which, if it were not stopped, would overrun all. " But I will stop that vein," was the reply. Owing to Edward Burrough's diligence in following up the matter, a mandamus was sent to Boston, compelling the cruel rulers to release their innocent victims.

After labouring in the neighbourhood of his birthplace, and visiting Thomas Ellwood who had been deeply impressed by his ministry, and was then ill of small-pox, in Oxfordshire, we find Edward Burrough once more in London. Then follows a visit to the Friends at Bristol; both in meetings and in private he exhorted them to " faithfulness and steadfastness to that wherein they had found rest unto their souls," and solemnly bade them farewell. " I am going to the city of London again," he said, " to lay down my life for the Gospel, and suffer amongst Friends in that place." Soon after his arrival he was violently arrested, whilst preaching at the Bull and Mouth Meeting-house, and committed by Alderman Brown to Newgate, in which filthy and frightfully crowded gaol his friend, Richard Hubberthorne—of whom he wrote a memorial—died, not long afterwards, in great peace; " That faith which hath wrought my salvation," he said, " I well know. . . . Out of this straightness I must go, for I am wound into largeness, and am to be lifted up on high, far above all ! "

Whilst confined amongst the vilest felons, Edward Burrough, in a letter to some of his friends in the country, says that it would be " too large to relate, and too piercing to their hearts to hear, the violence and cruelty which Friends had suffered : " he begs them to be ready also to die rather than deny Christ before men, or cease from the free exercise of their consciences. Slightly alluding to the extreme sufferings of his companions and himself—easy to read of, hard to realise—he adds, " but the Lord supports ! " King Charles, who greatly respected him, sent an order for his release, which Alderman Brown and others managed to evade.

It soon became manifest that neither his youth nor strong constitution could withstand the pestilential air. Calmly and patiently he awaited the close, night and day praying exceedingly for himself and his people whilst not forgetting his enemies, " Father, forgive them, for they know not what they do." Almost his last words were, " Though this body of clay must return to the dust, yet I have a testimony that I have served God in my generation; *and that Spirit which has acted and ruled in me shall yet break forth in thousands.*"

Truly, those who rejoiced at his death—in the belief that the cause which he had advocated would have been injured or destroyed thereby—made, as Sewel says, " a wrong reckoning." " Shall days, or months, or years," writes his friend Francis Howgill, " wear out thy name as though thou hadst no being? Oh, nay! . . . The children that are yet unborn shall have thee in their mouths, and thy works shall testify of thee in generations who have not yet a being and shall count thee blessed. . . . Oh, Edward Burrough! I cannot but mourn for thee, yet not as one without hope or faith. . . . I am distressed for thee, my brother; very pleasant hast thou been to me, and my love to thee was wonderful, passing the love of women."

When George Fox heard of the death of this " valiant warrior, more than a conqueror," so he calls him,— " being sensible how great a grief and exercise it would be to Friends to part with him," he wrote a few lines counselling them, in his deep spirituality, so to dwell in Christ as to " feel dear Edward Burrough among them," that they might thus " enjoy him in the life that doth not change, which is invisible."

It is difficult to bear in mind that the vast and varied labours of which this imperfect outline is given, were accomplished between the age of eighteen and of twenty-eight. Without any doubt whatever, Edward Burrough was endowed with a powerful intellect, a large amount of energy of character, and the good gift of physical strength: yet it would be in vain to attribute to these what Sewel speaks of as "his very glorious success." Surely it rather lay in this :—called and chosen, and faithful ;—conscious that, without Christ we can do nothing, and being well aware that "There can be nothing servile in the entire resignation of ourselves to be taught of Him, for He is the absolute truth—nothing unmanly in the yielding of our whole being to be wholly moulded by Him " *—he placed *himself and his all* at the disposal of his Lord.

In the words of his faithful friend, Francis Howgill, " his very strength was bended after God."

---

* Archbishop Trench.

ELIZABETH STIRREDGE.

> "God's love so walls us round about,
> How is it possible to doubt?"—Anon.

ELIZABETH STIRREDGE.

> She " had a Guide, and in His steps
>   When travellers have trod,
> Whether beneath was flinty rock
>   Or yielding grassy sod,
> They cared not, but with force unspent,
> Unmoved by pain, they onward went,
> Unstayed by pleasures still they bent
> Their zealous course to God."
>
> T. T. Lynch.

"I can truly say," remarks Elizabeth Stirredge, when describing the earlier years of her life—"That I never coveted heaven's glory, nor to be made a partaker of the riches, glory, and everlasting well-being for ever, more than I desired to walk in the way that leads thereunto. And I did as truly believe that the Lord would redeem a people out of the world and its ways." She was born in 1634, at Thornbury, in Gloucestershire, and was the child of God-fearing parents, Puritans, by whom she was very carefully brought up. The consistent life of her father, and his fervent prayers in his family, were long remembered by her. "There is a day coming," he would say, "wherein Truth will gloriously break forth; more glorious than ever since the apostles' days; but I shall not live to see it." In spite of many advantages the childhood of Elizabeth Stirredge — whose maiden name we do not know—was far from being a happy one. Naturally timid and pensive as she was, it does not seem unlikely that the training which might have suited a more vigorous mental constitution was scarcely adapted to her sensitive nature. She however gives no intimation of this herself, and probably when looking back at her early troubles she could thankfully set her seal to the truth of the blessed declaration, that all things shall work together for good to them that love God.

When only ten years old she felt that she could take no delight in the pleasures which the world offers. As she grew older she found satisfaction in intercourse with some religious people, and it was very delightful to her to listen to their conversation; but soon her sadness returned with the conviction that she was not living as the people of God did in former times. Unable to find relief in prayer, or comfort in reading the sacred Scriptures, she mourned because she had not lived in the days when the Lord spoke with Moses, in order that she might thus have known His will, or in the days when Christ was personally on earth, that she might have followed Him and sat at His feet; all unconscious that, even in the midst of her trials, He who had loved her with an everlasting love was drawing her into closer fellowship with Himself than any outward one could be. In reference to Satan's subtle snares she says:—

"The enemy will befool as many as he can, therefore look unto the Lord, and pray unto Him in the inward of your minds, though you cannot utter one word: know it assuredly that He is near to help His afflicted children at all times. Oh that I had known this in my young and tender years when the Lord was near me, and at work in my heart, and I knew it not! . . . I had many times a concern upon my mind which brought great heaviness over my spirit; but I knew not what it was, and I little thought it was the Lord who was ever good and gracious, kind, merciful, and slow to anger. I little thought He looked so narrowly to my ways. . .

He took me by the hand and led me when I knew not of it; and if I had not hearkened unto the enemy all would have been well."

When Elizabeth Stirredge was twenty years of age, she attended a meeting held by John Audland and John Camm. The ministry of the former sank to the bottom of her heart; and, leaving her companions, she walked home alone, the cry of her soul being, " What shall I do to be saved ? I would do anything for the assurance of everlasting life." Her earnest aspirations for a new heart could but be answered by Him who had redeemed her with His precious blood. To her children, in after years, she writes that they may " know the way to heaven's glory and to the enjoyment of true peace and satisfaction, because it is a straight and narrow way;" and she begs them to keep their hearts with all diligence, in order that they may be brought nearer and nearer unto the Lord and grow in fellowship with Him. "My very aim," she adds, "is to make you a little acquainted with the work of the Lord in my heart, and also with the subtle devices of the enemy; . . . his way is to set baits according unto people's nature, for therein he is most likely to prevail. And because I was of a sad heart and very subject to be cast down, therefore did he with all his might endeavour to cast me down into despair; . . . many things he cast before me that seemed too hard for me to go through." The precious consciousness of the comforting and sustaining presence of her Saviour which had for a while been her joy was withdrawn; and Satan insinuated that the sorrow which she felt at the loss of this sweet fellowship was most sinful, and that the fate of the murmurer was to fall in the wilderness.

Just at this time William Dewsbury [of whom there is a sketch in this volume] visited Gloucestershire. His soul was especially drawn out in sympathy for those who were passing through such sorrow as had at one time well-nigh overwhelmed himself. After hearing his comforting language in meeting, Elizabeth Stirredge felt a great longing to open her heart a little to him: and yet imagining that, stranger though he was, an insight would be given him of her spiritual state, she feared that he would speak to her about the hardness of her heart, and that such an additional affliction as this would be more than she could bear. She was not mistaken in supposing that he would understand her case. Before she had reached the spot where he stood the word in season was spoken. "Dear lamb!" he said, "judge all thoughts and believe, for blessed are they that believe and see not. They were blessed that saw and believed, but more blessed are they that believe and see not." "Oh," she writes, "he was one that had good tidings for me in that day, and great power was with his testimony; for the hardness was taken away, and my heart was opened by that ancient power that opened the heart of Lydia: everlasting praises be given unto Him that sits upon the throne for ever."

She seems simply to have accepted the truth that "emotion is not faith;" that when feeling is at its lowest ebb, faith—even from the fact of this great strain on it—may grow the stronger. "I can only say," she remarks, "that my heart and soul delighted in judgments. The Lord's end in chastening His children is to make them fit for His service." Not long afterwards Elizabeth Stirredge met with Miles Halhead, another minister in the newly-formed Society of Friends. Looking at her, he said, "Dear child, if thou continue in Truth, thou wilt make an honourable woman for the Lord; for the Lord God will honour thee with His blessed testimony." Ten years later, and soon after she felt called on to speak in meetings, he was again the bearer of a message to her soul. "My love and life is with thee," he said, "and that for the blessed work's sake that is at work in thee. The Lord keep thee faithful, for He will require hard things of thee that thou art not aware of: the Lord give thee strength to perform it; my prayers shall be for thee as often as I remember thee."

The cruel persecution to which the Friends were exposed had no terror for her on her own account, for her heart, she says, "was given up to serve the Lord, come what would come;" and she found that He in whom she trusted not only supported her under grievous trials, but so sanctified them as to cause her to rejoice that she was counted worthy to suffer for His sake.

In the year 1670 she was for a while deeply distressed; it seemed to be her duty to write an address to King Charles II., and to present it to him in person. Such a service seemed to her strange and wonderful, and, having a very low estimate of her own spiritual and mental gifts, she tried to think that Satan was endeavouring to ensnare her into something better suited to a wise and good man, and prayed that a more simple task might be assigned to her. But such sore sorrow followed this unwillingness that she was led to cry, "Lord, if Thou hast found me worthy, make my way plain before me, and I will follow Thee; for, Lord, Thou knowest that I would not willingly offend Thee." Yet, being now a wife and mother, most naturally, her heart yearned for her little children, and shrank from the thought that she might not perhaps be allowed to return to her family alive. But He who

> "—— Never yet forsook at need
> The soul that trusted Him indeed,"

comforted her with this assurance, If thou canst believe, thou shalt see all things accomplished, and thou shalt return in peace, and thy reward shall be with thee. The address was a very brief one, a solemn warning of what would be the consequences of the bloodshed and persecution of the righteous. This she placed in the King's hands whilst saying, "Hear, O King, and fear the Lord God of heaven and earth." He turned pale, but only answered in a sorrowful tone, "I thank you, good woman." On coming back to her family she found them well. "The Lord," she writes, afforded me His living presence to accompany me, which is the greatest comfort that can be enjoyed, and my coming home was with joy and peace in my bosom."

Not long afterwards a constable and other officers entered the shop of her husband, James Stirredge, to exact a fine from him for the attendance of himself and his wife at the meetings of Friends. This he declined to pay, at the same time saying that had he owed the King anything he would surely have repaid him. The constable leant his head on his hand, and remarked that it would be against his conscience to take their goods from them. Elizabeth Stirredge, on hearing this, said, "John, have a care of wronging thy conscience; for what could the Lord do more for thee than to place His good Spirit in thy heart to teach thee what thou shouldst do and what thou shouldst leave undone?" He answered that he knew not how to act; for, although he might take their goods once, the matter would not end there whilst they continued to go to meetings, as never had there been such laws. She replied, "John, when thou hast wronged thy conscience and brought a burden on thy spirit, it is not the rulers can remove it from thee. If thou shouldst say, I have done that which was against my conscience to do; they may say, as the rulers did to Judas, 'What is that to us? see thou to that.'" The officers, however, who were with him seized some of the goods, but with trembling hands, and compelled a poor man to carry them. "You force me," he said, "to do that which you cannot do yourselves, neither can I." When, a little later, a meeting was held to appraise the goods which had been taken from Friends, Elizabeth Stirredge felt, as she sat at work in her husband's shop, that it would be right for her to go to the room where the justices and others were assembled. She did not at all know why this was required of her, but the impression of duty became stronger while she hesitated. On entering the apartment she silently took a seat just within the door: some of those present repeatedly said that they could not go on with the business whilst she was with them, and ordered the owner of the house to turn her out; but he replied that he could not lay hands on her, which made one of the justices leave the room in a violent passion. On his return, " The power of the Lord," she writes, " fell on me with a very dreadful warning amongst them." A short time after this, two of the company died suddenly in the midst of the joviality of a feast.

In the year 1670 the persecution reached such a height, that it was at the risk of life itself that the Friends held their meetings. Grievous, indeed, was the outward suffering of those days, yet to Elizabeth Stirredge and many others this caused far less sorrow than did the unfaithfulness of a few of their brethren. As the door of the meeting-house was nailed up, the usual attenders felt it right to assemble outside : a bailiff and other officers, followed by an angry crowd, came with clubs to disperse the quiet congregation. But ONE was in their midst whose name is a strong tower ; and Elizabeth Stirredge and another Friend were enabled to speak words of encouragement to the company, and to praise Him who had given them a banner to display because of the truth. The power of the Lord so perceptibly prevailed that their cruel adversaries were awed, though at length they exacted a fine of twenty shillings from each of the attenders, most of whom, however, left the spot with rejoicing hearts. John Story, an influential member of the meeting, was much displeased when he found that he could not induce his friends to save themselves by privately assembling for worship; but, cost what it might, they felt they must confess their Lord before men. Then a second minister sent a message, suggesting the advantages that would arise from waiting on God in a quiet room instead of in the street. Can we wonder when we learn that some united in this view? But there were many in those sifting times, men, weak women and even children, who, with a heaven-taught fortitude, delighted in the thought that

"Love would have his children brave!"

Looking steadfastly at the strength of their Almighty leader, they—

"Said not, 'Who am I?' but rather
'*Whose* am I, that I should fear?'"

Century after century, in testing times such as these, has a simple trust in Christ, and an entire surrender of the soul to Him, triumphed gloriously, *overcoming the world*. How should we have acted had we lived in those stormy days? Yet surely such holy confidence is needed for the conflict with evil in every age. Very varied are the forms in which it confronts us. And is there less danger in passing over the treacherous marsh than in crossing the foaming torrent; or less cause now for closely cleaving to Christ with the confiding prayer, "Hold Thou me up, and I shall be safe,"—than at a time when the path of the pilgrim to the Celestial City did not at least lead him through the perils of outward prosperity?

Very earnest were the prayers of Elizabeth Stirredge by night and day that she might be enabled to hold out to the end, and that the Lord would "strengthen His weak ones, and make the little ones as strong as David." "And," she writes, "according to the day was our strength renewed; blessed be that Hand that never failed us, nor any that put their trust in Him." Above all she desired to know and to do her Lord's will. "Search my heart," was her prayer, "for I love to be searched and tried." She knew that God was calling her to be His messenger, to proclaim a warning in the ears of those who, whilst calling themselves His children, were denying Him before men; "which," she says, "made me tremble before the Lord, crying, 'Oh Lord! why wilt Thou require such hard things of me? Lord, look upon my afflictions and lay no more upon me than I am able to bear. They will not hear me that am a contemptible instrument. And seeing they despise the service of women so much, O Lord! make use of them that are more worthy.' . . . The answer I received was, 'They shall be made worthy that dwell low in My fear.'"

About this time Elizabeth Stirredge paid a religious visit to the Friends in Wiltshire, where John Story, to whom allusion has been made, was causing much trouble, especially by his efforts to persuade others to save themselves by the use of what he found it convenient to call "Christian prudence." The distress of Elizabeth Stirredge was great; and she dreaded attending meetings for fear of what might be given her to express. Miles Halhead, whose words had twice before sunk deeply into her heart, came to see her.

"He was," she writes, "wonderfully endowed with the power of the Lord, and with great discerning; he said, ' My love runs unto thee, and that for the work's sake that is in thee; for God will require hard things of thee; thou little thinkest what is at work in thy heart. The Lord God of my life keep thee faithful; my prayers shall be for thee as often as I have thee in remembrance. Thou art as my own life, and sealed in my bosom; I cannot forget thee, so, dear child, fare thee well. The Lord my God hath sent me forth once more, and when I return home He will cut the thread of my life in two!' And so it was. But, oh! the goodness of the Lord with that salutation overflowed my whole heart and melted me into tenderness."

A little later she went to Bristol, where John Story was much disturbing the meetings by his long and lifeless sermons. Her suffering became deeper and deeper.

"Many a time" she writes, "have I lain down in my sorrow and watered my pillow with tears. . . . I said, 'Oh Lord! if Thou wilt open my heart to declare of Thy goodness, and what Thou hast done for Thy people, and to tell of Thy noble acts, and Thy manifold mercies, how ready should I be to do it; but these are hard things, who can bear them?' . . . I knew what the Lord required of me as well as I knew my right hand from my left, and would not obey Him. I thought that if any one had borne a testimony before me, I could the better have borne it; but to be one of the first—I thought I could not do it. But what mercy did not do, judgment did; for the Lord was pleased to lay His hand heavily upon me, and with His correcting rod chastised me. And I did feel more of the displeasure of the Lord for my backwardness to His requirings than ever I did for my former transgression."

It was needful that the Lord should choose His own messenger, and also that the lesson of trustful submission should be learnt at any cost, till there should be a willingness to say—

"My soul the untried seas would dare,
Or sands of every waymark bare,
Should but Thy voice distinctly say,—
'Go forward, soul, there lies thy way.'"

But the Master whom Elizabeth Stirredge served is one who delighteth in mercy—who maketh sore that He may bind up, and woundeth that He may make whole. In her intense longing to be consciously restored to His favour, she now asked Him to exact from her whatever service He pleased, even if it should cause her to be hated of all men. It was on a Sunday morning that strength was given her to deliver a most solemn warning to those who, whilst still having the form of godliness, denied its power. Then a minister arose, beginning a sermon, remarkable for the heavenly power which accompanied it, with these words: "A living testimony is the God of heaven and earth raising up among the poor and contemptible ones, that shall stand over your heads for evermore." It would seem that the Holy Head of the Church saw fit on that occasion, in an unusual degree, to "take to Him His great power, and reign" manifestly over the assembly. "Oh! glory be to His everlasting name for evermore," writes Elizabeth Stirredge, "for His blessed appearance to us that day, who returned me a hundredfold into my bosom after all my unworthy consulting against the motions of the Spirit of so merciful and compassionate a Father, who, after He had corrected me, received me into favour again. Oh! the peace and comfort and consolation that I received from the Lord, was more to me than all the world and the friendship of it." She saw that it was in order to train her for His own service that the Lord had "tried her as silver is tried."

"There is no hearing of His gracious voice," she writes, "but by humbling under His mighty power, and subjecting the mind unto His will; *then* doth He make known His mind and will, and then blessed are they that hear His word and obey it. Oh! blessed be His eternal name for ever and for evermore, for all His mercies, and favours, and blessings, and good gifts, and tokens of His gracious love that He hath bestowed upon me ever since I have had a remembrance."

It is interesting to notice the frequency of passages of thanksgiving and praise in her journal. Doubtless she felt it was well worth while to endure the chastening which afterward yielded the peaceable fruits of righteousness; and in the very midst of her sorrows there were seasons when to her hungry soul bitter things were sweet; for she remarks: "I can truly say that my heart and soul delighted in judgment, though one woe was poured out after another."

In 1683 Elizabeth Stirredge found a cruel persecutor in Robert Cross, the clergyman of the parish of Chew Magna, Somerset, where her family had for some time resided. He was particularly enraged against her because, when visiting a neighbour who was ill, she had felt that a message from on high had been given her "to declare a day of mortality" to some who were in the room, which, she adds, accordingly fell out in two or three weeks' time. His anger increased when he found that she had spoken at the funeral of a young Friend when many of his congregation had been present. The following week another burial took place, and some officers were sent with a warrant to arrest any one who should venture to preach to the large company assembled. But no human authority could hinder the accomplishment of His will who has chosen the weak things to confound the mighty, and it was with a "spirit greatly enlarged by the power of the Lord, and drawn forth in love towards the people," that Elizabeth Stirredge addressed them; many faces were wet with tears, and not a few promised to amend their lives. By her side meanwhile was the officer with his warrant, which he unfolded with such trembling hands as to endanger tearing it. As he opened it he exclaimed, "Oh! that I had been twenty miles from my habitation, that I had not a hand in this work this day." When she was brought before the justices, one of them said: "You are an old prophetess; I know you of old." He had been present when, ten years earlier, she had been led to give an awful warning in their midst. To his violent threats she answered that she was not so much afraid of a prison as he imagined, though, if by sending her there he shortened her days, he would bring innocent blood upon his head. When he asked if she would keep the King's laws for the time to come, she said: "I do not know whether ever the Lord may open my mouth again, but if He do, I shall not keep silent." To the question whether a conventicle had not been held at the house of the deceased Friend, she made no reply until the justice said: "Why do you not answer? I knew she would be dumb." Then she told him that she was no informer, as Judas was when he betrayed his Master. The indignant justice, addressing the officer who had arrested her, said: "You silly fellow, you have let all the men go and have brought a troublesome woman here; you should have brought two or three rich men to have paid for all the conventicle." This officer, when asked what Elizabeth Stirredge had said at the burial ground, repeated some of her words, confessing that they had made his heart tremble, and that he had had no power to touch her until she had said all that she had in her heart to say. On hearing this another justice said: "Pray, neighbour Stirredge, go home about your business." She remarks that the honest confession of the man who had arrested her did her more good than her release. The clergyman, finding that few of his friends were willing to unite in his plans, sent to

Bristol for John Hellier, who was celebrated as a persecutor.

On a Sunday morning he and some others rushed into the quiet meeting at Chew Magna; they arrested those present in the King's name, set a guard over them, and then went to dine at the clergyman's house. During their two hours' absence, Elizabeth Stirredge says, "We had our solemn meeting peaceably, wherein we enjoyed the presence of the Lord to our souls' comfort, who never failed His children in a needful hour, but always gave them strength suitable to the day—everlasting honour be given to His holy name." Hellier and his companions returned from their feastings with faggots of wood, hatchet and axe, declaring that they were going to blow up the house and burn the Quakers; they especially threatened the children, though the treatment of others present was violent and brutal, and a mittimus was made committing them to Ilchester Gaol. When the clergyman was told that his work had been well done, he said that it would add years to his life. But very soon some of James Stirredge's neighbours entered his shop, exclaiming, "Now you may abide at home, for Mr. Cross is fallen down dead in the churchyard." Although apparently dead he slightly rallied for a few days, but reason did not return.

However there were others ready to carry out his schemes, and several Friends were confined in the common gaol with three felons who were under sentence of death. Some fellow-sufferers in the next room gave them, through the grating, two blankets, some chaff pillows, and a little straw. The weather was intensely cold, they had not even a stone to sit on, and the ground was damp. Here it was that most of the captives "*took their rest very sweetly.*" The black walls around them could not shut out Him in whose presence is fulness of joy, and they could say, as Richard Baxter did—

> " Heaven is my roof, earth is my floor ;
>   Thy love can keep me dry and warm ;
>   Christ and Thy bounty are my store ;
>   Thy angels guard me from all harm.
>
> " No walls or bars can keep Thee out ;
>   None can confine a holy soul ;
>   The streets of heaven it walks about,
>   None can its liberty control."

As Elizabeth Stirredge lay down in the prison she earnestly prayed that He, for whose sake they were suffering, would comfort them by the consciousness of His own presence. So abundantly did her Lord satisfy her soul with His goodness, that it was only the sight of her sleeping companions that prevented her from praising Him aloud. Several people gathered around the prison door when morning came to learn how many of the inmates were dead, and when they found that all were alive and well they exclaimed, " Surely they are the people of God if there are any ! " * A meeting was held in the prison. " The good presence of the Lord," writes Elizabeth Stirredge, " was with us, and filled our hearts with joy and gladness, insomuch that I was constrained to testify, in the hearing of many people, that we were so far from repenting our coming there, that we had great cause to give glory, honour, and praise to the Lord ; for His powerful presence was with

---

* The winter of 1683-4 was one of exceptional severity, when "Frost Fair" was held on the Thames.

us, and sanctified our afflictions, *and made the prison like a palace unto us.*" How long this imprisonment lasted we are not told. To Elizabeth Stirredge it appeared that even through these sufferings the Lord was honouring His steadfast servants by weaning them more and more from the world.

"Amongst all the blessed seasons of His love," she says, "*this was the greatest of mercies* unto me, for the God of heaven and earth was with us at our downlying and uprising. ... It seemed to me as if I had no habitation but the prison; *then* was the time for the Lord to reveal His secrets unto His children that He had tried and proved; ... for I cannot believe that he that is not true to a little will ever be made ruler over much. ... A great concern came upon me for many careless ones that had deprived themselves of that blessed benefit that our souls enjoyed with the Lord."

Most fervent were her prayers for such as these, as well as for the deliverance of her persecuted people; and whilst still with her husband in Ilchester Gaol, an assurance was afforded her that God would speedily proclaim liberty to the captives, who should declare His wondrous works that many might " hear and fear, and return unto Him." Night and day did she rejoice in her inmost soul at these glad tidings; and whilst wondering at the condescending goodness of God, she besought Him to preserve her in His fear for ever.

When the Friends were tried at the sessions of Browton, she fully believed that the time for their release was at hand, although a second jury had been called, whom the persecutors hoped would suit their purpose. When they returned to the court, the foreman was so much agitated that he could scarcely give the verdict, " Guilty of not going to church, but not guilty of a riot."

"Of not going to church," repeated the Bishop; "that is not the matter in hand. Guilty of a riot you mean." But other members of the jury said, "No, my lord; guilty of not going to church, but *not* guilty of a riot." Whilst the justices were dining, Elizabeth Stirredge says a great concern fell upon her to follow them. When the meal was over she addressed them, vindicating the innocency of the downtrodden Friends, and adding: "There is not a man here, nor any that draws breath in the open air, that shall escape the tribunal seat of God's divine justice," etc.

When, on the following morning, the prisoners were called into the court, they found that the Bishop had absented himself, and the behaviour of the judge was altogether changed. More than eighty persons were that day set free. "Men would ruin you, but God will not suffer them so to do," were the words of the Crier, who took an affectionate leave of the Friends whilst begging their forgiveness for the part he had to act in the court.

Elizabeth Stirredge spent the last fourteen years of her life at Hempstead, in Hertford. As her strength lessened, her labours of love were pretty nearly limited to that county, and were highly valued. When earnestly exhorting all to faithful dedication, she delighted to dwell on the wonders which "the great God of heaven and earth, that brought up the children of Israel out of Egypt's bondage," had wrought amongst her people as they put their trust in Him. To her children she writes: "Oh! what shall I say in the behalf of all the Lord's wondrous works that mine eyes have seen; but more especially the inward work of regeneration! Oh!

my tongue is not able to demonstrate the tenth part of it that He hath been pleased to bring me through!" She died in 1706, at the age of seventy-two.

Whilst pondering such lives as hers, shall we not remember that we have the same unwearied enemy to withstand, though now he may wield his weapons in a different way; and that still the only victory that overcometh the world is faith—that faith which can alone be exercised by the faithful follower of Christ? Therefore may it be the aim of each to give his whole heart to the Lord who died for him. The righteous in all ages could do *no more* than this, and why should any be content without steadfastly striving to do as much?

WILLIAM DEWSBURY: AND HIS WORDS OF COUNSEL AND CONSOLATION.

"Thy gifts are like Thyself
 Whom none divideth;
 Thy gifts are like Thy love
 Which evermore abideth;
 Thou givest all Thyself to him
 Who in Thy word confideth.

"Thy gifts are like Thyself;
 In round unending,
 The river from Thy throne
 Back to Thy throne is tending;
 And the Spirit that draws nigh Thee
 Is the Spirit of Thy sending."
      R. H. COOKE.

WILLIAM DEWSBURY; AND HIS WORDS OF COUNSEL AND CONSOLATION.

"A King shall reign and prosper; . . . and this is His name whereby He shall be called, THE LORD OUR RIGHTEOUSNESS."—Jer. xxiii. 5. 6.

"Whatsoever thou hungerest and thirstest for in His life, *thou art the heir* of it, and the Lord will satisfy thy hunger with His refreshings for His name's sake."—W. DEWSBURY.

THE early years of William Dewsbury's life were spent as a shepherd's boy at Allerthorpe, in Yorkshire. His father died when he was eight years old (probably about the year 1630), and whilst giving vent to his sorrow in tears, he seemed to hear a voice saying, "Weep for thyself, for thy father is well." Exceedingly powerful was the impression then made on his mind. "Deep sorrow seized on me," he says, "and I knew not what to do to get acquaintance with the God of my life." When about thirteen, having heard of some Puritans living near Leeds, his anxiety was great to meet with them, and he begged his friends to find him some employment in that neighbourhood, quite indifferent as to what it might be, if it only brought him amongst those who feared the living God, that he might "thus become acquainted with the God of his life." But disappointment awaited him; he found none who could tell him "what God had done for their souls in redeeming them from the body of sin. The flaming sword, the righteous law of God," he adds, "cried in me for a perfect fulfilling of the law, so that I could find no peace in that worship of God the world had set up." His health suffered from these spiritual conflicts, and he found it hard to carry out the requirements of the cloth-weaver to whom he was apprenticed, though doing his utmost to fulfil them.

When about twenty years of age he entered the parliamentary army. His biographer imagines that he had been led to believe that by this step he "would be going up to the help of the Lord against the mighty," and that "he was willing to give his body unto death, if by such a measure it had been possible to have freed his soul from sin. Failing to find the associates he longed for in the army, he visited Edinburgh, where, he tells us, that he only found formality; nor did his intercourse with Independents and Anabaptists bring light to his soul.

"Then," he says, "the Lord discovered to me that His love could not be attained to by anything I could do in any outward observances, and in all these turnings of my carnal wisdom, while seeking the kingdom of God *without*, thither the flaming sword turned to keep the way of the tree of life and fenced me from it. . . . Then my mind was *turned within* by the power of the Lord. . . . And the word of the Lord came unto me and said, 'Put up thy sword into its scabbard; if my kingdom were of this world then would My servants fight; knowest thou not that, if I needed, I could have twelve legions of angels from my Father?' which word enlightened my heart and discovered the mystery of iniquity; it showed the *kingdom of Christ to be within*, and that, its enemies being within and spiritual, my weapons against them should also be spiritual—the POWER OF GOD."

William Dewsbury now resumed his old occupation as a cloth-weaver, and whilst his hands were thus diligently employed, his mind was frequently engaged in waiting on the Lord. Carnal weapons were laid down, but spiritual weapons were wielded in a conflict more severe than any outward one; but being wielded in that faith, the trial of which is more precious than of gold that perisheth, he found that they were mighty through God to the pulling down of strongholds:—

> " He saw his sad estate, condemn'd to die;
>   Then terror seized his heart, and dark despair;
> But when to Calvary he turned his eye,
>   He saw the cross and read forgiveness there."

It was about this time that William Dewsbury married a young woman who, like himself, had passed through many inward conflicts. A few days after this event—when returning from a trial concerning some property, which had been unjustly decided against him—he was tempted with doubts about the propriety of his marriage, as it seemed likely that his wife might be brought to poverty. But having, through long and bitter experience, learnt how utterly powerless he was to overcome temptation in his own strength, he turned away from it to his Almighty Helper, with the prayer that the Lord " would make him content to be what He would have him to be." Immediately he felt in an overwhelming manner the presence of his Lord; so exceeding was the weight of glory that he thought that his mortal frame could not long endure it, and he heard as it were a voice saying, " Thou art mine; all in heaven and in earth is mine, and it is thine in Me; what I see good I will give unto thee, and unto thy wife and children."

It was at Synderhill Green, in Yorkshire, that William Dewsbury and George Fox first met. The latter writes in his Journal that, "At an evening meeting there, William Dewsbury and his wife came and heard me declare the Truth. And after the meeting, it being a moonlight night, I walked out into the field: and William Dewsbury and his wife came to me into the field, and confessed to the Truth and received it; and after some time he did testify to it." Sewel says:— "He was one who had already been *immediately* convinced, as George Fox himself was ; who coming to him found himself in unity with him."

In the year 1652, "The Word of the Lord," writes William Dewsbury, " came unto me, saying, 'The leaders of my people cause them to err, in drawing them from the light in their consciences (which leads to the anointing within, which the Father hath sent to be their Teacher, and would lead them into all Truth) to seek the kingdom of God in observances where it is not to be found. . . . Freely thou hast received, freely give and minister; and what I have made known unto thee in secret, declare thou openly." Six years earlier he had felt a strong inclination, as a public preacher of the Gospel, to invite others to come to the Saviour so precious to his own soul; but he was taught by the Holy Spirit that the time for this was not yet come, and that if he waited until a future year there would be a greater openness in the minds of the people to receive his message. Knowing the voice, and following his Shepherd, he quietly pursued his trade, holding meetings for worship in his own house and neighbourhood. But the "tongue of fire, when it came, made up abundantly for all delays."

This time of waiting was one of the most momentous

in his history; a time in which he learned what has been called "one of the hardest lessons we ever learn in our lives—that having Christ, we have salvation also; . . . having the fountain we have its issuing streams."* Like the Great Apostle he was led to cry, "Oh, wretched man that I am! who shall deliver me from the body of this death?" "As I was crying to the Lord," he says, "to free me from the burden I groaned under, the word of the Lord came to me, saying, 'My grace is sufficient for thee, I will deliver thee.' And by the power of this Word I was armed with patience to wait in His counsel; groaning under the body of sin in the day and hour of temptation, until it pleased the Lord to manifest His power to free me, which was in the year 1651." From his own sore and unavailing struggles with sin he was taught that the only victory which overcometh is faith in Him who "bare our sins in His own body on the tree, that we, being dead to sins, should live unto righteousness;" who is ever ready to take hold of shield and buckler, and stand up for our help. Knowing that neither height nor depth was able to separate him from the love of God, he did not fear to abandon himself fully, and trust himself wholly to His keeping, neither wishing nor daring to limit the Holy One of Israel in what He should do with him, exact from him, or *bestow upon him.* He believed that God "is able to do exceeding abundantly above all that we ask or think, according to *the power* that worketh in us," and according to his faith was it unto him. "Through the righteous law of the Spirit of Life in Christ Jesus," he writes, "I was

* Dr. Boardman.

and am made free from the body of sin and death; and through these great tribulations my garments are washed and made white in the blood of the Lamb, who hath led me through the gates of the city into the New Jerusalem, . . . where my soul now feeds upon the tree of life, which I had so long hungered and thirsted after, that stands in the paradise of God."

When on his death-bed, alluding to this period of his life, he said that he never afterwards "played the coward, but as joyfully entered prisons as palaces, telling his enemies to hold him there as long as they could; and in prison he sang praises to his God, and esteemed the bolts and locks put upon him as jewels."

> " Who that one moment hath the least descried Him,
> Dimly and faintly, hidden and afar,
> Doth not despise all excellence beside Him,—
> Pleasures and powers that are not and that are ? "

It is not the object of this brief sketch to give the details of the numerous hardships, sufferings, and long imprisonments which William Dewsbury willingly endured in the service of his Lord. Once he was confined in Warwick gaol for nearly eight years; and at a later period for six years more, when his little granddaughter, Mary Samm, though only twelve years old, left her father's home in Bedfordshire, that she might comfort him in his captivity; but a violent fever, most easily accounted for by the horrible state of the prison, soon ended her life. She appears to have been a child of remarkable character, and to have partaken of the religious fervour for which this era was specially distinguished. To her aunt, Joan Dewsbury, she said, "Not any one knows my exercise, but the Lord alone, that

I have gone through since I came to Warwick;" and the next day she remarked, "If this distemper do not abate, I must die: . . . O Lord, if it be Thy will take me to Thyself. . . . Oh! praises, praises be to Thy holy name for ever, in Thy will being done with me, to take me to Thyself, where I shall be in heavenly joy, yea, in heavenly joy for ever and for evermore." To her grandfather she said, "I do believe it is better for me to die than to live. . . . Dear grandfather, I do believe that thou wilt not stay long behind me when I am gone." "Dear granddaughter," he answered, "I shall come as fast as the Lord orders my way." To her mother she said, "My grandfather and I have lived here so comfortably together that I am fully satisfied as to my coming to him. . . . And, dear mother, I would have thee remember my love to my dear sisters, relations, and friends; and now I have nothing to do, I have nothing to do." "After which," William Dewsbury writes, "she asked what time of day it was. It being the latter part of the day, I said, 'The chimes are going four.' She said, 'I thought it had been more; I will see if I can have a little rest and sleep before I die.' And so she lay still, and had sweet rest and sleep; then she awoke without any murmuring, and in a quiet, peaceable frame of spirit, laid down her life in peace when the clock struck the fifth hour."

In 1657, when visiting Devon, William Dewsbury had a strong impression that a storm of persecution awaited him, and, at Torrington, he shortly afterwards had to encounter it. He was arrested, and brought before the mayor and other officers, some of whom he says, "were very cruel and wicked against the truth of

God, and did deal very rudely with me." But when, in reply to their questions, he "was free in the Lord to declare to them how he came to be a minister of Christ," one of the justices could not refrain from tears, and the clerk said, "If thou hadst spoken thus much before, there had not been this to be done." Yet he was sent back to lie on the bare floor of his prison. When next brought before them he tells us, "My God had pleaded my cause; . . . the man that said I should see his face no more until I was before the judge at Exeter, pulled the mittimus in pieces before my face, and said to me, 'Thou art free.' So did my God set me free."

The ministry of William Dewsbury is thus described in a little book by "that ancient servant of God, Thomas Thompson":—"O! how was my soul refreshed and the witness of God reached in my heart. I cannot express it with pen; I had never heard or felt the like before, . . . so that if all the world said Nay, I could have given my testimony that it was the everlasting truth of God."

It was said by one who intimately knew him, that "to the tender he was exceedingly tender," which those who have read his epistles can well believe. "Beloved are you," he writes, "that hunger and thirst after righteousness; for you are the children of the kingdom of my Father. With you my life is bound up." One of these pastoral letters has this superscription: "Let this go abroad amongst all the afflicted and wounded in spirit." The following passages are taken from it:—

"Oh, thou child of the morning, of the pure eternal day of the God of Israel, hearken no longer to the enemy who saith there hath none travelled where thou art travelling, neither drunk of the cup that thou art drinking. . . . In the word of the Lord God I declare unto thee, I drank the same cup, with my faithful friends, who are born of the royal seed; every one in their measure have travelled in the same path, and have endured the same temptations. . . . The Lord God, He will throw down the enemy of thy peace. . . . So in the power of His might, stay thy heart; and tread upon all doubts, fears, despairing thoughts, questionings, reasonings, musings, imaginations, and consultings. Arise over them all in the light of Christ. He will lead thee into the banqueting-house of the pleasure of our God. . . . And this shall be the portion of thy cup, if thou diligently hearken to the counsel of the Lord which calls thee to *trust in Him.* He will embrace thee in the arm of His love, and thou shalt praise His name for ever! God Almighty, in His light and life, raise up thy soul, . . . steadfastly to wait for His power to lead thee in the cross out of all unbelief."

At another time he writes:—

" Watch over one another, . . . opening your hearts in the free Spirit of God to them that are in need, that you may bear the image of your Heavenly Father, who relieveth the hungry, and easeth the burdened, and maketh glad in refreshing His, in the time of need. Even so be it with you in the name of the Lord."

Again, as an ambassador for Christ, constrained by His love, he writes:—

"*Oh, come away, come away, out of all your thoughts, desires, doubts and unbelief, which would turn you aside from the enjoyment of the love of God in Christ Jesus.* Let none stand afar off because of your littleness, lameness, blindness, weakness or infirmities, who cannot live at peace until you be healed by the blood of the Lamb. . . . Give up to the drawing spirit of life in the light of Jesus Christ. He will carry thee that canst not go, in the arms of His compassions; He will cause the lame to walk; and thou who art sensible of thy blindness to recover thy sight; yea, He will heal thee of all thy infirmities, who waitest in the light, to be ordered and guided as a little child by the washing and sanctifying

Spirit of the Lord Jesus. . . . Oh! what shall I say of the unspeakable love of God in Christ Jesus, the husband of the bride. Oh! ye sons of the glorious day, read and feel in the deep tastes of the unsearchable love, and you handmaids of glory, drink of the inexhaustible ocean which in the light flows over all opposition. This is the Son of the Father's love, . . . wounded for our transgressions! . . . Let all crowns be thrown down before Him, He alone shall have the glory. . . . Whatever the natural man most inclines to, when the temptations beset you . . . look up to the Lord and resist the devil with boldness in the first assault, and the Lord God will give you dominion over them, . . . that in the perfect freedom every particular individual may reign in the measure of the light, over every thought and desire that is contrary to the will of God. . . . You shall break down Satan under your feet, . . . and shall overcome through the blood of the Lamb; . . . and continually drink of the rivers of pleasure, the presence of the Lord Jesus, our Light, Life and Righteousness for ever. . . . Thou who lovest the light and bathest thy soul in the ocean of His inexpressible mercies, shall never more want the fresh springs of life. The Lord will keep thee in the safety of His power."

Early in 1688, William Dewsbury visited London. Very striking was a long sermon preached by him in Gracechurch Street Meeting, a few weeks before his death. He says:—". . . Become as a little child, humbled and slain as to thine own will. . . . Thou wilt not question, 'Shall I live a holy life?' but will give all that life thou hadst for that life which is hid with Christ in God. O! there is none come so far that ever miss of eternal life."

Some friends having met together in his room, about a week before his death (which took place at Warwick), he, notwithstanding his weakness, rose from his bed to address them. "Fear not, nor be discouraged," were some of his concluding words, "but go on in the name and power of the Lord; and bear a faithful and living testimony for Him in your day; and the Lord will prosper His work in your hand, and cause His Truth to flourish and spread abroad."

Of this faithful servant of God, may we not say that he, being dead, yet speaketh? Jesus Christ is the same yesterday, *to-day* and for ever. What William Dewsbury and other of the devoted early Friends were they were by the grace of God alone. And His promise to those who "chose the things that please Him, and take hold of His covenant," can be no less sure now than it was two centuries ago—"Even unto them will I give, in mine house and within my walls, a place and a name better than of sons and of daughters: I will give them an everlasting name, that shall not be cut off."

JOHN CROOK.

"I HAD long seriously thought with myself that besides a full and undoubted assent to the objects of faith, a vivifying savoury taste and relish of them was also necessary, that with stronger force and more powerful energy they might penetrate into the most inward centre of my heart, and there being most deeply fixed and rooted, govern my life."—JOHN HOWE.

JOHN CROOK.

"The longer I was in finding whom I sought,
The more earnestly I beheld Him being found."
BEDA.

" I WILL not serve thee, O Satan, but I will serve the Lord God of heaven and earth whatsoever I suffer, or becometh of me therefor." Such were the words vehemently spoken by John Crook, when a little lad of some nine or ten years. Although so young he was no stranger to spiritual conflict, and it was when on the point of yielding to a violent assault of the enemy that be became aware of a mightier power within him, strengthening him boldly to resist the temptation. But a child's heart is small for so sore a combat, and he soon felt frightened and bewildered at the "opposite strivings" in his soul; yet he at last thought that his deliverer could be no other than the Lord Himself. After this memorable hour he would, oftener than before, seek for some secret place to pray for help in the time of trial. Many were the tears shed at such seasons as he thought over his sins; for when alone he says that he was "sure to hear of his doings." Yet he found himself unable to keep the promises of amendment which he made, and his soul was often weighed down with sorrow.

When he saw the natural and healthy delight which other children took in play, he thought that they must be better than he, and that it was in anger that God was correcting him. Indeed, it would be strange if at so early an age he could have conceived that at times—

> "The sharpest discipline
> On best-loved child is laid."

His home, he tells us, was in the "North country," where he was born in 1618. At the age of ten or eleven he was sent to London and attended several schools there until he was about seventeen. He states that the family with whom he was "scoffed at all strictness," so he spent his spare time in solitude and prayer, weeping much from the sense given him of his sinfulness. During these years he did not — to quote his own words — "mind hearing of sermons, being little acquainted with any that frequented such exercises." However, when afterwards apprenticed in another London parish he often heard a Puritan minister; he read the Bible much, and other good books, and so earnestly poured out his soul in his prayers, that he afterwards found the family with whom he lived secretly listened to him.

"I remember," he writes, "when I was most fervent in my devotion, something in me would be still pulling me back, as it were, as if I would not wholly yet leave those evils I knew myself guilty of, but would gladly have them pardoned and forgiven, and yet would I continue in them, which at last made me conclude I was but a hypocrite. . . . I continued professing, and praying, and hearing, and reading, and yet I could not perceive any amendment in myself; but the same youthful vanities drew away my mind as before."

Working hard by day, and shortening his hours of rest, John Crook was often allowed by his master to attend religious lectures and meetings. Whilst listening to different sermons he felt himself "tossed up and down from hope to despair." He did not dare to tell any minister of his distress, lest he should be driven to despondency if another judged as hardly of his condition as he himself did. With his mind in this state one cannot greatly wonder at the singular determination he one day came to, nor doubt that the delivering hand of the Lord was then outstretched to help him.

"I resolved," he says, "one First-day afternoon, being full of trouble, to go that time which way I should be moved or inclined in spirit, whether it was up street or down street, east or west, north or south, without any predetermination or forecast, but only as I should be led." Wandering on in this strange manner he at length entered a church, where a young clergyman preached from the text, "He that walketh in darkness and hath no light, let him trust in the name of the Lord and stay upon his God," describing the state of one who, though fearing the Lord, yet walked in darkness, as if he had clearly known John Crook's distress, and was speaking to him only. Greatly was he comforted, and it was even with a rejoicing heart that he left the place; but this consolation did not last long, for he writes of trouble overtaking him "through some negligence and coldness which gendered to distrust and unbelief." He thus experienced that if the soul consciously withholds any allegiance from Christ it cannot at the same time exercise unwavering faith in His all-availing aid. When his misery was inexpressible, as he was one day sitting alone, he says:—

"On a sudden there arose in me a voice audible to the spiritual ear, 'Fear not, O thou tossed as with a tempest and not comforted, I will help thee; and although I have hid my face from thee for a moment, yet with everlasting loving kindness will I visit thee, and thou shalt be mine.' . . . I was filled with peace and joy like one overcome, and there shone such a light within me that, for the space of seven or eight days' time, I walked as one taken from the earth. I was so taken up in my mind as if I walked above the world, not taking notice (as it seemed to me) of any persons or things as I walked up and down London streets, I was so gathered up in the marvellous light of the Lord, and filled with a joyful dominion over all things in this world; in which time I saw plainly, and to my great comfort and satisfaction, that whatever the Lord would communicate and make known of Himself and the mysteries of His kingdom, He would do it in a way of purity and holiness. I saw then such a brightness in holiness, and such a beauty in an upright and pure righteous conversation and close circumspect walking with God in a holy life, . . that it sprang freely in me, that all religion and all profession without it were as nothing in comparison with this communion. For I remember, while I abode and walked in that light and glory which shone so clearly on my mind and spirit, there was not a wrong thought appearing or stirring in me but it vanished presently, finding no entertainment; my whole mind and soul was taken up with, and swallowed up of, that glorious light and satisfactory presence of the Lord thus manifested in me."

Long after, in a very beautiful letter of sympathy to Isaac Penington, John Crook says:—

"Be thou still in thy mind, and let the billows pass over, and wave upon wave; and fret not thyself because of them, neither be cast down as if it should never be otherwise with thee. The days of thy mourning shall be over, and the accuser will God cast out for ever. For therefore was I afflicted and not comforted, tempted and tried,—for this end —that I might know how to speak a word in due season unto those that are tempted and afflicted as I once was; as it was said unto me in that day when sorrow lay heavy upon me. By these things thou wilt come to live in the life of God, and joy in God, and glory in tribulation; when thou hast learnt in all conditions to be contented; and through trials and deep exercises is the way to learn this lesson."

Well had he learned how to give comfort and support. In the same letter he writes of his own sore sorrow until his eyes were opened to see his Saviour, and his heart to receive Him as his all in all.

"Sure I am," he says, "none can be so weary but He takes care of them; nor none so nigh fainting but He puts His arm under their heads; nor none can be so beset with enemies on every side but He will arise and scatter, because they are His own, and His life is the price of their redemption and His blood of their ransom. When they feel nothing stirring after Him, He yearns after them; so tender is the good Shepherd of His flock! *I can tell*, for I was as one that once went astray and wandered upon the barren mountains."*

At another time he writes:—

"Your God sees and beholds, and ponders all your trials. Leave them all with Him, and cast your care wholly upon Him; for by all your care not one cubit can be added to your stature. . . . He hath tempered your cups that you may say of the bitterest of them. *My God is the portion of this also.*"

Two or three years after the remarkable visitation already referred to, John Crook found that, whilst "dwelling more without and less within," winter had taken the place of spring-time in his soul, and little seemed left him but memories of that sunny season. Many questionings about worship and the ordinances arose in his mind, and he thought that he should be guilty of ingratitude to the God who had done such great things

---

* It is interesting to compare with this letter I. Penington's own words of encouragement to others in later years.—*Letters of Isaac Penington.* Nos. 3 and 73, etc.

for him, if he did not seek for the purest way of worshiping Him. At length he joined some persons whose views resembled those of the Independents, and who, like himself, hungered and thirsted after righteousness. A blessing rested on their meeting whilst, as John Crook says, they "were kept watchful and tender, with minds inwardly retired, and words few and savoury;" in which frame of spirit, he adds, they were preserved by communicating their experiences one to another week by week. But, as might be feared, after some years, this became a mere form; questions about their "Church state," etc., arose; the sweet fellowship was no longer felt, and at last they wholly gave up meeting together, and some of them completely cast off the yoke of Christ.

John Crook could not go so far astray as some of his acquaintances, and at times his unhappiness caused him to resume religious reading and prayer. Much as he was tempted to adopt dangerous principles, the strong sense of his former wonderful deliverances and consolations, as well as the taste he had had of joy unspeakable, made him sure that there was (to quote his own words) "a far better state and condition to be known and enjoyed in this world by walking with God in holiness and purity, than by all licentious and voluptuous living, or covetous gathering of riches together, to get a name in the earth." Neither could he doubt that obedience to what his conscience told him was the will of God would bring him more peace than any outward observances could do.

It was at this crisis, and when John Crook was about thirty-six years of age, that he was providentially led to the spot where William Dewsbury was preaching, though had he known that he was a Friend he would have avoided hearing him.

"His words," writes John Crook, "like spears, pierced and wounded my very heart; yet so as they seemed unto me as balm also. . . . I remember the very words that took the deepest impression upon me. . . . He implied the miserable life of such who, notwithstanding their religious duties or performances, had not peace nor quietness in their spirits, . . . and wanted a spiritual understanding of that which might then have been known of God within; which afterward I came to know and behold. . . . Whereby I understood certainly that it is *not an opinion, but Christ Jesus the power and arm of God*, who is the Saviour,—and that felt in the heart and kept dwelling there by faith; which differs as much from all notions in the head and brain as the living substance differeth from the picture or image of it. . . . I came to see what it was that had so long cried in me upon every occasion of serious inward retiring in my own spirit; so that I could say of Christ, 'A greater than Solomon is here.'"

With such wonderful power did the minister's words sink into his inmost soul, that to him it almost seemed as if one of the old Apostles had arisen from the dead. He saw now that the victory could be gained over the sinful desires which resisted what he calls those "little stirrings and movings after the living God." In allusion to this time he speaks of receiving the earnest of the inheritance and seal of the covenant. The light which now shone around him seemed to illumine the painful path he had trodden in the past. And as he called to mind the "sweet refreshings" granted him all along in the midst of his sorrowful pilgrimage — his frequent neglect of the tender wooings of his Lord, and ingratitude for His marvellous mercies — he was ready to cry out, "*What! was God so near me in a place I was not aware of?*" And with a heart melted and overcome by the great love of his Father in heaven, realising that he was a child, an heir—even a joint-heir with Christ—he felt that nothing less than his all would be an offering worthy of being laid upon the altar. Now were the mysteries of the kingdom more and more revealed to him by the Holy Spirit, and it must be from his own blessed experience that, long after, he could write for the encouragement of others :—

"Lift up your heads, you that have come, through and beyond all outward washings, unto the Lamb of God *that your robes may be washed white in His blood; that thereby you may overcome*, and then sit down in the kingdom with weary Abraham, thoroughly-tried Isaac, and wrestling Jacob."

"O, the many devices," he elsewhere writes, "that the enemy useth. . . . That now we had lain long enough in the furnace, and nothing was left but pure gold; but he lied unto us. . . . We saw we must into the furnace again, and there continue all the appointed time of the Father, till indeed we were changed into the state of the precious sons of Zion, truly comparable to fine gold."

Nothing had ever seemed harder to him than the having to "lay down all weapons and crowns" at the feet of his Lord. But when this had been done he found that the cravings of his soul were satisfied at last; and that it was refreshed by "a most sweet shower," while formerly it had only been revived by "summer drops ushering in a greater drought afterwards." Possessing now the riches of the glory of the inheritance of the saints, he says that a cry often arose in him that he might be kept poor and needy, in daily dependence upon his Saviour.

Soon he found that he was called to publish to his

fellow-men what he "had seen, felt and handled of the word and work of God." When he did not yield to this conviction, sorrow was once more his portion; and some other who was present would now and then speak the words which had been in his heart. But when he simply followed the guidance of the Holy Spirit a rich blessing followed, as he went from place to place, and he does not scruple to say that many were converted who lived and died in the faith.

" I found God," he adds, "always to be larger in His goodness than I could expect, and more abundant in pouring out of His Holy Spirit than my faith could reach, even to the breaking of my heart many a time before Him in secret. . . I was constrained to obey the Lord, taking no thought what I should say, but cried to Him often in my spirit, 'Keep me poor and needy, believing in Thee, and then I shall speak from Thee and for Thee.' . . From the deep sense I had of God's majesty and purity in my heart, I spoke of Him as I felt His requirings thereunto, and His rewards were in my bosom as a most sweet comforting cordial, that did lift up my spirit above all discomfortings from the enemies within and without, although both ofttimes sorely beset me. . . . I might swell a volume with this subject, but this is spoken to the glory of the Almighty God, that the all-sufficiency of His Holy Spirit may be trusted in and relied upon, as the only supplier of His ministers and people."

Strongly as his strong faith was tried, he found that the Comforter had truly come to abide with him for ever. "Never did the word of promise fail,"—though he was imprisoned ten times, was once tried for his life, and also incurred the sentence of premunire in 1662. John Crook had himself been a Justice of the Peace, and was well aware of the illegality of the sentence undergone by his companions and himself; and on being remanded to Newgate he wrote an account of the trial, calling it

"The Cry of the Innocent for Justice." This was printed, together with the Latin indictment, in which he pointed out many errors. One would fancy that his judges must have been taken aback by his bold words at the bar, and his accurate acquaintance with some details of law. When they told him that they had power to tender the Oath of Allegiance to any man, he answered, "Not to me upon this occasion, for I am brought hither as an offender already.... I am an Englishman, as I have said to you, and challenge the benefit of the laws of England, for by them is a better inheritance derived to me than that which I receive from my parents; for by the former the latter is preserved." It is not known for how long this imprisonment lasted.

In one of John Crook's epistles, written in Huntingdon Gaol, "To those that are in Outward Bonds, for the Testimony of a Good Conscience," he says:—

"Love nothing more than God, but let Him be thy whole delight, and count it thy glory and thy praise that thou hast anything to lose, or part withal, for His sake. Account His chains as thy ornaments, and His bonds as thy beauty, and His prison as thy palace.... You may not disparage your descent, nor undervalue the race from whence you sprang, for you are become companions with all that are born from above, who walk with God, and have fellowship with Christ through the Spirit, with all the royal race amongst the living."

Such animating words, from one himself in captivity, must have carried comfort to many hearts.

It is related of John Crook that, in consequence of preaching in a meeting, he was brought, late one evening, before a Justice of the Peace, who, being a kind-hearted man, was unwilling to send him at such an unseasonable hour to the distant prison; so bidding the informer to call in the morning, he offered the offender a night's lodging, telling him, however, that, as he had company at the time, he could only spare him a room which one of his servants said was haunted. But haunted chambers had no horrors for John Crook, abiding, as he did, under the shadow of the Almighty, and he gratefully accepted the invitation. Not only was he courteously and hospitably treated, but opportunity was also cordially given him for religious conversation with the company, in which they were much interested. The Justice kindly showed him to his room, which was at the end of a long gallery, and he slept soundly until about one o'clock. When he awoke, it was with even an unusually vivid sense of that love which passeth knowledge—of being compassed with God's favour as with a shield. Just then a rattling noise was heard in the gallery, and when, after a time, it ceased, a shrill voice three times said, "You are damned." Quite undismayed, John Crook answered, "Thou art a liar, for I feel this moment the sweet peace of my God flow through my heart." All was again quiet, and he soon fell asleep, not waking until his usual hour for rising. Finding that his host had not yet come down stairs he took a walk in the garden, where he was soon joined by a manservant who, falling on his knees before him, said that it was he who had tried to alarm him in the night, and that his heart had been pierced by John Crook's words. He asked for his forgiveness and his prayers, going on to say that for some years past some of his fellow-servants and himself had been in the habit of secretly robbing their master, and, in order to facilitate their plans of concealment, had pretended that one part of the house was haunted. At John Crook's request he confessed his crime to the Justice, who pardoned him, and also gave his guest a dismission from the informer. The impression made that night on the servant's heart was a lasting one, and we learn that he afterwards became "an honest Friend and a minister."

Four years after John Crook had become a Friend, a general Yearly Meeting was held at his house in Bedfordshire. It continued for three days, and was attended by George Fox and so many others from most parts of England that the inns in the neighbouring towns were crowded. John Crook has been described as an Apollos, eloquent and mighty in the Scriptures, and by his ministry not a few were turned from darkness to light; but no detailed record of this is left by himself, nor does he give many particulars of the persecutions which he suffered. He speaks of how God has made prisons to be schools for prophets and nurseries for divines. "He that would build high," he remarks, "must lay the foundation deep. There is flesh as well as spirit in us all, as the Apostle saith of himself (Gal. v. 17). Therefore there is great need of a strict watch to be kept 'with all keeping,' as the margin hath it, lest we forget there is going out of the truth by many unsuspected ways as well as goings in by Christ, the door." Again, in his eighty-second year he writes:—

"Perfecting holiness in the fear of the Lord is so far from lessening or undervaluing the merits or conquests of Christ, that it manifests Him to be able to save to the uttermost all that come to God by Him. Not only from the guilt, but from the filth of sin also, . . . to make them whole every whit as He did those He cured outwardly."

Writing of faith, he says:—

"By this living faith Abel saw beyond the sacrifice unto Christ, the first-born of God, beyond the firstling of the flock which he offered; and therefore God had respect unto Abel and his offering. But God rejected Cain and his offering, though he had faith to believe it to be his duty, yet sticking to the form, *and not flying on the wing of faith unto Christ, the One Offering*, he missed the mark. . . . We believe that faith to be only true and saving that flies over self-righteousness as well as filthiness into the fountain of life in Christ, which faith hath nothing of man in it, but is as the breath of life by which the soul lives: not a bare assent to the truth of a proposition in the natural understanding, but the soul's cleaving unto God out of a naturalness between Christ and the soul, . . . *not looking at its doing to commend it, but God's love and bounty in Christ, the Light, to receive it; and yet holiness is its delight*, and it can no more live out of it than the fish upon the dry land. This faith keeps the mind pure, the heart clean, through the sprinkling of the heart from an evil conscience by the blood of Jesus."

Not long before his death he writes:—

"Let not your outward concerns prevent your religious meetings and services on the week-days, lest the earthly spirit get up again; but meet in the faith that *you shall meet with God*, whether you hear words spoken outwardly or not."

On another occasion his words are:—

"Watch, my dear friends, against the enemy of your souls that you may be preserved out of all its snares. . . . So will you delight to meet together, and the joy of the Lord will be your strength, and you thereby encouraged to wait upon Him. And His sweet and precious presence will be manifest among you, unto the building up and strengthening one another in the faith of the Gospel, unto the vanquishing of your fears and scattering of all your enemies."

During the latter part of his life, John Crook suffered from intense bodily pain, which he bore with the utmost patience, though he admitted that, did he not feel the upholding arm of his Lord, he could not live under it. In a letter of advice to his grandchildren, he bids them embrace afflictions as messengers of peace. He counsels them to "wait upon God," adding—"I have had more comfort and confirmation in the truth in my inward retiring in silence, than from all words I have heard from others, though I have often been refreshed by them also." Although at so advanced an age his spiritual strength seemed unabated; yet he rejoiced at the thought that he would soon be free from his suffering state. "Many of the ancients," he would say, "are gone to their long home; they step away before me, and I, that would go, cannot. Well, it will be my turn soon also!" About three weeks before his death he very emphatically said, "Truth must prosper, Truth shall prosper; but a trying time must first come, and afterwards the glory of the Lord shall more and more appear."

He died in 1699 at Hertford, which had been his home for many years. He leaves no details of his domestic life, but we learn from Sewel that some of his children were a cause of sorrow. He might well say that he had been afflicted from his youth up— yet he also knew what it was to glory in tribulation. Growing from one degree of grace to another, it was granted to him to experience, by faith, that the child of God is translated out of darkness into the kingdom of God's dear Son; and the eyes of his understanding were enlightened to know the riches of the glory of this inheritance. Realising as he did the exceeding greatness of God's power to those who believe, neither persecution nor pain, neither grief nor care, could debar him from the privileges of his citizenship in the New Jerusalem. For—to borrow the words of George Fox— "All that dwell within the grace, and truth, and faith, and Spirit, which are the wall of the city, dwell within that city," even the Zion of the Holy One of Israel.

STEPHEN CRISP AND HIS SERMONS.

"PURIFYING their hearts by faith" (Acts xv. 9.)

"FAITH is the victory over that which separated man from God; by which faith he hath access to God. And it is faith that sanctifies."—GEORGE FOX'S DOCTRINALS.

STEPHEN CRISP AND HIS SERMONS.

Christ hath bound Himself to those that trust in Him.
STEPHEN CRISP.

It was in the spring of 1655, when Stephen Crisp was about twenty-seven years of age, that the town of Colchester where he lived was visited by James Parnel * (a minister of the newly-formed Society of Friends), whose labours had already been greatly blessed although he had not attained his twentieth year. Night and day had Stephen Crisp been longing that the Gospel might be preached in his native place by one of the Quakers; for though he knew that they were a hated and persecuted people, he was well aware that this had often been the lot of the faithful followers of Christ. He had, however, heard that one of their

---

* James Parnel's services at Colchester, where many thousands came to hear him, are thus described by Stephen Crisp:—" He spent that week in preaching, praying, exhorting, turning the minds of all sorts of professors to the light of Jesus, which did search their hearts and show their thoughts, that they might believe therein. . . . Many did believe, and others were hardened. . . . To one that struck him with a great staff, saying, 'There, take that for Jesus Christ's sake,' he returned this answer, 'Friend, I do receive it for Jesus Christ's sake.'" He died about a year later, the victim of most cruel treatment coupled with close confinement, in Colchester Castle. "Here I die innocently," he said; "I have seen great things. Do not hold me; but let me go." During his captivity he writes:—" Be willing that self shall suffer for the truth, and not the truth for self, . . . all you that would follow the Lamb to the land of rest, and through many trials you will wax strong and bold and confident in your God; *for God is not known what a God He is until the time of trial.*"

tenets was, that sin might be overcome in this life, which at first seemed to him to be a great mistake; for —although from childhood he had taken a deep interest in religion, and as he grew older had made acquaintance with several sects, and had tried many ordinances and many means in the hope of finding a power which would give him this victory—"his arm," he says, " was never so long as to reach thereunto."

Conscious of his own good abilities, his knowledge of the sacred Scriptures, and of numerous old philosophical works, Stephen Crisp thought to find an easy task in opposing the argument of the young stranger. He sought an opportunity for conversing with him, and on the same day attended a meeting in which he heard him preach the Gospel in the name and authority of the Lord. This he at once felt that no wisdom of his own could withstand. His reason also was convinced, and with all its strength he was soon to uphold and valiantly defend the views he had heretofore resisted. Hard indeed would it be for him thus to humble himself, but "a strong hand gave the stroke." " I was," he writes, "hewn down like a tall cedar. . . . The eye that would see everything was now so blind that I could see nothing certainly but my present undone and miserable estate." In touching words he tries in his journal to give some idea of the exceeding sorrow of those days, in which all trust in his own righteousness was swept away. In a sermon preached in after years, he speaks of how it is God's will that "man shall be beholden to Christ for all. . . . One would think it should be no great matter," he adds, "for men to lay aside their own works and duties and submit to Christ;

but I tell you it is very hard, and I found it hard myself." But He who has made the depths of the sea a way for the ransomed to pass over, did not suffer His servant to sink into utter despair. Dawn followed the midnight darkness, and he felt a hope that this was the forerunner of that light in which the blood of Jesus Christ is known to cleanse from all sin. Weary of warfare, watching and waiting, he yearned to know how long this discipline must be borne; yet he had to learn that even this seemingly lawful desire must, like all other self-will, be laid down.

"Upon a time," he writes, "being weary of my own thoughts in the meeting of God's people, I thought none was like me, and that it was but in vain to sit there with such a wandering mind as mine was, while, though I laboured to stay it, I yet could not as I would. At length I thought to go forth, and as I was going the Lord thundered through me, saying, '*That which is weary must die*,' so I turned to my seat, and waited in the belief of God for the death of that part which was weary of the work of God. . . . And the cross was laid upon me, and I bore it; and as I became willing to take it up I found it to be to me that thing which I had sought from my childhood, even the power of God. . . . Oh! the secret joy that was in me in the midst of all my conflicts and combats; . . . manifold and daily were God's deliverances made known to me beyond all recount or remembrance of man. . . . And as the word of wisdom began to spring in me, and the knowledge of God grew, so I became a counsellor of them that were tempted in like manner as I had been, yet was kept so low that I waited to receive counsel daily from God, and from those that were over me in the Lord."

About four years after James Parnel's memorable visit to Colchester, Stephen Crisp felt the love of God so shed abroad in his heart as to reach to the whole human family, with earnest desires to share with them the unsearchable riches of Christ. He longed to be made willing to go whithersoever the Lord should send him, and he thought that he was so; but when the call came to leave wife and children, father and mother, in order to visit the churches in Scotland, he found to his cost that "all enemies were not slain indeed." Gladly would he have excused himself on the easily-found plea of unfitness, or the care of his family and his service in Colchester Meeting. He spoke of the subject to some faithful ministers and elders, half hoping that they would dissuade him from the performance of this serious and arduous work; but, on the contrary, they urged him to be faithful in the carrying out of what seemed to him to be his Master's will. This he made up his mind to do, and, notwithstanding the sore trial of his wife's opposition, he was kept in much patience and quietness. As winter drew near he would fain have put off his mission until the summer, but was taught that the Lord's time must be his time; he wished to go by sea, but had also to learn that the Lord's way must be his way, and the event proved that there were fields for him to work in before reaching Scotland.

His faithful obedience was rewarded; and, as he was more conscious of his Lord's presence than usual, his journey became "joyful," though he was "weak, poor, and low." He writes: "In every place my testimony was owned, and divers were convinced of the everlasting Truth: then I marvelled and said, 'Lord, the glory alone belongs to Thee; for Thou hast wrought wonders for Thy name's sake.'" With a heart constantly warmed by the constraining love of Christ, he cheerfully pursued his winter pilgrimage on foot, undaunted by many dangers and difficulties caused by the movements of the English and Scottish armies.

He had indulged the hope that, this mission accomplished, he should be able to come back to his family and quietly follow his calling; but the Lord had need of him to "be His witness unto all men of what he had seen and heard." He was now about thirty-two years of age, and the remaining half of his life was chiefly spent in active and devoted labour for his Saviour; and probably, George Fox alone excepted, no one person was so active in caring for the newly-formed churches as Stephen Crisp. A few days' rest at home and a short visit to the Friends in London were followed by another northern journey, in describing which he alludes to many being turned from darkness to light, and writes of peace and joy as his portion, yet also of trials within and without; the latter including his imprisonment when two hundred miles away from home. But the Lord, to whom he looked for aid, suffered not his faith to fail: yet, as he writes of finding the work every day more and more weighty, can we wonder at his owning that the hope of being freed from bearing these burdens lived long in him; but, simply and faithfully doing his Master's bidding, he learnt to love the labour more and more—until "nothing in the world seemed so desirable to him as the spreading and publishing of His truth through the earth;" and a longing filled his heart to be "as serviceable as possible in his generation, and to keep himself clear of the blood of all men."

Fearless and forcible were his words of warning; several of the remarkable sermons preached by him in

London were taken down in shorthand by one of his hearers, who was not a Friend, in one of which we read the following passage :—

"How strangely doth the man talk, will some say, concerning the Christian religion! The Christian religion is all England over; go to any meeting in London and they will tell you they are Christians. I would to God they were; that is the worst I wish for them all! . . . There are many in this city urging this very command of loving God with all their hearts, and their neighbours as themselves, as fervently as I can do, or anybody else; and yet they will tell you in the next breath that no man in London or in the world can do this." At another time he says, "Is not man God's creature, and cannot He new-make him and cast sin out of him? If you say sin is rooted deeply in man, I say so too; yet not so deeply rooted but Christ Jesus is entered so deeply into the root of the nature of man that He hath received power to destroy the devil and his works, and to recover and redeem man into his primitive nature of righteousness and holiness; or else that is false to say that He is able to save to the uttermost all that come unto God by Him. We must throw away the Bible if we say that it is impossible for God to deliver man out of sin." And again, "When you hear truth preached, there is an assent and agreement with it in your minds; but when a command comes to be obeyed, and a cross to be taken up, and self-denial to be shown, or some interest of trade lies in the way, let truth go where it will, you must follow your interest."

In a sermon preached a few weeks before his death the following remarks occur :—

"What if I live in the truth, that will not serve *thee;* and if I be a holy man, that will not sanctify *thee;* thou must hearken to truth's speaking in *thyself;* thou mayst hear it speaking it in thy own heart before thou be an hour older. . . . If thou join with the truth and with that which is holy, thou shalt have strength and ability to withstand temptation, and overcome it; and (I may speak with reverence) *Christ hath bound Himself to those that trust in Him.*"

In 1663 Stephen Crisp crossed the sea on the first of the thirteen or fourteen visits made by him to the Low Countries, where a large number of persons had adopted the views of Friends; a mission which "the unknown land and unknown speech" did not hinder him from accomplishing in cheerfulness and peace, and with very satisfactory results. When, four years later, he again felt himself called to go there, he found "a dear companion" in Josiah Coale, who died in the following year at the age of thirty-five—his constitution prematurely worn out by the persecutions and hardships which he had encountered in the service of his Lord, though long borne up by a manly, dauntless spirit. Many were the seals set to Josiah Coale's ministry, which was of a very striking character; and most ardent were the longings implanted in his soul for the prosperity of Zion. Just before his death, when George Fox and other of his friends were around him, he said, "Be faithful to God and have a single eye to His glory, and seek nothing for self, . . . then will ye have the reward of life. For my part, I have walked in faithfulness with the Lord. And I have peace with Him. . . . His majesty is with me, and His crown of life is upon me. So, mind, my love to all friends." Soon afterwards he said to Stephen Crisp, "Dear heart, keep low in the holy seed of God, and that will be thy crown for ever."

It was in this year (1688) that Stephen Crisp was imprisoned in Ipswich Gaol, where one of his valuable pamphlets—"The Plain Pathway Opened"—was written. Sewel speaks of visiting him during his captivity, which he bore with great cheerfulness and perfect contentment. His ministry had been the means of considerably adding to the number of Friends in Ipswich, to whom he still preached the Gospel when they came to see him. A heaven-taught submission to all God's will concerning him had altogether taken away the sting from sorrow: bearing the image and superscription of Christ, fervent were his desires to "render unto God the things which are God's." Thus, when he writes in his journal of the presence and power of the Lord leading him from country to country, he adds, "I was obedient thereunto, not of constraint now, but of a willing mind; counting His service a freedom, feeling myself freed from the cares of this life, having now learnt to cast all my care upon Him."

In the spring of 1669 he went, at the bidding of his Lord, from the Netherlands into Germany, apparently at the peril of life itself while passing through lands shrouded with the darkness of superstition. Yet he was safely led on to Griesham, near Worms, where he found a blessed service in speaking a word in season to many who were weary with long years of trial for conscience' sake: amongst these sufferers, others, whilst hearing him, were constrained to cast in their lot. One cause of trouble was the imposition by the Palsgrave of an annual fine on Friends for their meetings, which they did not feel it right to pay, and three times the amount was taken from them, an exaction borne with "great joy and gladness," for the sake of Him who had suffered for them, and who now called them to display His banner because of the truth. Stephen Crisp had an interview with the prince, in consequence of which the persecution was checked.

The following extracts from his sermons show the value set by Stephen Crisp on spiritual worship and Christ's own teaching:—

"Travail on in the faith committed to you and you will be more than conquerors; . . . your communion will not be in words and doctrine and principles of faith; but your communion will be with God the Father and His Son Jesus Christ. And so in all your meetings together the joy of the Lord will be your strength, and the joy of His great salvation your covering; and He will manifest His gracious presence with you. . . . When a man or woman comes to this pass, that they have nothing to rely upon but the Lord, then they will meet together to wait upon the Lord. And this was the first ground or motive of our setting up meetings; and I would to God that this was the use which all that come to them would make of them. . . . People cry out of the bondage of corruption and of their subjection to sin and Satan. I would they were in earnest! . . . Now, if there was but a willingness in every one of us freely to give up ourselves to that Power that created us, to obey His will, I am sure there is never a man or woman among us shall long be without a knowledge of it. . . . But methinks the sound and noise of flesh and blood grows loud here: I would be subject to God, but I would not have Him cross my interest and deprive me of that I love and thirst after. . . . If you will become spiritual, and partake of spiritual blessings and benefits, I would advise you to turn from all kinds of reasonings that come from the pit of darkness. . . . As many as are led by the Spirit of God they are the children of God. . . . *As soon as a man comes to adhere and join to the power of God revealed in his soul, he sees the coming of the kingdom of God;* he sees it at a distance: he saith within himself, ' I will follow my Captain—I will become subject to the kingdom of Christ.'"

Again, in relating the manner in which he and his friends had grown in grace, he says:—

"Jesus was our great minister; we waited upon Him and trusted in Him, and He taught us Himself. He hath ministered to us at our silent and quiet waiting upon Him those things that were convenient for us: He hath not only given strong meat unto men, but hath ministered of the sincere milk of His word unto babes that lived in sincerity and self-denial, loving God above all things. And He taught and conducted us in our way—this way of simplicity—until our understandings came to be opened; until our souls came to be prepared to receive the mysteries of His kingdom."

In a sermon preached a few days before his death he says:—

"*When a man or woman come to a meeting to worship God and hear the word spoken outwardly, they must pray for something that may be for their good:* Lord, give me something that may support my soul, and something that may withstand temptation. People should have their minds thus exercised; and they should think upon the name of the Lord according to their particular necessity; they should pour out their supplication to the Lord: this is such worship as God looks for, and such as He likes and is pleased with. He will deliver those that thus pray to Him out of temptations, so that they shall not prevail over them. . . . There are none of you, if you would not be lazy and idle, but you might be delivered every day and have experience in your own souls that, when the devil comes and tempts, the Lord is at hand to deliver you by His grace and power."

As Stephen Crisp was now able to preach in the Dutch language, the meetings which he had in Holland were very large. "Some present," he says, "were overcome by the power of Truth, and the overflowings of my cup made many glad." A journey to the southern part of Germany, where a great weight rested on his spirit on account of the wickedness which abounded, was followed by a visit to the Friends at Frederickstadt, whom he found assembled at their week-day meeting, and with whom he was refreshed in the "fellowship of the blessed

Gospel." Meetings especially for the public were also held here, and were very striking ones, leaving a marked effect on the city, which was afterwards visited by William Penn and Thomas Green. Before leaving, Stephen Crisp and his companion Peter Hendricks, met with their friends early in the morning in order to commit one another to the Lord's care; while the final parting, "in that love which never changeth," took place at the river Jider, without the city.

In 1673 some six months were spent by Stephen Crisp in London and its suburbs, where the Lord, he says, was with him daily, to the rejoicing of thousands. "By His mighty power were many strong oaks bowed, and many subtle foxes prevented of their prey, and many wandering sheep brought home who had for a long time longed to find the fold of rest; and whose souls will ever live with my soul in His covenant, to praise Him world without end."

During his next mission across the seas he was led to visit "that hard-hearted city of Emblen," where a physician named Hasbert kindly welcomed him, and even offered his house for the holding of meetings, which were well attended. After a while some "were drawn in love to God" to assemble there regularly for spiritual worship. When this became known in the city sore persecution followed; a few were banished sixteen or twenty times, spoiled of their goods, stripped of their clothing, and then driven through the streets to the ships in which they were to sail: "all which and *much more*," Stephen Crisp remarks, " by the mighty power of the Lord, did these innocent, harmless lambs, bear with great patience and quietness, and were not dismayed at all these cruelties." A year or two later, on revisiting Emblen, he found that a fine of £25 was to be imposed on any one who should harbour a Friend in his house; whereupon he wrote a book of "sharp and sound judgment" to the rulers and priests, who, however, did him no harm; for, as he says, *a power came over them.* Nor was the labour lost, for we find that the Friends soon had more freedom than formerly. At other times also he successfully pleaded on behalf of his persecuted brethren : yet throughout his constantly-renewed Continental labours no hand was laid on him, although, when in the Spanish Netherlands, he could but boldly bear his testimony against the grievous idolatry which weighed down his soul.

During an exceptional winter, chiefly spent at his home at Colchester, he visited the neighbouring meetings—a service accomplished with "much joy of spirit," in spite of severe bodily suffering :—

"I found," he remarks, "that though through long experience my senses were exercised in the service of God, yet I had nothing to trust to how and after what manner to minister to the Church of Christ, but the same that led me in the beginning—even the immediate operation of the power that brings forth, in the will of God, all things suitable to their season, that the glory might be to the power, *and the praises to Him that gives it, for ever and for evermore.*"

Again, he speaks of returning to his

"place in the will of God, remaining as a servant *waiting to be ordered,* and as a child waiting to be fed."

To the faithful disciples who thus wait will not service of some sort be surely sent by the Lord of the harvest ?

Two or three years later Stephen Crisp's life was threatened by a severe fever. God's presence was with him, and into His hands he confidingly committed himself. When he found that his days were to be prolonged he was well content that it should be so, as the one aim of his soul was still to spend them "in the service of God and His dear people." Apparently no meeting of Friends in the nation was left unvisited by him.

In 1682, a sense having been given him of the suffering soon to befall the Friends who lived in Norwich, we find that at harvest-time it came into his heart, "in the dear love of God," to go again to that city. Whilst worshipping with his brethren there on the day of his arrival, the assembly was violently broken up by a justice and constables, accompanied by a rabble who seemed ready to devour their prey. Stephen Crisp and about a dozen other Friends were brought before the mayor and aldermen. Strong was their desire to get him into their hands, but the Lord, who had hitherto helped him, taught him how to avoid the snares carefully set for him. As his mission to the city was still unfulfilled, it would seem that the possibility of any other course than that of performing it did not enter his mind. Such simple faith and obedience could not be exercised in vain : in the two large meetings which were held, the power of the Almighty wonderfully prevailed over all. It must have been consoling to him at this time to foresee that, though the fiery trial of persecution was about to test the faith of the Friends here, they would be ready for the conflict, being clad in the impenetrable armour of God.

In the following year his beloved wife died. Although

for thirty-five years her love and sympathy and trust in Christ had been invaluable to him, grace was given in his time of need to murmur not, but rather to praise the holy name of Him who had made her what she was.

His second marriage took place in 1685, and was a most happy union, though of short duration, for he writes:—"It proved the pleasure of the Lord to try me, whether I could part with, as well as receive, this great mercy. . . . She was a woman beyond many, excelling in the virtues of the Holy Spirit with which she was baptised." Heavy as was the stroke, it was softened by the share which was granted him of the joy into which she had entered.

In 1689, in spite of many bodily infirmities, Stephen Crisp, in company with other Friends, successfully appealed to Parliament for the suspension of those laws which had caused sore suffering for conscience' sake. After describing the failing of his physical power, he says: "Yet the word of the Lord lived in my heart, to the refreshing of my soul, and the souls of many tender babes that lived and grew up by the milk of it." This may be imagined by those who read the remarkable sermons delivered by him during the last few years of his life.

"There are," he says, "many that have had some taste of great joy, and apprehensions of heavenly things to which they have not attained, *but they know what they are waiting upon God for;*—not that they may have a little joy which passeth through them, but come to have that joy and tranquillity which will accompany them in all their doings, and their whole conversation. . . . Let such go on and follow that guide by whom they have been directed, and they shall at last come—through the Divine Spirit of Grace which they followed, and so closely cleaved to—to have an entrance administered to them abundantly into the salvation of God."

And again:—

"If it be truth which you own, *then exercise faith upon it*—and whatsoever sin or temptation assaults you, say, I shall overcome in the name of the Lord Jehovah; I shall bring thee under, be what lust, passion, or corruption, soever thou wilt; *in the name of the Lord* I shall overcome thee."

In the spring of 1692 it would seem that he felt the time of his departure was at hand. When taking what proved to be his last farewell of Colchester (before leaving for London), in several meetings his ministry both to Friends and others, was of an especially powerful and exceedingly striking character; he spoke of his wish to be clear of the blood of all men, and of his belief that he was so. In private families, also, the Lord did indeed make manifest the savour of His knowledge by this good and faithful servant, whose mouth was "as a well of life" to many a thirsty soul.

A few days before his death he preached at considerable length at Devonshire House. When increasingly ill, he was carried in a litter to Wandsworth (where in early life he had acted as usher in the celebrated college of Richard Scoryer). To George Whitehead he said: "I have a full assurance of my peace with God in Christ Jesus.* . . . Dear George, I can live and die with thee." When George Whitehead was parting from him, he asked: "Dear Stephen, wouldst thou anything

---

* "For my part," was Stephen Crisp's strong language in one of his sermons—"for my part, my tongue shall as soon drop out of my mouth as oppose the doctrine of being justified by faith in Christ; but let me tell you this may be misapplied. . . . If a man hope to be saved by Christ, he must be ruled by Him. It is contrary to all manner of reason that the devil should rule a man, and Christ be his Saviour."

to friends?" But his life's labour was ended now, and he only answered: "Remember my dear love in Christ Jesus to all friends." He died at Wandsworth, 1692, aged sixty-four years, and was buried at the Friends' burial-ground, Bunhill Fields.

A fitting conclusion to this short sketch of Stephen Crisp and his Sermons will be found in his own words in Gracechurch Street Meeting:—" I have considered many a time that *there are many brave men and women in this age that might have been eminent witnesses of God in this world, and borne their testimony to His truth, but their faith has been weak and ineffectual;* they have discovered their unbelieving hearts, and have joined with the common herd of the world, because they thought such great things could never be done; that the kingdom of Satan could never be pulled down and destroyed, and the kingdom of Christ set up within us. But I would hope better things of you, things that accompany salvation; and that He that hath begun a good work in you will carry it on to perfection."

JOHN BANKS.

"I saw with wonderful clearness that we attain this nearness of access, not by struggling and agonising with ourselves, . . . but simply by ceasing to struggle and yielding the mind *in trust* to the care of the living Saviour."—J. M. WASHBURN.

JOHN BANKS.

"The soul that has made the discovery that it has nothing in itself to hang upon, must hang upon Christ."—DEAN GOULBURN.

ON a winter's day in 1711 William Penn, whilst walking, cane in hand, up and down his room, dictated the preface to the autobiography of John Banks, whom he had known for more than forty-four years, and had, in the earlier days of his own religious experience, found to be "an ordinance of strength to his soul." This proved to be the last of Penn's literary productions. "Friendly reader," he begins, "the labours of the servants of God ought always to be precious in the eyes of His people; and for that reason the very fragments of their services are not to be lost, but gathered up for edification. I hope it will please God to make them effectual to such as seriously peruse them, since we have always found the Lord ready to second the services of His worthies upon the spirits of their readers."

John Banks was an only child, and was born in Cumberland, in 1637. When only fourteen, after having made a good use of seven years' schooling, he was employed as a schoolmaster. A year later, in order to please his father and some others, he held a weekly service in a chapel-of-ease near Pardshaw, where he read the Bible and homily, sang psalms, and engaged in prayer. One of his hearers, a highly educated but very intemperate man, told him that he read well, and added that he ought to use a form of prayer, offering to send him one in a letter. No sooner had John Banks made use of this form, than his mind was powerfully impressed with the Apostle Paul's description of the Gospel which he had to preach: "I neither received it of man, neither was I taught it but by the revelation of Jesus Christ." He knew that he had had this form from man, and, moreover, from "one of the worst of many." The end of the year was approaching when payment for his services would be due to him, but he felt that he must refuse it, and that he could not read in the chapel again.

"The dread of the Lord fell upon me," he writes, "with which I was so struck to my very heart that I said to myself, I shall never pray on this wise. And it opened in me, 'Go to the meeting of people in scorn called Quakers.' It pleased the Lord to reach my heart by His great power and pure living Spirit, in the blessed appearance and revelation thereof, in and through Jesus Christ; whereby I received the knowledge of God, and the way of His blessed Truth, by myself alone in the field before I ever heard any one called a Quaker preach. But the first day I went to one of their meetings the Lord's power so seized upon me that I was made to cry out in the bitterness of my soul, in a true sight and sense of my sins that appeared exceeding sinful; and at evening, as I was going to the meeting, I was smitten to the ground with the weight of God's judgments for sin and iniquity, and I was taken up by two friends. Oh! the godly sorrow that did take hold of me that night in the meeting."

There was very little ministry, but a Friend, who deeply sympathised with John Banks' distress, was, as he said, "made willing" to read a paper suitable to his condition, and which was the means of giving him a little comfort. He now remembered that in the midst of his wildness and dissipation he had felt a restraining influence in his heart, but had given no heed to it.

"I did not," he continues, "only come to be convinced, by the living appearance of the Lord Jesus, of the evil of sin; but by taking true heed thereunto, I came, by one little after another, to be sensible of the work thereof in my soul in order to tame and subject the wild nature in me, and to cleanse me inwardly from sin that I might be changed and converted." If the upward progress was slow, it was also sure; the few following years of his life might not have been marked ones in his outward history, yet doubtless they were of deep importance in the sight of One who, having redeemed him to God by His blood, had entered his tempest-tossed heart, and with

> "An unseen hand was building
> For Himself a temple there."

During this time he found neither body nor mind adapted to the "good and lawful" calling of a schoolmaster; he therefore diligently employed himself in learning his father's trade and a little husbandry, living meanwhile with his parents, who, to his great joy, he says, also "came to receive the Truth." Some of his spare hours were spent alone in the woods, in great distress from the temptation to despair. But the enemy was not suffered to uproot the grain of faith which had been sown in his soul; and there were times when, conscious of the sincerity and steadfastness of his endeavours to follow his Saviour, he could even ask himself, "What evil have I done since I received the truth?"

"So," he writes, "through faith in the power of God, and shining of His glorious light in my heart, I overcame the wicked one; through a diligent waiting in the light and keeping close unto the power of God; in waiting upon Him in silence among His people, in which exercise my soul delighted. And oh! the days and nights of comfort and divine consolation we were made partakers of together; and the faithful and true in heart to God, still are; but it was through various trials and deep exercises."

Although he does not yet appear to have fully learnt that lesson—which seems very hard to learn—of trusting in the Lord with *all* the heart, he thus reveals the secret of his steady growth in grace: "Now the way of my prosperity in the Truth and work of God, I always found was by being faithful to the Lord in what He in the light manifested." After a while his mind became more peaceful, and he began to hope that the sore struggles with temptation were nearly ended; and great was his grief when he found that, though much evil had been overcome through the grace of God, Satan was well able to invent new allurements when old ones failed to ensnare. Yet, after all, victory must have been nearer than he imagined, for he was becoming

"Confident in self-despair."

"Oh!" he says, "how was I humbled and bowed, and laid low. Wherefore I took up a godly resolution in His fear—'*I will rely upon* THE SUFFICIENCY OF THY POWER, *O Lord, for ever.*' So that about six years after I had received the Truth by believing therein, I came to be settled in the power of God, and made weighty in my spirit thereby." Thus did he

"——— venture his all upon Christ,
And prove Him sufficient for all."

He refers to the conflict he passed through with regard to his call to the ministry, but adds, "The Lord through His power wrought me into a willing witness."

When he was about twenty-five, he was one day attending a meeting of Friends held out of doors near Coldbeck, when the congregation was disturbed by a justice of the peace, who rudely rode into the group as they sat on the ground. John Banks—who had knelt down to pray—he violently struck with his horsewhip over the head and face, and then ordered his man to take him away, which he did by dragging him down the hill by his hair. John Banks and three others were committed to the common gaol, where they were kept for several days without bread or water, because they could not pay the covetous gaoler eightpence for every meal. He told them he would see how long they could live without food; and as he would not allow their friends to provide them even with straw, their only bed was the prison window, where, on the cold stones of the thick wall, there was room for one person to rest at a time. Their companions are thus described by John Banks: "A Bedlam man and four with him, for theft; two notorious thieves called Redhead and Wadelad; two moss-troopers for stealing cattle; and one woman for murdering her own child." Bad enough such company must have been at the best; but soon these poor creatures were freely supplied with drink by some visitors, and began to abuse their quiet fellow-prisoners. "In that very close, nasty place," writes John Banks, "we were nearly stifled." Happily, the next day they were removed to another room. The hearts of his parents must have yearned for their only child; but in loving letters he begs them to be "not at all dejected or cast down concerning him, but rather to rejoice. All I desire is that you may come to say in truth, 'The will of the Lord be done!'" He gives no details of outward sufferings to add to their sorrow, but says that he "*never knew the worth of a prison so much before, to his sweet peace and inward consolation.*"

About twelve months after his release he married; and four years later went with John Wilkinson to visit the south and west of England, being made truly willing, he says, "to leave his dear wife and sweet child, and go forth in the power and spirit of the Lord Jesus." They had many meetings on their way; in Yorkshire these were held daily, and were eagerly flocked to by the people, who seemed to be hungering and thirsting after righteousness. To his wife John Banks writes:—

"The further I am separated from thee, the nearer thou art unto me, even in that which neither length of time nor distance of place shall ever be able to wear out, or bring a decay upon. . . . I have been under weakness of body, but nevertheless I have faith to believe that whatsoever the Lord is pleased to exercise me in, He will give me ability to perform, and nothing shall be able to hinder it; and therefore I am truly content whatsoever the Lord may suffer to come upon me, because hitherto He has kept me, to His praise and glory, and to my sweet peace. . . . The Truth of our God prospers; yea, very many are coming in to partake thereof; for people in many places are weary of the hireling priests and dead formal worship, and their assemblies grow thin."

Meanwhile his wife was brought low by a violent fever, but writes that she is "well in mind and spirit, and desires nothing more than that the will of the Lord might be done in all things." The meetings held during this journey were very large and satisfactory, and John Banks says that to his companion and himself it had been a sweet and precious time.

It was his desire that a brief record of what he was enabled to do and suffer for Christ should "be kept on record *for the good of ages to come.*" Twelve times he crossed the sea to Ireland, often in violent storms. After he had sailed a few times from Whitehaven, the sailors became very anxious to have him for a passenger, saying, "You are the happiest man that ever we have carried over sea, for we get well along when we have you."

He lived to see large results from his diligent and protracted labours in eight meetings in his native country, as well as in many other places. Besides perils by sea, he tells us he had to brave " robbers by land, bad spirits, and false brethren; . . . yet, through the strength of the power of God was well kept and preserved in and through all, *having faith therein.*"

At the time of John Banks' second visit to Ireland he thought it would be right to attend the half-year's meeting at Dublin, so two days before it began he went to Whitehaven, from which port he wished to sail. Finding that the wind was from a very unfavourable quarter, his wife and friends asked him to delay his voyage; but his simple answer was that he "could not," and that he might rely upon Him who had power to command the winds and seas. He then spoke to the captain of a vessel and requested some of his crew, if the wind became fair before the morning, to call for him, which they said they would do with all their heart, though apparently thinking it very unlikely that such a speedy change would take place. But at daybreak the hasty summons came, and the passage was an excellent one, enabling him to attend the "glorious, heavenly meeting," to which his heart had been drawn. He felt himself especially directed to hold a meeting on the following Sabbath at Wicklow, where great excitement was caused by the announcement that an English Quaker was going to preach, a priest having done all in his power to prejudice the people against him. The landlady of the inn where he and his friends lodged begged him to walk to the carpenter's shop, where the meeting was to be held, by a back way, as a guard of musketeers was waiting at the Cross to take him; but this he did not think it right to do, saying that he had a testimony to bear for the Lord in the town. Almost as soon as he had taken his seat in the meeting, a sergeant, with no warrant but his halberd, followed by the musketeers, ordered John Banks to appear before the Governor, who had been persuaded by the priest and his wife to imprison him and his friends. A crowd of people followed them to the gaoler's house, which he allowed them to enter although they occupied two or three rooms. "So," writes John Banks, "in a little time my mouth was opened in the demonstration of the Power and Spirit of God, and I preached the way of life and salvation to the people in and through Jesus Christ His Son, . . . and it was a blessed, heavenly day for the Lord and His truth; for His heavenly power broke in upon many, and several were convinced." When the priest told the sheriff of this gathering, he added that he feared unless something was done all the town of Wicklow would be Quakers, and then there would be "no abiding for him." Notwithstanding many threats, the gaoler allowed John Banks so much liberty that almost every hour during the three days of his imprisonment he had religious conversation with numerous visitors, whose hearts the Lord had opened to receive his message; and he was only sorry that he had not a longer time to spend with them. When told by the Governor that he should be set free if he would never again hold meetings at Wicklow, he declined making this promise, but added: "If I do—if thou hast power so to do—thou mayest put me in prison again, and I believe I shall be as willing to suffer then as now." They separated in a friendly manner, the Governor saying, "God keep you in that mind you are now in, for I think you are in a good mind." Whilst John Banks' parting words were, "Governor, fare thee well; and in so saying, I truly desire the welfare both of thy body and soul."

Before leaving Ireland, believing that his work at Wicklow was not altogether accomplished he returned there for a short time, and in spite of threatened opposition " a blessed, heavenly, peaceable meeting " was held. When, two years later, he re-visited this town and called on some Friends who were confined in the prison, the gaoler said: " Oh, Mr. Banks, are you come again ? I think you need not to have come any more, for you did your business the last time you were here, for I think all the town of Wicklow will be Quakers." After two years more had passed away a still greater change was manifest; the Governor was in England. The soldiers had left, the priest was dead, a Friends' meeting was established, and, as John Banks says, " Truth still prospering." In company with some others he had arranged to hold a meeting in a private house at Antrim, but being prevented by a constable, he addressed the people in the street, "turning their minds to the teachings of God in themselves." The angry constable made violent efforts to drag him out of the assembly, but all power to do this seemed to be taken from him, and also from another strong man whose services he had enlisted. A violent storm was also raging, the rain pouring down in torrents, "a true figure," remarks John Banks, "of their raging, persecuting spirit." Yet he could describe it as "a glorious, heavenly day, for the Lord's power and heavenly presence in a most glorious manner did appear in the meeting, and many were convinced and several came clearly forth to own and receive the Truth."

In 1675, John Banks attended the Yearly Meeting, which he says that he would not have missed for all that could be mentioned in the world. "Oh, how near," he writes, " were we to the Lord, and how near and dear one unto another, in the unity and fellowship of His holy, blessed Spirit! . . . Oh, that I may never be forgetful of this glorious, heavenly, and living appearance of our God with us, by His glorious power and life-giving presence." He tells his wife that he cannot fix the time for his return home, his secret cry to the Lord being, "Let me not go hence except Thy presence go with me;" and expresses his hope that already his labour of love had been blessed to many souls.

The following year, John Watson being his companion, "many precious and heavenly meetings" were held in Ireland, although, as John Banks says, they were sometimes disturbed by " the *collegianists* rushing in like so many wild beasts out of the forest; but the Lord," he adds, " by His power is pleased so to tame them that they are put to silence and made to be quiet. . . . Our travels and exercises are made very comfortable unto us, because of the power and presence of the Lord that doth go along with us." In the same letter he writes: "Oh, that Friends might live in love . . . and whatsoever would arise among them that in anywise tends to the breaking of their heavenly unity and brotherly fellowship, and sowing of dissension in the churches of Christ, may be nipped in the bud." Afterwards his friend and himself crossed in a half-decked boat to Scotland, and we read again of "the Lord's power chaining down some wild scoffing people at two heavenly meetings" in Edinburgh. Before reaching Douglas the travellers lost their way on a mountain amidst snow and ice, not reaching that town until late at night; but the meeting held on the morrow with the few Friends there was a time of refreshing from the presence of the Lord.

Soon after returning home John Banks suffered from a severe pain in the shoulder, which, passing into the arm and hand, increased until they became powerless, and began to wither, and medical aid proved unavailing. At length, one night whilst asleep, he " saw in a vision " that he was with George Fox, and thought that he said to him, "George, my faith is such that if thou seest it thy way to lay thy hand upon my shoulder, my arm and hand shall be made whole throughout." For two days and nights his mind was strongly impressed with the idea this was, as he says, "a true vision," and that he ought to go to George Fox, who was then at his home at Swarthmoor Hall. We certainly cannot wonder that he felt this to be " a near and great trial of faith," and that it was only after much mental conflict that he became willing to do so. After attending Swarthmoor Meeting he went to George Fox's residence, and, in a private interview with him in the hall, told him of his dream and the impressions which had followed, at the same time showing him his arm. They walked together silently for a short time, until George Fox turned, and laying his hand on John Banks's shoulder, said, "The Lord heal thee within and without." Then they parted, John Banks going to Marsh Grange, the residence of Thomas Lower (a son-in-law of George Fox); as he sat down to supper he suddenly discovered that he had raised his hand and was using it, just as he had been wont to do three months before; at which he says, his "heart was broken into true tenderness before the Lord." The recovery was complete, and on the following day he went to his home. George Fox's remark when they next met was, "John, thou mended? Thou mended?" and on receiving an affirmative answer he added, "Give God the glory," which indeed John Banks was most ready to do.*

During a meeting held at a private house at Dullverton, an informer entered and took down the names of some who were present, being also very abusive to them, and to John Banks who was preaching; and who was constrained to pause and say, "Friends and people, mark and take notice of the end of that wicked man." After a while this man was hung for the murder of his wife.

---

* "Every true revival of religion," remarks a recent writer, "is unquestionably accompanied by signs which are not trickery. . . . No great popular return to the habits of piety has ever been made, from the time of the Apostles, without the occurrence of certain spiritual phenomena which cannot be entirely explained away by any theory."

In 1678 John Banks was, he says, "moved to give forth a paper" which was read in many meetings; a few extracts follow. After alluding to Christ as "the High Priest of our profession, our Redeemer and Restorer, our Captain, King and Lawgiver, our everlasting Shepherd," he continues:—

"Although many have been our trials both within and without, the Lord by the all-sufficiency of His power hath wrought our deliverance through all, as we have and do rely upon the same, so that sorrow and sighing is fled away, and everlasting joy is sprung up; even because of the glory and excellency of the power which hath appeared, which is all-sufficient to work our deliverance, and that throughout; *yea endless joy is known here, endless comfort and satisfaction.*"

The following counsel seems peculiarly fitting from one who himself faithfully followed his Saviour :—

"Oh the great care and tenderness God hath had over us. Did He call us to be idle? Surely nay. Did He give a gift unto male and female that we should hide it in the earth, and not improve it to His glory? Oh, nay. Hath He done what He hath done for us that we should always be as children, when we could neither speak nor act as a man? Oh! surely nay. But that we should grow up in stature and strength before Him as perfect men and women in Christ Jesus our Holy Head; that we might all work together as a body fitly framed in holy order in His heavenly power and pure spirit."

In the same epistle we find this practical advice :—

"Be faithful, careful and diligent in keeping of all your meetings in the name and power of God; and cry not, 'My business, my business, my work and my trade,' when you should go and wait upon, worship, and do service for the Lord; but mind the *Lord's* work and business, and live by faith, and you will have time enough to do your own."

About this time John Banks felt that "a peculiar

testimony" was given him against what he calls "a wicked spirit of separation," for he believed that Satan, being envious of the progress of the Redeemer's cause, was doing all the mischief in his power; in one, especially, of the thirteen meetings held by Christopher Story and himself on their way to the Yearly Meeting in 1679, John Banks was conscious of this separating spirit, but felt that it was "chained down by the Lord's eternal power." In a letter to his wife, from London, he remarks that such was the glorious appearance of the Lord in all the meetings that his heart broke into tenderness whenever he thought of it. In the week preceding the Yearly Meeting peaceful and quiet meetings, apparently held for the public, were attended by thousands.

Of a different character were the meetings he afterwards had in the country, which greatly distressed him on account—he says—of "that spirit of separation and division which had sown much discord in the Church of Christ." In Wiltshire this trial reached its height. One night, sleep having entirely forsaken him, Christopher Story, who was still his companion, kindly said to him in the early morning: "Dear heart, John, I think thou hast slept none this night; I will get up and walk abroad, perhaps thou mayst get some sleep." "I find no want of sleep," was the reply; "howbeit, thou mayst do as thou hast a mind." Soon John Banks fell asleep, to dream vividly that he was desperately attacked by "three ugly, serpentine creatures;" having overcome two of them, he was in the midst of a terrible struggle with the last when he awoke. He was sure that this vision indicated the opposition which would rise against him that day, and earnestly prayed for help. As he sat in meeting three men entered, who were strangers to him, yet he felt certain that bitter enmity dwelt in their hearts; and, as soon as he was constrained to speak against the evils of dissension, their hatred very plainly showed itself, by their angry countenances, and by their rising in turn with the intention of interrupting him; one of them even went up to him whilst he was still preaching, and unbuttoned his coat, apparently with the intention of resorting to physical force. But, as John Banks says, the Lord's power was too strong for them; they silently resumed their seats, and we read that in the latter part of the meeting "Friends were abundantly comforted in the living enjoyment of the Lord's power and presence."

Early in 1684, John Banks having conscientiously refused to pay tithes (amounting to 6s. 8d.), he was committed to prison at Carlisle, where he was confined for nearly seven years! But he was still the Lord's freeman, and, constrained by His love, he preached from the casement window, notwithstanding the menaces of clergymen, mayor, aldermen, and gaoler, of which he says that he took no notice, knowing the furthest of all their power, and trusting in the all-sufficient power of God. Very violent measures were frequently taken by the cruel gaoler to put a stop to his ministry; but he writes that the Lord never failed in the hour of greatest need to bear up the spirits of his fellow-sufferers and himself "with courage and boldness, for His own name's sake, whose power and presence was daily manifested amongst them." John Banks' words to the infuriated mayor were: "The Lord has opened my mouth, and thou and all the assistance thou canst get in the city cannot stop it;" and, in reply to a further threat, he added: "I neither fear thee, thy gag, nor the common gaol." He told the gaoler that wherever he might place him, as a prisoner he would be subject to him, but in what the Lord required he was resolved in His name to stand faithful; that he well remembered the joy and gladness with which, twenty years before, he had been enabled to suffer confinement in the common gaol; "and thinkest thou, man," he continued, "I will play the coward now after so many years?" He confesses that not only was his body bruised, but that his health was also impaired by the gaoler's cruelty; yet he can tell his wife in a letter that he has "great peace and soul-satisfaction from the Lord," and, as usual, writes in a strain of praise and thanksgiving:—

> "Happy is he whose heart
> Hath found the art
> To turn his double pains to double praise."

One summer evening the gaoler carried out his threat of confining John Banks (who had been ill for some time) in the common gaol, which was so crowded already that there was barely space enough for the prisoners either to sit or lie. The first night John Banks and a Friend who was with him could only find a place close by a disgusting sink, the gaoler tauntingly telling them that if there was not room for them by it they might go into it. Here they were kept for a fortnight, and "the Lord," writes John Banks, "was pleased to make it as a place of healing and restoration of strength to me; . . . endless praises, honour, and glory be given to

Him." Even whilst detained in this dark gaol, he employed himself, as was his wont throughout his long imprisonment, by working at his trade of glover and fellmonger. He was at length liberated in 1691, by William III.'s Act of Grace.

> "How came it, men of faith, to pass
>   That ye were mighty handed?
> How brake ye down the gates of brass,
>   When few of ye were banded?"
>
> .   .   .   .
>
> "How was it, lovers of your kind,
>   Though ye were mocked and hated,
> That ye with clear and patient mind
>   Truth's holy doctrine stated?
> In God, as in an ark, ye kept;
>   Around—and not above you—swept
> The flood, till it abated."

After his liberation he took a religious journey to the west of England, where the Lord so blessed his labours that his "travel and exercises were made very sweet, comfortable, and delightsome." Writing to his wife and children from Bristol, he remarks: "it is such who are kept near unto the Lord in their hearts, who are kept living, fresh and tender; for He causes His heavenly rain and gracious showers to be poured forth upon them, that they are made to say, 'What manner of love is this, wherewithal the Lord our God hath loved us? And what manner of persons ought we to be?'"

In the latter part of this year John Banks' wife died. Although this was "the greatest trial that ever he had met with, above anything here below," the Saviour in whom he steadfastly trusted bore up his sorrowing soul. The warmth of his domestic affections, the earnestness of his solicitude for the welfare of his children, his loving interest in his servants, are abundantly shown in his numerous letters. His travels in England alone were very extensive, and a list of even the counties he visited would be too long for insertion here; allusion has already been made to Scotland, and to his repeated voyages to Ireland; his labours were greatly blessed to many, some of whom became in their turn faithful ministers of the Gospel.

In 1696 John Banks thought it would be best for him to take up his residence in Somersetshire, and in the same year he entered into his second marriage. During the last fourteen years of his life he often attended the London Yearly Meeting, and undertook many religious visits to the north and west of England, even reaching the Land's End. In the latter part of his life he suffered intensely from gout: at one time his neighbours were called to the house, as it was thought that his last hour was come; but to his own soul these words were applied: "Thou must not go hence yet, thou hast not wholly finished the work of thy day," and from that moment he felt no doubt that he should rally for a time. Great as was his affliction, even more than he was able to express, so also, he says, the tender care of his Heavenly Father was beyond utterance. As he was now unable to walk to the Meeting-house, the Friends assembled for worship at his house, where the Monthly Meetings were also held. The following extract is from a letter written to an intimate friend:—

"That which makes us near and dear one to another is because we have received certain knowledge that we are the children of one Father, begotten again to a lively hope in and through Jesus Christ by the quickening of His eternal power and spirit. . . . As a tender Father He has always waited and still doth, to be good and gracious unto us, with His gracious rain and heavenly dew that He hath caused many times to fall upon us, that we might grow from one stature and degree of holiness to another—that so we might come to answer the good end wherefore He has done what He has for us, and made us a people that were none. . . . Happy are they who can say in truth that what they do in His service, they do it as unto the Lord."

Two months before his death, although very weak, he attended several neighbouring meetings—at a Monthly Meeting preaching for an hour and a half to the comfort and refreshment of his friends, whom he earnestly exhorted to a holy zeal for God. His exhaustion was such that he needed the support of two men when going to his lodging; but he was very cheerful, and on the evening of the same day had a meeting to which the public were invited.

Notwithstanding the extreme pain which accompanied his last illness, the praise of the Lord was still his theme. "I am rich," he said, "in faith towards God, and my cup is full of the love of God." He addressed a young man who came to take leave of him with these words: "The Lord be with thee, and I desire thee in His love to give up in obedience to the workings of the Spirit of God in thy heart, and then He will do great and glorious things for thee." The intimate friend who gives the account of his last illness, adds: "He earnestly desired Friends to keep in the unity of the Spirit which is the bond of perfect peace, with a great deal more good advice and counsel; it being attended with the living divine power of the great eternal God, which did tender the hearts of many of those present. . . . . He said that he had nothing to do but to die; he was very sensible to the last, and after all his violent pains he had a very easy passage, and so died in peace the 6th of the Eighth Month, 1710, aged seventy-three years, and is undoubtedly entered into the rest which remains for the people of God. The Lord prepare us all more and more for the entering thereinto, through the alone merits and mediation of His dear Son, our Lord and Saviour Jesus Christ."

In lives which, like John Banks', have steadily shed light around them, because they reflected the rays of the Sun of Righteousness, we see the blessed result of an implicit trust in Christ, and a full and practical belief in the direct and perceptible influence of the Holy Spirit. "Where people," writes John Woolman, "are divinely gathered into a holy fellowship and faithfully abide under the influence of that Spirit which leads into all truth—they are the light of the world. Now holding this profession to me hath appeared weighty, even beyond what I can fully express."

HUMPHRY SMITH AND HIS WORKS.

"TEACH us that as we yield ourselves wholly to be possessed of the Spirit in which Thou didst bear the Cross, we shall be made partakers of the power and the blessing, to which the Cross alone gives access."—ANDREW MURRAY'S "ABIDE IN CHRIST."

HUMPHRY SMITH AND HIS WORKS.

" With Himself God hath and doth daily gratify me with a full reward for all, and all manner of, my manifold trials and daily sufferings and exercises. . . . Him alone it was that my broken heart was by the power of His constraining love resolved to follow for ever, even through the greatest difficulties, and the hardest straits, trials, and hardships, with all manner of outward and inward sufferings, that might be permitted to happen unto, or fall upon, any one of the children of men."—*From a letter of Humphry Smith, dated from Winchester Prison.*

WHEN Benjamin Seebohm was preaching in Bradford Meeting-house in 1846, for the last time before his departure for America, he said that " his mind had been carried back to a period two hundred years ago, when a remarkable visitation was extended to the people of this land, and men were stirred up to exhibit Christianity to the world, not only in its fundamental principles, but in its practical bearings. . . . They were much misunderstood by those who, however sincere in adopting their own modes of serving God, failed to draw the same inferences from the same premises. But believing they were under the influence of the Spirit, that it was God Himself who spake to them in the secret of their hearts, they dared not say to Him, 'Thus far shalt Thou go and no further.' . . . The life-blood of religion circulated not only at the heart, but to the extremity of every limb ! . . . What tenderness to good lay at the root of their supposed stubbornness and obstinacy : *that which is pliable to good will be unbending to evil.*"

In the long roll of names which might be given from the earliest ages to the time of the Apostle Paul, and from the time of the Apostle Paul to the present day, as exemplifying the words last quoted, it would not perhaps be easy to find a more appropriate one than that of Humphry Smith. Yet little can be learnt about his life, except from allusions now and then made by himself in his works. These, whilst still in manuscript, he had bound, and presented the volume to his only son, writing within it the request that it should be kept safe and unspoiled, so that his love to Christ might be read and seen in years to come. After his death this book was published " by Andrew Sowle, at the Crooked Billet, in Holloway Lane, near Shoreditch, in 1683." Only a very few copies are, it is said, extant.

Some idea of his holy constancy may be formed from the following words of his own, written whilst a prisoner: " How can I but declare the Lord's wondrous works, and proclaim His Name wherever I come, and confess Him before men, though I should suffer much more prisoning, dungeon, and whipping, than I have done? Surely His Name I will declare in the world . . . His love constraineth me, whose name is called Jesus, who hath and doth save from sin, for whose Name's sake I have been brought before Rulers, haled and beat out of the synagogues, numbered amongst transgressors, tried at Assizes as an offender, yet there denied the liberty of a murderer; being six times imprisoned, twice stripped naked and whipped with rods, and since put into Bridewell. Once put into and kept long in a dungeon for praying; often abused in prison; sometimes near death; in trials often, in perils often, in loss of goods, in daily reproaches, and in that which has been greater than all these things; and yet I have been preserved unto this day by the power of Him who is the Light, and the only Son of God, to whom be eternal glory."

The place and date of Humphry Smith's birth are both unknown; but in his address "To all Parents of Children" we find a few particulars of his early days, when the first words in the Bible which, to use his own forcible expression, "pierced his heart, and remained as a thing printed and sealed there from the pure love of God," were "He hath filled the hungry with good things, and the rich hath He sent empty away." His young heart was often tender and contrite, and his parents' utter absence of sympathy, and the harshness of his father, which, even at the age of six or seven, was the almost daily cause of bitter crying, must have been a crushing trial.

When reviewing his infancy, he apparently feels that their conduct had provoked him to wrath, and had thus hindered him from coming to Christ. Yet this could not have been altogether the case, for he writes of God's love being exceeding prevalent upon his little tender heart, and much more precious than anything of the world. Sometimes," he adds, "as I went along the way when it came into my heart, then should I even as it were beg and cry, with many tears, and had boldness towards God, as towards a familiar friend, though much in submission and fear." And when, poor child, he could find a place where he felt quite sure of being undiscovered, he would kneel in earnest prayer; and he remarks that he certainly never knew the kingdom of righteousness and peace until he again became as he was when a little child.

If a companion struck him, he would not return the blow; and great was his distress when, notwithstanding his earnest pleadings, he was compelled by his father or mother to destroy a puppy or kitten. "My life in me was grieved to do it," he says, "which may be a warning to all parents that they be not the cause of the hardening of their children's hearts, for that which hardens the heart separates from God, who is love, and from Christ, who comes to save the life." Some advice follows on moderation in discipline, which is more applicable to Humphry Smith's day than to our own, which has, perhaps not altogether inappropriately, been called "the age of obedient parents."

Even at this early period he strongly disapproved of infant baptism. When he one day said that he should never stand as a godfather, some one who was present swore at him, and replied that it was a pity any one did it for him. He answered, "I matter not if they had never done it, for I was never the better."

When he was about ten years old his father sometimes sent him to market to sell things, and he was often called a fool and dunce because he would not ask more for the goods than the price at which he was allowed to sell them. He often got into trouble from his parents' dislike to his quietness and silence when his heart was filled with serious thoughts. Now and then he would retire to the woods to wait on God.

"Sometimes the love of God," he says, "would break through me, and His Word would make my heart soft, and I felt the same then which now is my life; and now I know that those that wait on the Lord renew their strength; and though it is written the Lord was weary of the people's sacrifices and with their words, yet it was never written in

Scripture that the Lord was weary of those that waited upon Him. . . . The Lord hath not left Himself without a witness in every conscience; and it is Christ that is given for a witness (Isa. lv. 4). And certainly my soul was cut off from the Life when I was forced from hearing His voice in me; and I do affirm in the presence of the Lord God that I had not returned out of the degenerate state which I was hurried into, if I had not waited in and been obedient unto the light of Christ which was in me of a child. . . . The Lord knoweth I was long not knowing where to find the rest, having been hurried and led out from my true Guide."

When, at the request of others, he used a form of prayer every night, instead of praying for himself, he found that he had exchanged "a honeycomb for dry heath." It seems to have been God's will that he should fully learn, from personal experience, the utter emptiness of a form of religion when altogether unaccompanied by its living power. The clergymen to whom his attention was now turned must have been perfectly unfit for their responsible office, or he could not have had cause to make this strong assertion—"As true as the Lord God of heaven and earth liveth, priests and sermons did me more harm than all the rest." In his paper entitled, "A Word to all Professors," he writes:—

"Now in the world there are sects, schisms, judgments, and opinions, and according to the number of their fancies so are there ways of worship. . . . Now, Friends, all you that have looked after me and other men for teaching, now I can write unto you what I know, that none teacheth like Him who is now my Teacher indeed; and will be yours if you are made willing and obedient to be taught, directed, and guided by Him who is gathering His out of all nations, kindreds, and tongues.* . . . Oh! leave all for Christ. You cannot serve

---

* Elsewhere Humphry Smith shows his appreciation of the true preaching of the Gospel. In his address "To the Tender-hearted

two masters; you cannot be of the world and of God; you must witness a separation. . . . The sword is drawn against the Man of Sin, to cut it down root and branch, and to set up the kingdom of Christ in righteousness and true holiness. And this work of the Lord shall certainly go on, and Men, Devils, or the Gates of Hell shall never prevail against it."

George Fox describes him as "a worthy soldier and follower of the Lamb, who kept his habitation in Christ Jesus;" and George Whitehead writes:—"I have this testimony nakedly and in the sight of the Lord to bear, that he was a man fearing God and hating iniquity, fervent and zealous against deceit and hypocrisy, and endued with a heavenly gift." Another tells us that "He never murmured at the exercises that he met withal through wicked and unreasonable men." And one who for a year shared with him "that straight, noisome prison of Winchester," says that the love of God constrains him to testify that "he was a man that loved the Lord with an upright heart, and that it was as meat and drink to him to do the will of God, desiring to spend and be spent for the Gospel's sake." Whilst his devoted and enthusiastic friend, Nicholas Complin—who also ended his life in prison—writes: "Is thy holy, innocent, pure life to be buried in oblivion as not to be remembered by us any more? Are thy sufferings, with all thy valiant engagements with the enemies of thy God to be blotted out of the record of the children of the Most High? Oh! what

---

Lambs of Christ" he says, "The Lord in His power gave utterance to His servants and messengers, and then were the words of His Truth as food to the hungry, and with much gladness of heart was the sound of the way of life by many received. . . . Then did the Lord visit such again and again in His lovingkindness by His servants."

saith my soul? Nay, nay, let let it be had in living remembrance among the followers of the Lamb, and let it be written upon the tables of their hearts even to all generations." And again, after describing him as being very meek and of a quiet spirit, he says, "If any knew not the Light which condemns the sin, then in the meekness of love everlasting he would open unto them the way thereunto, and labour mightily to bring them to the knowledge of it. Oh! how great was his love to the eternal Truth which abounded in his heart! And how would he groan for the lost sheep! Surely his love was more than my tongue can express; and his courage did abound in a great measure."

It was at a time when Humphry Smith had abandoned manifest ungodly habits, and was greatly engrossed with his farm, "loving outward goods (as he says) more than Christ," a man of note in his town, and a popular preacher (although, to quote his own words, "not according to the knowledge of the cross of Christ,") that the secret voice of the Saviour called him to forsake all and follow Him. He says that the strivings of his soul can never be declared, for he knew that if he gave up his heart to God he should be called on to testify against the unrighteousness, not only of the people, but also of their rulers, of clergy as well as laity; and it was given him to foresee the hardships, torture, and imprisonments which would ensue. But he writes:—"The powerful Life of God did so much break through me with such unspeakable love that I was even willing to leave all and walk with God." As he pondered the promise, "They that turn many to righteousness shall shine as the stars for ever and ever," the redemption of souls seemed so precious to him that he thought that if, in the course of his life, he could but convert one to God, it would be worth while to undergo any amount of suffering; and his fears concerning his unfitness for the work seemed to be answered by the words, "Who is it that openeth the mouth? Is it not I, the Lord?"

But soon Satan showed his skilfulness in transforming himself into an angel of light, by causing Humphry Smith to suspect that the mighty work which the Holy Spirit had been performing within him was a delusion, and even that it was the effect of the very transformation which the Tempter had made before laying this new snare. Then another temptation arose: "I have seen children, wife, farms, and oxen," he writes, "to hinder from the Kingdom of God; that which hindered most was the love of outward goods." Yet, having tasted of the bread of heaven, and drank of the living water, some time elapsed before the united influence of the world, the flesh, and the devil, could prevail to make him "drive the power of God" from him; and when he did succeed in overcoming what he calls "the strivings of the sweet and lovely Spirit of Truth," he was so assailed by inward and outward trials that, being unable to conceal his despair, it was reported he was becoming mad. "I could neither pray nor believe," he says, "but concluded that I was accursed from God for ever—and that which disobeyed *was* accursed—and, being in a sad, miserable condition, resolved to write a warning to all people that they might take example by me and never resist the Spirit as I had done." Before this was accomplished, however, the Lord, who does not afflict willingly, caused some rays of hope to pierce the dense darkness which surrounded him. Yet it was not soon fully illumined by the Sun of Righteousness, for, to use his own suggestive words, he was still striving "to keep two kingdoms;" but, in proof of His unfailing love, the chastening hand of God was so heavily laid on him that he at last told his wife and children that he could bear it no longer, but that he must leave off following the ways of the world with them, and devote his life to the Lord. In after years, when referring to God's dealings with him during this period, he says, "In the Lord's judgments I now rejoice for evermore." Whilst far from needlessly neglecting his outward avocations, or separating himself from his family, Humphry Smith seems to have been almost literally called on to forsake all for Christ; but none of the sufferings through which his onward path lay caused him to regret the choice he had made. On the contrary, he writes, "I have found the promise true, for *a hundred times hundred-fold have I already received*, blessed be the Lord for ever."

Widely different as are the circumstances of the disciple of the nineteenth century, does he not also find, at certain stages of his spiritual pilgrimage, that there is a something—such habits or pursuits as constitute the spirit of the world *to him in his own particular position*—which, if not abandoned, may greatly hinder or altogether prevent his upward progress; and that, hard as the sacrifice may seem, Christ can give all the strength that is needed for its accomplishment, and "can and does," as Humphry Smith says, "with Himself make up for all," in a manner which must be experienced in order to be understood?

"The true desire," he writes, "of my present enlarged heart for your eternal happiness is, That as the Lord of Heaven and Earth hath counted you worthy of His call, in the power of His grace which bringeth salvation unto all, you may not judge yourselves unworthy of the Kingdom of God, but may cleave unto His Truth in the inward parts, leaving all that which hath kept you from it, whatsoever it be; and all that which hath hindered you, and doth hinder from the life and virtue of it in your own hearts—this all to leave behind you for ever, to give it away freely, and as freely willing as a man would part with dross for gold!" Again, he remarks, "Such as knowingly deny their obedience in anything to the light of Christ, He will deny them His power in all things."

It is interesting to find that before this momentous change had taken place, when daily preaching in one pulpit or another—although, as we have seen, he was by no means indifferent to worldly possessions—he conscientiously declined receiving any sort of remuneration, and felt that even had he lacked food and clothing he could not do otherwise. On one occasion, when offered £100 per annum, he refused it, saying, that he would "rather go in sheepskins and goatskins, and eat bread and drink water." The last time that he preached before the complete change in his views with regard to ministry, he remarked to the congregation, "My mouth is stopped at this present, but if ever the Lord shall open my mouth again, I shall preach indeed!" In allusion to the ministry he writes:—

"Though Christ, after His resurrection, said, All power in Heaven and in earth is given unto Me, go ye, therefore and teach—yet they were to tarry until they had the power in themselves; and when that was come, then with that they went and taught the nations, from the sensible feeling of that which taught them how to teach. . . . So the power and virtue of the Holy Spirit coming forth from Christ, being sent of the Father and received by the disciples (who, with much desire, waited for that), empowered them to do that which before they were commanded to do. . . . And as Christ commanded them to go and teach, He also required them to tarry—and so not to go—until they had received power so to do; and so it was the power of the Holy Ghost in them which made them ministers; these were, and such are, truly ordained ministers. . . . Then they went to teach the nations, and converted thousands! Thus it is with Christ's followers now; they are not satisfied until they are filled with that which they heard of, and their souls thirsted after; and so it was with them then, they were filled with what they wanted before; and then from that which they were filled with, they spoke forth."

Again, he asks,

"How can your hearts be restrained from an inexpressible yearning after the advancing of the living Truth of God, which He hath so freely made you partakers of?"

Humphry Smith's own ministry was remarkably blessed; George Fox says that, "he did convert and turn many to the Lord Jesus Christ, that had been outward professors, as he himself had been, to the possession of Christ; so that he did see, and was comforted in the fruits of his labours in Christ." Not unfrequently he felt himself commissioned to speak and write—

"As one to whom is given,
To know the wrath of outraged Heaven,
And to pour it forth."

"He spared not," writes Nicholas Complin, "but cut on the right hand and slew on the left, and made the arrows of his quiver to strike into the bowels of God's enemies; but he preached peace to the captive." Another of his contemporaries alludes to the many seals to his ministry; one of whom, Edward Waldren, says that he hopes he shall never forget Humphry Smith, or the memorable day on which he went with some others to visit him in a prison, where he had been confined after holding a largely-attended and remarkable meeting at Andover, in which the opposition of rude soldiers could not hinder the free course of the word of the Lord. Edward Waldren was in deep mental distress, and, to quote his own phrase, "void of the saving knowledge of Jesus," and, having heard of Humphry Smith, greatly longed to see him, and therefore attended a meeting which was held in the prison. He writes, "I have cause for ever to praise the Lord in the behalf of this tender, innocent, faithful man to God's truth and people; his memorial cannot pass into oblivion by any that had the true knowledge of him,—dear Humphry Smith!" These words were written twenty years after his death, and whilst Edward Waldren was a prisoner in what he terms, "This close, straight, nasty, stinking prison, or county gaol in Winchester," in which Humphry Smith had laid down his life.

From the manner in which his friends describe him, as well as from his own writings, one would imagine that he knew well how to comfort the faint-hearted, and to speak a word in season to his fellow-believers; but his own conviction was that God sent him "rather to call home the lost sheep than to nourish them which were already brought home." Addressing such on the love of God, from Winchester Bridewell, he writes: "He spreadeth forth His arms to gather them that ask not for Him. He giveth gifts to the rebellious, and He is grieved with those that receive not the tenders of His love. . . . . *His Light of Life hath shined in you to let you see the want of a Saviour.*"

In His earnest appeal " to the Sons of Men," he asks, " Did you never feel a seed in you cry aloud for life, though it lies in the death ? Are you quite dead and past feeling? Nay, nay, there is many of you are not so far hardened. Hearken and hear a little. He that makes an end of sin is come near unto you. Resist Him not, lest the things which belong to your everlasting peace be hid from your eyes for evermore, and you left desolate, only having the Scriptures of Truth, and not the Truth in the inward parts, where the knowledge of it makes me free." How far he was from underestimating the value of the Bible will be seen by the following extract :—

"Do I in the least contemn, slight, vilify, or deny the Scriptures? God forbid. Nay, I had rather my pen might fall out of my hand, or my arm from my shoulder, or my tongue cleave to the roof of my mouth for ever, than I should go about to make void the Scriptures of Truth, which was given forth from that which is my life, which is hid, not in the Scriptures, but with Christ in God" (Col. iii. 13). . . . " Nay, rather I establish the Scripture in directing all people unto that which the Scriptures testify of, and were given forth from " (John v. 39).

In allusion to the Holy Spirit, he writes :—

" Christ, when He was upon earth, did often speak unto His followers of what was yet to come, and I do seldom read or take notice that He did so often preach and repeat any one thing unto them as that of the Spirit to come, saying that it (mark, the Spirit) would lead into all Truth. And seeing their weakness and unbelief, He, by the often repetition thereof, did, as it were, the more chiefly engage their hearts to wait for and seek after the incomes of that which should comfort them and abide with them when His body was gone from them."

It was probably in 1654, whilst residing at Little Cawerne, Hereford, that Humphry Smith cast in his lot with the persecuted Friends, and the following summer we find him a prisoner in Evesham dungeon, for refusing to take the Oath of Abjuration, which was tendered to him after many efforts to ensnare him by a long examination in points of doctrine had failed. He was at first confined in the gaoler's house, where he was repeatedly engaged in prayer, and all who were present listened with silent awe. Soon he was sent to the common gaol; the infuriated mob threw water and heavy stones into the prison, and treated him with the greatest indignity. But in his opinion, the magistrates were far more to blame than the untaught people. Meetings were often held in the street outside the prison, and were largely attended on market-days. Many hearts were stirred, and blessed results began to appear. But the Mayor of Evesham vowed that he would break up the Quakers' meetings; and several Friends were violently arrested whilst holding one, some being placed in the prison, others in the stocks, whilst three—one of whom was Humphry Smith—were thrust into a loathsome dungeon.

At the previous sessions the judge had said to him, "You have been kept very high all this while; but I shall take a course ere I go hence that you shall be kept shorter." The mayor caused them to be deprived of the bedding with which their friends had supplied them, and although one of the prisoners, who was suffering from severe toothache, begged leave to keep his pillow, he was not allowed to do so. The gaoler coolly told them, he could do what he liked with them, for they would have no benefit from the law, and no lawyer dared to plead for them; had they been imprisoned for theft or murder—regarded, seemingly, as less glaring offences than that of holding meetings—he could, he said, have given them more liberty. The dungeon was not twelve feet square; light and air were only admitted by an aperture four inches in width, through which the prisoners received their food. So intolerably impure was the air which escaped through this opening that sometimes the people in the street could not venture to stand by it. Once, at Humphry Smith's request, a Friend asked the mayor if the dungeon might be cleansed, but his petition was refused, and he was placed in the stocks. In hot weather the captives found it difficult to breathe, and in cold weather they had not space enough to use exercise in order to warm themselves. Here Humphry Smith was confined for fourteen weeks.

One day, two men from the country, who were passing by with their teams, asked why the Friends were kept in prison; the gaoler induced them to enter, then locked them in, and refused to open the door until some money had been given him. Two Friends, named Margaret Newby and Elizabeth Quorte, after holding a meeting at Evesham in a private house, visited some of their captive fellow-believers. The mayor ordered that they should be seized and put into stocks, which were so constructed as to cause great suffering by only an hour's confinement; but at his request they were kept in them, during a freezing night, for fifteen hours. "I have thought," says Humphry Smith, "that Paul's forty stripes save one were not so bad." Of course he could but keenly feel the barbarity and injustice of the cruelty to which his friends and himself were subjected, and at times he gave expression to his righteous indignation in very strong language. But it was the sin, not the sinner, that he hated. Concerning the persecutors, he writes:—"Had the Lord left us where they are, then might we have been this day as ignorant of the way of peace towards enemies, and of the path of innocency and righteousness, as they. The God of Heaven forgive them, and defend us! . . . A remnant He hath whose hearts He enlargeth with prayer, and some of them with strong inward desires and groans, and some with utterance to declare the goodwill of God unto others in your assemblies, and some steadfastly to believe in God that He will never leave us—and all this ascends up before the Lord as one sacrifice. . . . Oh! how shall He forget us now we are His people, and are purchased with a ransom more precious than all the gold in the world?" Again, he says:—" Behold the goodness of God is unutterable! Yea I have not words to express it; and such that feel it may taste of it, and drink of the fulness thereof, beyond the narrowness of my broken speech; and let such draw near unto me, . . . for my heart is filled with love, and my dwelling is enlarged with boundless borders of peace. . . . And if the will of God should be so that my body suffer in this close unsavoury prison at Winchester many more months or several years longer, yet shall the Lord be my God for ever, and my rest unto the end of troubles."

The Parliament convoked by Cromwell in 1656 passed an Act against vagrants. As this term included all persons who when absent from home could give no satisfactory account of their business, cruel advantage was taken of the measure by many magistrates, who were but too ready to lay hands on those who were travelling at their own expense to preach the Gospel. Soon Humphry Smith and another Friend, when riding together near Axminster, were arrested and carried before a justice of the peace, who, after consultation with a clergyman, ordered them to be whipped; their books and papers were burnt, and their money was taken from them.

In 1658, two years before the accession of Charles II., whilst Humphry Smith was confined, as he says, "in a filthy prison and place unfit for men, at Winchester," he wrote his "Just Complaint of the Afflicted against the Rulers who oppress the Innocent," a prophetic warning to the persecuting magistrates, in which he tells them that his eyes have been filled with tears and his heart with sorrow because of the woes which awaited them. From the same place he wrote an epistle to his fellow-sufferers in Ailsbury Gaol. In it he remarks:—

"When I have beheld the plants of the garden of God in their fresh, green, growing, flourishing, united state, my heart hath often been refreshed. Then hath my life sounded forth the precious praises of the Almighty in the assemblage of the upright; and my heart, broken therewith in the delightsome love, hath poured forth thanksgiving with tenderness and tears in secret. . . . Dear lambs of the fold of Heaven, my heart and soul salutes you, my love is dear unto you, my life hath long reached out itself towards you. . . . How shall I salute you in that which cannot be declared? Behold, I may become as a babe herein, and be silent as a child yet learning utterance; lest in reaching forth of my strength I should signify my weakness to unfold the undeclarable infiniteness of the virtue, wisdom, meekness, life, and love—from the measure whereof my simple words most certainly do at present proceed —as some few will surely perceive, who yet daily yearn after a fuller enjoyment of God, and the increase and preservation of His precious truth. . . . Behold the God of Heaven is my refuge, and the daily incomes of that which doth truly comfort is as marrow to my bones; yea the Lord hath prolonged my days, enlarged my borders, and beautified the place of my dwelling! . . . Let not your hearts be sad, neither be ye discouraged by reason of anything that the Lord suffereth to come to pass, who in His secret wisdom bringeth forth good unto such, who in all conditions and under all trials, do truly love and cleave unto the Lord their strength."

In 1660 Humphry Smith had a remarkable vision with regard to the destruction of the City of London, which he published the same year as a warning-call to repentance. It will be remembered that the Great Fire occurred six years later. During the interval Humphry Smith died. "As for the city herself," he writes, "and her suburbs, and all that belonged to her, a fire was kindled therein. . . . And the fire consumed foundations, and the tall buildings fell, and it consumed all the lofty therein, and thus she became a desolation. . . . And the vision hereof remained in me as a thing that was secretly shewed me of the Lord. . . . My counsel is therefore that thou fear the Lord and turn from the way that thou art in. Let all thy inhabitants, O, thou great City! from the highest to the lowest, take good heed unto their ways." It was also in 1660 that

Humphry Smith wrote his address "To the Great Flock of the Imprisoned Servants of God Almighty." Some extracts follow :—

"*This we are most assuredly assured of, that the Lord is become ours, yea even our own, and we have a part in Him, and He hath bought us with the price of that which puts away sin.* . . . When I enter into the chambers of secrecy, where the hidden wisdom is treasured up, I have been even ready to shut up all the outgoings, and to dwell where the unutterable treasures are treasured up abundantly for ever, and say in my heart unto the yet scattered ones, Oh! that ye would come and see my dwelling, and find out my resting-place, and abide in the beautiful habitation, and rest in the munition of rocks. . . . Were I in one day bereaved of all, yet enjoying the Lord and His presence, so should it be well with me, and so may it be well with you. . . . He knoweth our intents. He hath given many of us an heart to say, 'Lord, if Thou shouldst suffer us to perish we will not leave Thee; and whatever becomes of us we dare not deny Thee.' *Let your eyes be more upon the Lord than upon those things which in this day of trial are suffered to come to pass by Him.* . . . And, Friends, let not the enemy prevail through unbelief; there is no greater danger than that of unbelief. You have a spiritual enemy to war with which flies not but as he is resisted; and in the time of your weakness and inward trouble is his time to prevail, if ever; and if thou canst stand then, full easy mayst thou walk when refreshings come. . . . And this know, that a storm lasteth but for a time, and winter is but for a season, and the night remains not always."

How many a struggling, sinking heart, must have been upheld and reanimated by these efforts of Humphry Smith to draw out his soul to the hungry, and to comfort the sorrowful with the comfort wherewith he was comforted of God; and thus giving the cup of cold water to others, it is evident that he in no wise lost his reward, but that his own soul was as a well of water whose waters fail not. A controversial pamphlet of

Humphry Smith's, " The Wandering Star discovered," is a reply to a book entitled, " The Quaker's Blazing Star," by a clergyman named Edmund Skipp, who resided at Bodenham. As Humphry Smith, in an early part of it, states his intention of " laying open some of the former and yet lived-in deceits of this open enemy, and also some of his lies which he hath written against the Truth of Christ," the reader's mind is prepared for its style, thoroughly characteristic of the age. But we find that " a tender letter in love to his soul" was also written; and in the latter part of the pamphlet, Humphry Smith says, " Now I charge thee, in the presence of the living God in as much love to thy soul as ever, that thou return to the light of Christ in thy own conscience. I tell thee, man, in love, there is something yet in thee which will witness me to be true."

It seems that Edmund Skipp had some time earlier been convinced of the truth of many of the views held by Friends. At one time he had acknowledged that for two years he had been acting in opposition to his conscience with regard to tithes, and yet, though admitting that he groaned under the burden of them, he said that he meant to receive them for another year. But Humphry Smith had, as he says, thoughts to the contrary, and plainly expressed this opinion to the clergyman, whom he met at a private house. On the following Sunday he sent his man to Humphry Smith with these few lines : " Brother Smith, the Lord hath done a strange work in me this morning, and I shall alter strangely this day ; therefore pray earnestly for me, and make what haste thou canst to come unto me." Once or twice he had told his whole congregation that he had "long spoken after the manner of men, but now they must expect no more such from him; that now he should wait to pray in the Spirit and speak by the Spirit." For a time he gave up receiving tithes, and even entertained the thought of resigning the glebe-land and building on his own. But he confessed to Humphry Smith that he had not faith enough to carry his convictions into effect, and was "confident that the devil would steal all from him again."

In Humphry Smith's pamphlet, "Hidden things made manifest," he remarks: "There are many that are now come to peace, dominion, and the land of Rest, who did once know the judgments of God upon Cain's nature, which then cried out that his punishment was too heavy to bear, . . . and yet have they not started aside like a broken bow, neither have they suffered unbelief to prevail, but in love to Him who was made a curse, in patience have endured. . . . Those come to know that notwithstanding the Law must be received, yet by the works thereof no flesh shall be justified, but by the obedience of faith towards God in the Blood of His Son, by which all that is done away which transgressed the law ; and so not of works, nor of merits, but of faith and love is the law fulfilled."

In the latter part of 1661, Humphry Smith told the Friends whom he had been visiting in the neighbourhood of London, that he had a narrow path to pass through, and foresaw that he should be imprisoned, and that it might cost him his life. Then, having taken leave of them, he set forward, we learn, "in the will of the Lord westward." Bonds and afflictions he knew awaited him, but God was with him and taught him to fear none of those things which he should suffer. In his bold address to Judges and Rulers, called, "The Voice of God's Mighty Power," he says, "Your long tyranny will never weary out the patience we have received, neither can you inflict more punishment than the Lord has enabled us to bear. And as you are filled and moved with envy, we are much more filled and overcome with the power of the Father's Life. We have given up our bodies and souls a living sacrifice unto God, to do or suffer His will. And him that kills the body we fear not, much less those that can but whip or imprison for a few months; for *our Life you cannot reach;* neither can you disturb their rest whom the Lord hath crowned with honour, who out of the world are redeemed and bought with the price of blood most precious."

When on his way to visit his son, he held a meeting at Alton, after which armed men were sent to the house were he was staying, who arrested him and took him to the Deputy-Lieutenant of the county, by whom he was committed as a "Ringleader and one of the chief of the Quakers," to Winchester Gaol, of the state of which his own strong adjectives have already given a slight conception. His pockets and boxes were rifled of papers, and the felons who were his companions sometimes took his food from him and abused him in other ways; yet his fellow-prisoner, Nicholas Complin, states that he was "very quiet, and lay down content." But knowing how illegal his imprisonment was, he wrote an answer to the mittimus. At the next Sessions he laid his cause before the justices, but unavailingly.

When told by Judge Terril at the Assizes that he should be released if he would hold no more meetings, he of course declined to accept freedom on such terms. As the judge was leaving the court, Humphry Smith, who was at the bar among the felons, said to him: "Friend, remember I have been a whole year in prison and no breach of any law proved against me." A little later he was attacked by the illness which, after a while, terminated his life, and which his close and cruel confinement would quite account for.

About two months before his death, he wrote a piece entitled, "One Hundred and Forty-four lines of secret, inward Melody and Praise to the Lord," the style of which is shown by the following stanza:—

"Behold His glory shines unto His jewels rare,
He visits them betimes, when they in darkness are.
Behold His heart is bent towards His little ones;
His love their hearts hath rent, and in His virtue comes."

But the last time in which the use of his pen is recorded, is on the occasion of his writing a letter to his "nearly-related friend Elizabeth Smith, of Little Cawerne." A few extracts will give an idea of its character:—

"My strength, life, and refuge alone is He whose service I have no cause to decline, and whose precious, powerful call He never gave me cause to repent. Oh! that I could now sufficiently declare His goodness, as the Lord hath given unto my heart to desire of Him to be made use of, in the declaration or manifestation thereof in this my day unto the sons and children of men. Surely, when I am writing of Him, and of His unutterable goodness and power, my words and lines are all so short of setting forth the virtue and fulness of the most unexpressible divine excellency thereof, that sometimes I am rather ready to dwell in silence with and in the fulness thereof—which overcomes with unutterable virtue—than to be writing of that which in itself can never be written; though what is written may be by, and with, and from the overflowings of the same; and so be as drops or little streams of heavenly water to refresh the dry and thirsty land. Yea, He is certainly mine, and I am His; and my soul doth magnify Him, and my spirit doth yet breathe farther to sound forth His praises—not only all the days of my life, whilst in this earthly tabernacle, *but likewise in the hearts of thousands of them yet unborn, by my faithful, upright testimony and the record thereof* which may remain when the God and Father of my life hath gathered me, with the rest of His servants of old, to live with Him in the delightsome Ocean of the Infinite Fulness, the streams whereof already are as the free issuings forth of Life Eternal. . . . And this is that thou and others may hear from me, and know that I remain in the service of God, and in faithful long-sufferings for the Gospel of His Son as at this day, being the 6th of the Seventh Month, 1662. In the straight prison of Winchester, where I am known by this name, Humphry Smith."

This form of signature was a favourite one of his; for possessing, as he did, the "new name which no man knoweth saving he that receiveth it"* (Rev. ii. 17) that which he bore amongst his fellow-men appeared to him of but little importance. This letter recalls a striking passage of an earlier date:—"Shall we not be contented if the Lord should suffer us to be deprived of all things but Himself, that we might have none other thing to have union with, but only Him alone? Surely this would be His love, and *great would be the unity between such and Him!*" Do not these last words reveal

---

* Dean Alford thus comments on this text:—"It is a revelation to a man of his everlasting title, as a son of God, to glory in Christ, but consisting of, and revealed in, those personal marks and signs of God's peculiar adoption of *himself*, which he, and none else, is acquainted with."

the secret source of the holy constancy of many to whom "it is given in the behalf of Christ not only to believe on Him, but also to suffer for His sake,"— including some

> "Who little dream
> Their daily strife an angel's theme,
> Or that the cross they take so calm
> Shall prove, in Heaven, a martyr's palm."

It was about three weeks after the Assizes that Humphry Smith became ill with ague, soon followed by violent fever. He sent a letter to Judge Terril, informing him of the severity of his malady, yet little was done to ameliorate his condition. No doubt the extreme hardships and cruelty of which he had so frequently been the victim had left him but little rallying power; but even a vigorous constitution would surely have found it hard to resist the prostrating influences of fever in that pestilential place. More than one of his friends, the sharers of this imprisonment, bear witness that no suffering could wring from those patient lips "one unsavoury word." He was given up to the will of the Lord, either in life or death, he said; but patience had had her perfect work, and he who, even in the midst of great tribulation, had so often realised fulness of joy in the presence of the Lord, was soon to behold the King in His beauty;

> "And he may smile at troubles gone
> Who sets the victor-garland on!"

He remarked that his heart was filled with the power of God: and was heard to say, "Lord, Thou sentest me forth to do Thy will, and I have been faithful to Thee in my small measure." A short time before his death he poured out his soul in prayer that the Lord would deliver His people from their enemies, and would Himself be the Teacher of those to whose souls he had been made a blessing. "O Lord, hear the inward sighs and groans of the oppressed, and deliver my poor soul from the oppressor. O Lord, hear me. O Lord, uphold and preserve me. I know that my Redeemer liveth. Thou are strong and mighty, O Lord." To the last his mind was unclouded. He died in 1663.

As we lay down the records of the lives of those who, having wholly yielded their hearts to Christ, feared not that He would suffer their faith to fail; and, undaunted by dangers and difficulties innumerable, carried out to the utmost their belief of the requirements of a Christian profession—let us remember that Christianity cannot be THUS practised in *any* age without making what has been termed "a tremendous innovation on this work-a-day world."

> "Breathe on us for the passing day,
>   The powers of ancient story;
> Then we with joyful heart shall say,
>   Though Wisdom's head be hoary
> His heart is fresh, undimmed his eyes;
> And in the old we must be wise,
>   If we would win new glory."

MARY FISHER AND HER FRIENDS.

"WE need God to make us understand God; we must be in union with Him in order to obey Him."—J. R. H.

MARY FISHER AND HER FRIENDS.

"The practical Christian life in the individual, is it not more the result of direct spiritual influence than of any letter, or rule, or law? Is it not emphatically the product of a divine power on the heart—of the operation of the Holy Ghost? . . . . The transforming power of the Gospel lies . . . . in a sympathy of man's spirit with the spirit of Christ, by which the Gospel becomes to man not merely a new demand of duty but a new endowment of power, and a law which he can fulfil through love."—*Myers' Catholic Thoughts on the Bible and Theology.*

It was on a spring-day in the year 1656 that the good ship *Swallow* sailed into Massachusetts Bay. Her arrival caused no small consternation, and the Deputy-Governor, Bellingham, deemed it needful to summon a Special Council. This alarm was caused by the rumour that Simon Kempthorn, the "master" of the *Swallow*, had brought into the jurisdiction two dangerous heretics, who had come with the express purpose of propagating their blasphemous errors. They were English women, named Anne Austin and Mary Fisher, the former an elderly matron, the latter unmarried and about the age of thirty-two. The Governor being absent, Bellingham gave orders that they should be held in custody on board the ship, and that their boxes should be searched. About a hundred books were taken from them, which the Council deliberately decreed should be "forthwith burned and destroyed by the common executioner"!

Their next edict was to the effect that the "said Anne and Mary" should be kept in close confinement, no one being allowed to have communication with them without leave, until they were sent out of the country. Simon Kempthorn was enjoined to transport them "speedily and directly" to Barbadoes whence they came, and to discharge all the expenses of their imprisonment. If he refused to give security for the effectual carrying out of these orders he was to be committed to prison. The magistrates moreover threatened to inflict a penalty of £5 on any person who should expose himself to the contaminating influence of the strangers by conversing with them through the window of Boston Gaol, which, for the sake of still greater security, was afterwards boarded up. The prisoners were deprived of their writing materials, and forbidden the use of a candle. So little food was allowed them that Nicholas Upsal, an old inhabitant and "freeman" of the city, fearing that they might be starved, paid the gaoler for permission to send them provisions; and at one time their lives were imperilled from the cry of witchcraft.

At the end of five weeks they were banished from Boston and sent back to Barbadoes, the captain of the vessel being bound, under a penalty of £100, to convey them thither without allowing them to land anywhere in New England, nor to have any intercourse with the inhabitants of that country. When, on returning to Boston, Endicott, the Governor, heard of these proceedings, he said, "If I had been present I would have had them well whipt." Ample opportunities, however, for the infliction of barbarous scourgings on others also guilty of being Quakers, were soon forthcoming, for scarcely had Anne Austin and Mary Fisher sailed from the shores of Massachusetts, before the arrival of the

Woodhouse from London, with eight Friends on board,* of whom Francis Howgill thus quaintly writes:—
"Four from London and four from Bristol are gone towards New England; pretty hearts; the blessing of the Lord is with them, and His dread goes before them."

Anne Austin and Mary Fisher were the first Friends who visited the New World with the hope of making known the doctrines of Friends. The former is described as being at this time "stricken in years," and the mother of five children. Her home was, apparently, in London. Persecution was again her lot after her return to her native land, and in 1659 she was imprisoned in one of the loathsome London gaols for preaching in the religious assemblies of her own Society. She died of the plague in 1665, and was interred in Bunhill Fields Burial-ground. From Barbadoes, where Anne Austin and Mary Fisher first landed, the latter wrote a letter to George Fox which bears evidence of being written in the days when "spelling was a matter of private opinion."

The name under which she addresses him is very suggestive; since—

"Whoe'er hath fanned the flickering torch of faith,
  Or bade the mists of fear and doubt retire;
  Or nerved our souls to meet the approach of death—
  To him we give the endearing name of *sire*."

She writes:—"My deare father . . . . lett me not be forgotten by thee, but lett thy prayers be for me that I may continuue faithful to the end if any of our

---

* See *The Martyrs of Boston*.

friendes be free to come over they may be servisable, here is many convinsed, and many desire to know the way; so I rest MARY FFISHER."

Mary Fisher was born in the north of England, and at the time when she became a Friend her home, it seems, was at Pontefract. The three years before her western voyage had been much devoted to the ministry of the Gospel in the intervals left by frequent imprisonments, and no small share of suffering had been her lot. For sixteen months she had been confined in York Castle; almost as soon as liberty was restored to her she visited the south-eastern counties with a Friend named Elizabeth Williams, who was also a minister. At Cambridge they "discoursed about the things of God" with the young collegians, and preached at the gate of Sidney College. But soon the mayor gave orders that they should be taken to the Market Cross and "whipped until the blood ran down their bodies." No Friend had been publicly scourged hitherto, and the assembled crowd marvelled at the patient fortitude of the sufferers when this command was executed with barbarous severity; and still more at the Christ-like spirit they manifested by their prayers that their persecutors might be forgiven. "This is but the beginning of the sufferings of the people of God!" Mary Fisher afterwards remarked.

A second imprisonment in York Castle, this time for six months, soon followed, and was shortly succeeded by one of three months' duration. In Buckinghamshire she was imprisoned for the offence of "giving Christian exhortations to the priest and people." She possessed much intellectual ability, and, dedicated as it was to the service of Him who enabled her to speak with power, it is easy to imagine that she was regarded as a formidable foe; especially when she dwelt on such unpalatable themes as the freedom of the Gospel ministry and the disuse of religious ceremonies. Henry Fell, who met with her in Barbadoes on her return from New England, says, in a letter to Margaret Fell, "Truly Mary Fisher is a precious heart, and hath been very serviceable here."

She afterwards visited the West Indies, but her name is chiefly associated with her journey to the East, undertaken from the conviction that it was her duty to seek for a religious interview with the Sultan Mahomet IV. Although only eighteen years of age, he was at the height of his power, and Turkey was viewed with dismay by the nations of Christendom.

> "The Sultan dreamed of boundless power
>   To wield the conquering sword,
> And make the unbelievers own
>   The prophet of the Lord:
> To fling the banner of His faith
>   O'er Islam's ancient reign,
> Above the valleys of Castile,
>   The mountain heights of Spain;
> In the great temple of the Cross
>   Marshal his Moslem force,
> And make its sacred fane at Rome
>   ' A stable for his horse!'"

"This English maiden," writes Gerard Croese, "would not be at rest before she went in person to the great Emperor of the Turks, and informed him concerning the errors of his religion and the truth of hers!" Having visited Italy, Zante, and Corinth, she arrived at

Smyrna. The English consul there, when he learnt her intention—not recognising her heavenly commission—very naturally advised her "by all means to forbear;" and when he found that his warnings were wholly unheeded, and that no milder measures would avail—recoiling from the idea that a woman should expose herself to such a perilous journey and hazard the unrelenting cruelty of oriental despotism—he placed her on board a vessel which was bound for Venice, giving orders that she should be conveyed thither.

But Mary Fisher was not to be so easily withheld from her holy errand. She induced the captain to land her on the Morea, and,

> "Bearing God's message in her heart,
> Her life within her hand,"

alone, knowing neither the route nor the language, she travelled on foot along the Grecian coast, through Macedonia, and over the mountains of Thrace, until she at length reached the beautiful plain, watered by the wide Maritza, on which Adrianople stands. Here the Sultan was encamped with so great an army and retinue, that even that spacious tract of land seemed barely large enough for them. Even now a less steadfast faith would have wavered, for how was an abhorred Christian to gain access to the Mohammedan monarch—"Shadow of God," as he was at times entitled? Having told her errand to some of the citizens, she asked them to bear her company to the royal camp; but their dread of the Sultan's displeasure forbade them to yield to such a request. So alone—yet not alone—

> "In the still temple of her soul,
> Communing with her God."

she went hither, and thither, until her diligent quest was rewarded by finding some one who was bold enough to speak to the Grand Vizier, Achmet Bassa, on her behalf. Through him the Sultan was informed of the arrival of an English woman who had "something to declare to him from the great God;" and she was told that she might have an interview with him on the following morning.

She spent the night in the city and went back to the camp at the appointed hour, where the Sultan awaited her, surrounded by his chief officers, as was his wont when giving receptions to ambassadors. By one of the three interpreters who were present, he asked her whether it was true that she had a message from the Lord God? On her answering affirmatively, he bade her "Speak on." Waiting for the summons of her Lord she did not at once address him, which led him to inquire whether it were her wish that any of the company should withdraw before she spoke? When she replied that she did not desire this, he told her to speak the word of the Lord without fear, since they had "good hearts" to hear it; strictly enjoining her, moreover, to say neither more nor less than the word she had from the Lord, since they were willing to hear it, be it what it might. With great gravity the whole assembly gave heed to her earnest ministry, and when she became silent the Sultan asked if there were nothing more she would like to say? When she inquired whether he had understood her, he answered, "Yea, every word, and it is truth!" He then expressed his desire that she should remain in his dominions, and when she declined this proposal, offered her a guard to escort her to Constantinople, as he would be greatly grieved if any harm should befall her in his empire. But she courteously refused this offer, trusting in the Lord alone.

May we not hope that one who had, for the moment, ignored the great national contest between the Crescent and the Cross, and—far beyond this—had laid aside the prejudices of the exacting faith of his fathers in his readiness to hear "the word of the Lord," albeit from the lips of a woman—was upheld by Him when some thirty years later he lay dying in prison? His abdication was demanded by the Turkish soldiers after the dreadful and unsuccessful siege of Vienna. Certainly his conduct stands out in strange contrast to that of the professing Christians of Boston, who would no doubt have despised him as an infidel.* Mary Fisher arrived at Constantinople, we learn, "without the least hurt or scoff," and finally reached England in safety.

Not long after her return from her oriental journey Mary Fisher was married to a sea-captain named William Bayley, well known in the Society of Friends as a powerful preacher and writer. He had once been a Baptist minister at Poole, in Dorsetshire; but in 1655—the year in which Mary Fisher set sail for the Western world—that place was visited by George Fox, whose ministry led him to become a Friend. It seems that he had previously longed for deeper spiritual instruction, and had vainly sought for it in a careful

---

* "In this town
They put sea-captains in the stocks for swearing,
And Quakers for not swearing."
—*Longfellow's New England Tragedies.*

perusal in the works of Jacob Behmen, from whose "reveries and rhapsodies" it must have been a relief to turn to the pure elevated spirituality of Christianity as pourtrayed by George Fox, whose aim was, as he himself said, "with and by the Divine Spirit of God, to bring people off from all their own ways to Christ the new and living Way; and from their churches, which men had made and gathered, to the *Church in God*, the general assembly written in heaven which Christ is the head of; and off from the world's teachers to learn of Christ."

Persecution was soon William Bayley's portion. In 1656 he was committed to Exeter Gaol in consequence of the unfair use often made, in that day, of the law against vagrants by magistrates who chose to apply it to Friends who were travelling to preach. In the following year, when in Hampshire, he was imprisoned with some other Friends, by a mittimus which falsely stated that they were accused of several offences. A few years later he made one of a group of Friends who, when quietly standing in the street near the Bull and Mouth Meeting-house in London, were arrested by some soldiers and taken before that notorious persecutor of the Friends, Alderman Brown. He ordered that their hats should be removed, and repeatedly struck William Bayley with his fist. But William Bayley's wife was with him, and, patiently as she had been wont to bear persecution herself, she now reproved the magistrate for his violence to her husband; whereupon he struck her also and threw her on the ground—William Bayley's remonstrances with respect to such treatment of a woman only causing a repetition of it. Then, without the least pretext for such a step, he bade his servant and some other men take William Bayley to Newgate.

Twelve months later he was arrested at a meeting at King's Langley, and committed to Hertford Gaol, where —having refused at the Quarter Sessions to take the Oath of Allegiance—he was retained a prisoner for some years. His remarkable warning to Charles II. and his Parliament was written from Hertford in the latter part of 1664, when, as the event proved, the war with the Dutch, the Plague, and the great Fire, were not far distant. Brief extracts from this lengthy document follow :—

"But what shall I say unto you? If ye will not believe our faithful testimony (or the testimony of God through us) and the innocency of our cause and sufferings, neither will ye believe if one should rise from the dead and declare it unto you. For many tender visitations and timely warnings and gentle reprehensions have you had from the pure Spirit of the Lord God. . . . And as for my part, who am one of the least of the thousands of Israel, I could willingly have been silent as towards you at this time, but the Lord hath laid it upon me to warn you, once more, for whose sakes I have borne a burden. . . . The more you strive with the Lord and oppress His people, the more will they multiply and grow stronger and stronger ; and you shall wax weaker and weaker ; for life and immortality is risen, and the power of God is risen in the hearts of thousands.

"I tell you plainly that such fruits and doings among you that profess yourselves Christians, have made the very name of Christ and Christianity a proverb of reproach through nations, and have caused the God of heaven to be blasphemed. And how could it be otherwise, seeing you, who profess the most knowledge of God, and have talked of converting the heathen (as some of your leaders have done), are found the least in the life and fruits thereof? But to what would they convert them? . . . The very heathen or infidels, as ye call them, do judge and condemn you concerning these your proceedings. . . . Friends, tell me what ye have justly to charge against this people (whom ye so furiously pursue, to the loss of the lives of so many of them; by which the children are made fatherless, and tenderhearted women mournful widows); and declare it abroad to the whole world, and speak the truth, and nothing but the truth! . . . What is become of all your promises of liberty for tender consciences? God's curse and vengeance will come upon you, and His plagues, to destruction will pursue you if ye proceed in this work; and your wives will be widows and your children fatherless. The Lord hath spoken it! . . .

"God Almighty, cut short Thy work in Thy righteousness, . . . and let the kings of the earth lay down their crowns at the feet of the Lamb; that through Thy righteous judgments they may partake of Thy tender mercies, which endure for ever; that their eyes may be no longer blinded by the god of this world, but that they may come to see Thee who art invisible, and enjoy the same precious life of pure unfeigned love which abounds in the hearts of Thy hidden ones; and receive Thy peaceful wisdom to be governed, and to govern therein; then would they surely know that we are Thine. . . . So, friends, ye are, and have been, warned again by the faithful servants of the Lord in love to your souls; and you are left without excuse, if words should never more be mentioned unto you. . . .

"A lover of the welfare of all your souls, thus far clear of all your blood.

"WILLIAM BAYLEY."

William Bayley was present at Gracechurch Street Meeting, one day in 1670, when an attempt was made to bring a clergyman to officiate there; the latter, coming from an adjacent ale-house, approached the meeting-house; but, although protected by soldiers, he did not like the idea of performing the task which had been set him, and took the undignified course of giving his escort the slip. The sergeant, running after him, persuaded him to return; but when he reached the door of the meeting-house his heart once more failed him, and he turned away. The soldiers, however, entered; and arresting William Bayley, who was preaching, carried him before the Lord Mayor, who committed him to Newgate for "abusing the priest and disturbing him in his office"!

Of violent outrage, as well as absolute injustice, William Bayley was at times the victim. Not content with the infliction of blows, his persecutors on one occasion stained the ground with his blood, as they dragged him over it, wrenching open his mouth, and wounding him in other ways. After trampling on him, in order to take away his breath, one of his persecutors ordered the gaoler to "put him in some nasty hole for his entertainment and cure." "And," remarks John Crook, in his preface to William Bayley's works, "had not the

God of Israel been his physician there, he had been taken from us long before this." After alluding to his bold and zealous ministry, his diligence in it,—and to his courageous endurance of suffering, John Crook adds: "Methinks how once I saw him stand at the bar to plead his innocent cause (like Stephen) in the Senate-house, when the threats of his persecutors, crying out with a hideous noise, resembled the showers of stones falling upon that blessed martyr; and yet all this while he changed not his countenance, except by the additional ornaments of some innocent smiles."

In a work jointly written by William Bayley and John Crook, the following remarks occur:—"We do in the sight of God really own the blood of the Son of Man, . . . both as bespeaking the remission of sin past, through faith in it, and as sprinkling the conscience of true believers, and cleansing them from all sin. . . . By all which it is manifest to be of infinite value. . . . *But because we testify that it is not the bare, historical, and literal belief of those things that justifies or makes us really free from that wrath which comes upon every soul of man that doeth evil; but only the life and virtue of this blood, received into the heart by that living faith which Christ alone is author of: therefore we are branded with slighting the blood of the man Christ, etc. Though we testify that without the life and virtue of this blood there is no remission.*"

During his occasional voyages it was William Bayley's aim to avail himself of all suitable opportunities for ministerial service, and his labours were not in vain. He died at sea in 1675, when on a return voyage from

Barbadoes. "*Death is nothing in itself*," he said, "'for the sting of death is sin.' Friends at London would have been glad to see my face; tell them I go to my Father and their Father, to my God and their God. Remember my love to my dear wife; she will be a sorrowful widow; but let her not mourn in her sorrow, for it is well with me. I have left my children no portions, but my endeavour hath been to make God their Father. Shall I lay down my head on the waters? Well, God is the God of the whole universe."

Mary Bayley subsequently became the wife of John Cross, of London, and emigrated with him to America. In 1697, when residing at Charlestown, she gave a hospitable reception to her fellow-countryman, Robert Barrow, whom she nursed in the illness caused by the great hardships and privations which he had undergone after his escape from shipwreck on the coast of Florida. Early yielding his heart to the Lord, Robert Barrow had for many years earnestly laboured and patiently suffered for his Redeemer's cause. After much diligent ministerial service in Britain, in 1694 when old age was approaching, he sailed from his native land with Robert Wardel, of Sunderland, going forth "in the love of God" to preach the Gospel in the New World. Strengthened by Him these two aged ministers travelled through nine provinces, in which they held 328 meetings, and afterwards had much service in Antigua, the Bermudas, and Jamaica.

In the latter island they suffered from the extreme heat of the climate, and soon Robert Wardel was attacked by the illness which, after a few days, terminated his life. To the Friend who nursed him he said, "The Lord reward thee for thy tender care; it makes me think of my dear wife. I know not whether I may ever see her more, but, however, the will of God be done. I am, and was, willing to be contented with the will of God, whether life or death before I came hither." He exhorted the Friends who came to see him to "*answer God's love in them.*" He knew not what trials he was spared, and which were to be the lot of his beloved companion during the year that would elapse before he also reached his heavenly home.*

Four months after the death of his friend, Robert Barrow embarked for Pennsyvlania on board the *Reformation*, with two friends named Jonathan and Mary Dickenson, and their infant son; one other passenger, the captain, his negro crew, and some negro servants made up the ship's company. One night, whilst in the Gulf of Florida, they were driven ashore in a great storm. When daylight came Jonathan Dickenson succeeded in finding a nook with a few bushes, among the dreary sand-hills; for shelter was greatly needed from the violence of the wind and rain, especially by Mary Dickenson, her ailing baby, Robert Barrow, who had been ill, and the captain, who had broken his leg a few days earlier.

Soon two very fierce-looking Indians made their appearance, and on seeing the strangers rushed towards them, literally foaming with fury, and armed with long knives, with which they had been supplied by the

---

* For the incident in Robert Wardel's boyhood which led to his becoming a Friend, see Sketch of William Edmundson.

Spaniards; they immediately seized the first two men they met, who were carrying corn from the wreck to the bank on which Jonathan Dickenson stood. Some of the crew wished to get their guns in order to shoot their assailants, but Jonathan Dickenson counselled them to put their trust in the Lord, who was able to defend them to the uttermost, and also pointed out the impolicy of the proposed measure. He told his wife and friends of the approach of the Indians, and then the idea occurred to him of offering the ferocious-looking strangers some pipes and tobacco. Eagerly snatching them from him, and sniffing the air like so many wild beasts, they turned from him and ran away.

He rightly surmised that they had gone to fetch their comrades, a crowd of whom soon arrived, running and shouting. The greater part of them set to work to plunder the vessel, but about thirty, headed by the Cassekay, their chief, and armed with knives, fell upon the shipwrecked band, and with countenances which betokened extreme ferocity, cried out, "Nickaleer? Nickaleer?" They had an especial hatred of the English, and by this question tried to ascertain if the strangers were of that nation. Some they seized by the head, and, with outstretched arm and knife in hand, seemed only to be waiting for the Cassekay to begin the slaughter. Meanwhile most of the little group thus suddenly placed in the utmost peril, continued quietly sitting on their boxes and trunks, or on the ground, some of them, as Jonathan Dickenson records, "in a good frame of spirit, being freely given up to the will of God." Deliverance was at hand. In a moment these savages changed their demeanour, and stood spell-bound, as silent and almost as still as statues for about a quarter of an hour. Yet afterwards they not only emptied the chests of their contents, but proceeded to strip the owners of their clothing.

On coming again the next day, the chief addressed the direct question, "Nickaleer?" to Robert Barrow, who, avoiding the evasions as well as the false replies of which some of the party had made use with respect to their nationality, answered, "Yes." His clothes, which had hitherto been left him were now stripped off. The Cassekay had a smattering of Spanish, and the fact that Robert Barrow did not use that language—which had been employed by one of the crew — probably strengthened his suspicion that the white men were of English birth. At mid-day the Indians, having gathered together their plunder, loaded the lawful owners with it, and, forming a guard around them, summoned them to march to their village—a toilsome journey, five miles in length, to be performed barefoot, over deep sand, and under a burning sun. The captain, in consideration of his broken leg, was allowed the aid of his negro Ben, but Mary Dickenson was obliged to carry her baby herself; for, whenever any of her friends attempted to take it from her, they were told they should be shot if they laid down the load they already had. The wigwams being at length reached, the captives were offered food, but fear deprived some of appetite, and others, although hungry, were naturally disinclined to eat, because they thought it highly probable that the Indians—of whose habits they had heard—gave them food for the sake of afterwards feeding themselves upon them.

On the following day their fears were increased by

the arrival of another band of natives, armed with bows and arrows. That evening the aged Robert Barrow addressed his fellow-sufferers with deep feeling from the text, "Because thou hast kept the word of my patience, I also will keep thee," etc., and afterwards fervently besought the Lord that, if it were consistent with His blessed will, He would deliver them from a barbarous people; that their names might not be buried in oblivion, and that he might lay down his body amongst his faithful friends. An assurance was given him that this prayer would be granted, and some of his companions also were "livingly refreshed and strengthened."

After spending five days at this place they were allowed to depart, and directed their course towards St. Augustine. The dangers and hardships they encountered during the following six or seven weeks are far too numerous for record here. Three or four of the negroes perished, being unable to endure the wilderness journey, the perils by sea, the floods, the scanty and loathsome food, and the excessive suffering caused, in their unclothed and unsheltered condition, by the biting blasts of the north-west wind, which produced an extremely severe frost. At one time, when the cold was so intense that the strongest of the company doubted if they should outlive that day, it was thought best that those who could make speed should do so without waiting for others. Jonathan Dickenson, of course, remained with his wife and infant and Robert Barrow. The poor baby, although black with cold from head to foot, "was not froward," we are told. No doubt, unless it were absolutely impossible, his mother devised some sort of wrap for him, for the Indians had violently snatched off his clothes, "as though they would have shaken and torn him limb from limb."

At length St. Augustine was reached, and a most hospitable reception was given to the exhausted travellers by the Governor, who provided them with the food and clothing they so sorely needed; and when they set out for Carolina he furnished them with an escort. On their embarkation, embracing some of the company, he said, "You will forget me when you get among your own nation; but if you forget me, God will not." Some weeks later Charlestown was reached, and here Robert Barrow, in his great weakness and weariness, became the guest of Mary Cross. Writing from her house to his wife he says, "It pleased God I had the great fortune to have a good nurse; one whose name you have heard of, a Yorkshire woman born within two miles of York. Her maiden name was Mary Fisher—she that spake to the great Turk—afterward's William Bayley's wife. She is now my landlady and nurse." After spending some time at her house, Robert Barrow sailed with Jonathan Dickenson and his family for Philadelphia, where Jonathan Dickenson entered into business as a merchant. He was greatly beloved and respected, and for some years filled the office of Speaker in the Assembly, and was also Chief Justice of Pennsylvania.

When, at eight o'clock one evening, the vessel arrived at Philadelphia, several Friends came on board to greet Robert Barrow and conduct him on shore, but they found that he was too weak to be removed that night. Yet it rejoiced his heart to see them, and he spoke of how God had granted his prayer that he might lay down his bones in that place. His heart was strong, he said, and he hoped to go to their meeting again; the Lord had been very good to him, consoling him with His presence in all his trials. On the following morning some of the Friends from the city helped to bring the vessel up to a wharf, and, wrapping Robert Barrow in a blanket, carried him to the house of a Friend.* "The Lord has been very good to me all along to this very day," he remarked, "and this very morning hath sweetly refreshed me." Two days later he expired, after telling his friends that he had nothing to do but to die. Very early that morning he had asked a Friend who was with him to write to his "dear wife," to tell her of his travels, his arrival at Philadelphia, and that the Lord was with him.

Mary Cross was now a widow, and about seventy-three years of age. It would be interesting to trace her history to the end, but apparently no particulars of her last days have been left on record. It is probable that she died in South Carolina, where Sophia Hume, who was the grand-daughter of William Bayley and herself, was born.

Sophia Hume's father was not a Friend, and in her early days she allowed herself to be much absorbed in

---

* Samuel Carpenter, who (William Penn excepted) was considered the most wealthy person in the province. During a previous residence in Barbadoes he had suffered much from distraints, and in consequence of his conscientious objection to bearing arms. In 1693 he was made a Member of the Assembly, becoming, a few years later, one of the Council, and, finally, Treasurer of Pennsylvania. His benevolence, ability, and energy, won him much love and esteem.

empty worldly pleasures. Indeed half a lifetime had passed away before she awoke to the sense of the impossibility of being satisfied by such aimless pursuits. Her judgment was first convinced on this point, but it was not until she was about the age of forty that she fully yielded her heart to her Redeemer. She one day took up "Barclay's Apology" to search for some material for conversation, and being too much interested in it to lay it hastily down, its perusal led to her joining the Society of Friends, amongst whom she became a very remarkable minister. In later life, when London had become her residence, she thought it right to revisit her native land, to declare what God had done for her soul, and to call others away from those things which had for so long a time ensnared her own soul, but out of which she had been "brought and redeemed by the powerful hand of God." She died when in her seventy-third year, and was interred in the Bunhill Fields Burial-ground.

As we turn from the lives of any of our forefathers, who, "*through faith*, . . . wrought righteousness, obtained promises, . . . out of weakness were made strong, waxed valiant in fight, turned to flight the armies of the aliens,"—it may be well for us to ponder over the words of a writer of the day, who views the Society of Friends from an outside standpoint, whilst we remember that if our privileges are great the need for a faithful stewardship is but increased thereby:—"In its absolute recognition of the sacredness of individual responsibility, . . . above all in its intense recognition of a great spiritual force—call it by what name you will—which a man can lay hold of by faith and make his own, Quakerism stands alone and unrivalled. . . . St. Theresa said when she set to work to found a much-needed house of mercy with only three halfpence in her pocket, 'Theresa and three halfpence can do nothing; but God and three halfpence can do all things.' In this practical recognition of a great ever-present spiritual force, the power of the Holy Spirit, has not Quakerism still got much to teach the Church at large, and, once learnt, might not a new era dawn on Christianity?"

MARTYRS OF BOSTON AND THEIR FRIENDS.

"Not victims merely, they were willing sacrifices; they were not slain, they offered up themselves. . . . Willing submission, springing from trusting love, may indeed raise any sufferings into sacrifices, for God loveth a cheerful giver. In all sacrifices it is the offering up of self, not of things, which is precious—the love, and not the mere act."—"The Martyrs of Spain, and Liberators of Holland."

THE MARTYRS OF BOSTON AND THEIR FRIENDS.

"The blood which makes the robes of martyrs white, is not their own."—*The Author of " The Schönberg Cotta Family."*

"WHAT a God have the English, who deal so with one another about their God!" was the exclamation of an Indian chief after offering a "warm house" to Nicholas Upsal, who, notwithstanding the infirmities of old age, was exiled from Boston in the winter of 1656. He had ventured to remonstrate with the rulers of Massachusetts, on their passing a law for the banishment of "that cursed sect of *heretics* lately risen up in the world, commonly called Quakers," and prohibiting all commanders of ships, under penalty of a heavy fine, from bringing them into that jurisdiction. Leaving his wife and children, and the colony in which long before he had taken refuge from persecution at home, the old man at length reached Rhode Island. Although during many years he had taken deep interest in the particular Puritan congregation of which he was a member, he had found that forms and ceremonies could not satisfy his soul, and on hearing of the doctrines held by Friends he was "much refreshed." Probably some suspicion of this spiritual sympathy with the "heretics," increased the bitterness of his persecutors, who held the creed that,

"Toleration is the first-born child
Of all abominations and deceits."

Only a few months after the banishment of Nicholas Upsal, a vessel from London sailed into Boston Bay, on board of which were two Friends named Mary Dyer and Ann Burden. Both had left Massachusetts some twenty years earlier as Antinomian exiles, and Mary Dyer had taken a prominent part in that secession, whilst her force of character and vigorous understanding, no doubt, caused her to be regarded as a formidable opponent by the orthodox Puritans.

Her husband and herself took refuge in Rhode Island, which the new sect, with the assistance of Roger Williams, purchased of the Narragansett Indians. In this young colony it was decided that "none should be accounted a delinquent for doctrine." During a visit to Great Britain Mary Dyer became a Friend, and was a minister in that Society at the time of her return to the forbidden port of Boston. She is described by Croese as "a person of no mean extract and parentage, of an estate pretty plentiful, of a comely stature and countenance, of a piercing knowledge in many things, of a wonderful sweet and pleasant discourse—fit for great affairs." Ann Burden was a widow, and was desirous to collect some debts due to her husband's estate. But, as might be anticipated, both she and her friend were at once seized and cast into prison, and at the end of three months Ann Burden was banished to England. When Mary Dyer's husband, who was not a Friend, heard of her imprisonment, he came from Rhode Island, and succeeded in obtaining her release and leave to take her home, after becoming "bound in a great penalty not to lodge her in any town of the colony, nor permit any to have speech with her on the journey."

But no Puritanical power, no human hand, was strong enough to suppress the heaven-implanted and divinely-directed zeal of the Friends to share their spiritual treasure with others. About this time six of those who had been driven from Boston the preceding year, believed that the Lord was calling them thither again, and were assured that He would give them grace to endure any suffering they might have to pass through. But the practical difficulty was how to obtain a passage to New England, for the enactment of the Court of Boston naturally deterred the owners of vessels from taking them on board. This trial of faith was not a long one. A Friend and minister named Robert Fowler, who resided in Yorkshire, had been engaged in building a small bark, and had meanwhile been impressed with the idea that it was God's design that it should be used for the promotion of His cause. New England came before his mental vision, but imagining what might be involved by such a voyage, and dreading the parting from his wife and children, he at first thought he would as soon die as face the perils which would in all probability ensue. But after a while he was, we learn, "by the strength of God made willing to do His will," having been "refreshed and raised up by His instrument, George Fox." Accordingly he sailed to London, and there consulted a Friend who was deeply interested in the visits of ministers to distant lands; and wholly unsafe as it might seem to cross the Atlantic in so small a craft as the *Woodhouse*, no doubt was felt that this was the right mode of transit for the Friends who were anxious to return to Massachusetts. They were joined by five other ministers of the Society, one of whom was a young London merchant, named William Robinson.

In the summer of 1657 Robert Fowler received, he tells us, "the Lord's servants aboard, who came with a mighty hand and an outstretched arm with them." At the Downs William Dewsbury visited them. "When I came off," he writes to Margaret Fell, "they did go on in the name and power of the Lord our God. His everlasting presence keep them in the unity, in the life, and prosper them in His work: for many dear children shall come forth in the power of God in those countries where they desire to go."* Whilst the *Woodhouse* was waiting in Portsmouth Harbour for a fair wind, William Robinson addressed a few lines to Margaret Fell:—"My dear love salutes thee in that . . . which was before words were, in which I stand faithful to Him who hath called us. . . . I know thee and have union with thee, though absent from thee. . . . I thought good to let thee know the names of them that do go. . . . Humphrey Norton, Robert Hodshon, Dorothy Waugh, Christo. Holder, William Brend, John Copeland, Richard Doudney, Mary Weatherhead, Sarah Gibbons, Mary Clarke. The Master of the ship, his name is Robert Fowler, a Friend." He writes this letter from Southampton, where he had landed with another Friend in order to

---

* In the following year the first Yearly Meeting of the Society was held at Scalehouse, in Yorkshire, at which it was recommended that a general collection should be made in aid of Gospel Missions, "to be speedily sent up to London as a free-will offering for the Seed's sake;" and an Epistle to this effect was drawn up, in which, also, deep sympathy is expressed for those who had "so freely given up their friends, their near relations, their country, and worldly estates, yea, and their own lives."

hold a meeting, for—as Robert Fowler quaintly says in reference to this delay—"the ministers of Christ were not idle, but went forth and gathered sticks, and kindled a fire, and *left it burning.*" The voyage of the little bark was a very remarkable one.

For fifty leagues they were accompanied by three ships bound for Newfoundland, which speedily took a northward course on seeing the approach of a man-of-war. Humphrey Norton told the captain that early in the morning it had been shown him that enemies were near, and also that the Lord would preserve them from harm; and by means of a strong wind they were delivered from their dangerous position. Left alone on the wide ocean, they earnestly sought guidance from God, and believed that He bade them "cut through, steer their straightest course, and mind nothing but Him." "Unto which thing," says Robert Fowler, "He much provoked us, and caused us to meet together every day, and He Himself met with us, and manifested Himself largely unto us. After we had been five weeks at sea, wherein the powers of darkness appeared in the greatest strength against us, having sailed but about 300 leagues, Humphrey Norton, falling into communion with God, told me that he had received a comfortable answer; and also that about such a day we should land in America, which was even so fulfilled." They likewise felt that the circumstances attending their landing in the New World wonderfully manifested the loving care of their Lord. Blessed will be the result if we their successors, crossing "Life's solemn main," with a like faith "steer the straightest course" through its varied avocations, hallowing all by performing them under God's guidance and in the light of His countenance.

As the vessel was entering a creek between Dutch Plantation and Long Ireland, "the power of the Lord," writes Robert Fowler, "fell much upon us, and an irresistible word came unto us, *That the seed in America shall be as the sand of the sea:* it was published in the ears of the brethren, which caused tears to break forth in fulness of joy." He was also able to rejoice in the evidence granted him that the prayers of the Church at home did indeed ascend on their behalf. Five of the Friends landed at New York, whilst the remaining six went on to Rhode Island. Soon after their arrival, John Copeland says in a letter to his parents:—"Take no thought for me. The Lord's power hath overshadowed me, and man I do not fear; for my trust is in the Lord, who is become our shield and buckler, and exceeding great reward." Thus did God prepare His youthful servant to suffer for His sake.

A few weeks later, Christopher Holder and himself were lying in Boston gaol, without bedding, or even straw, fearfully lacerated from the effect of thirty lashes barbarously inflicted with a knotted scourge. For three days the gaoler refused to supply them with food or water, but they were upheld by their Saviour, and enabled to rejoice in His manifested love. Being accused as "blasphemers, heretics, and deceivers," they issued a declaration of faith, containing the following sentences:—

"In Him do we believe, who is the only-begotten Son of the Father, full of grace and truth. And in Him do we trust alone for salvation; by whose blood we are washed from sin; through Whom we have access to the Father with boldness, being justified by faith in believing in His name. Who has sent forth the Holy Ghost, to wit, the Spirit of Truth, that proceedeth from the Father and the Son; by which we are sealed and adopted sons and heirs of the kingdom of Heaven. . . . Believe in the Light, that you may be children of the light; for as you love it and obey it, it will lead you to repentance, bring you to know Him in whom is remission of sins, in Whom God is well pleased; Who will give you an entrance into the kingdom of God, an inheritance amongst them that are sanctified."

But the Governors would not allow any such assertion to alter their opinion that Quakerism was a dangerous heresy, and, terribly rigorous as was the law against its promulgators, it was not sufficiently so to satisfy them; for Endicott and Bellingham gave orders that all the Friends then in prison should be severely whipped twice a week. But the humanity of the inhabitants of Boston revolted at this decree, and the sympathy thus aroused led to the release of the sufferers, who were at once banished from the colony. Soon afterwards John Copeland and his friend William Brend were sentenced to a severe scourging when passing through New Plymouth. The age of the latter awoke no compassion in the hearts of the persecutors; the following year, after holding several meetings with William Ledra, of Barbadoes, he was imprisoned at Boston, and received such brutal beatings—inflicted with a pitched rope, by a gaoler who had previously kept him without food for five days, and most cruelly fettered him for many hours—that he appeared to be dying.* Endicott being alarmed at this, sent a physician to him, who thought

---

* W. B. had refused to work, not thinking it right to submit to prison discipline, as his confinement was unjust.

his recovery impossible. But the hand of an unseen Healer was laid on him, and he must have been at least ninety when, eighteen years later, the following burial note was made out:—"William Brend, of the Liberty of Katherine's, near the Tower, a minister, died 7-vii. 1676, and was buried at Bunhill Fields." Before returning to England he laboured in Rhode Island and the West Indies.

In 1662 he was one of the many hundred Friends confined in Newgate, fifty-two of whom died in consequence of diseases caused by the loathsome state of that prison. We may form some idea of the heavenly consolation granted to this venerable pilgrim, in that hour of need, by his beautiful "Salutation to all Friends," from which a brief extract follows:—"It hath been upon my heart when in the sweet repose of the streams of my Father's love and life, by which my heart hath been overcome, to visit you with a loving salutation from the place of my outward bonds." After bidding them "flock together into our Father's fold, to get into His tent of safety, and lie down in the arms of His dear love," etc., he adds: "Oh! in the love and life of the Lamb, *look over all weakness in one another*, as God doth look over all the weakness in every one of us, and doth love us for His own Son's sake—in so doing peace will abound in our borders, it will flow forth amongst us like a river, and it will keep out jars, strifes, and contentions."

As the Governors of Massachusetts were regardless of old age, so were they of the weakness of women: we read of the astonishment of the people of Boston at hearing Sarah Gibbons and her young friend, Dorothy

Waugh, offering praise and thanksgiving for the gracious support granted them during a cruel scourging, three days before and three days after which they were kept without food. A little later Endicott sentenced Hored Gardner, of Rhode Island, to the punishment of the knotted scourge: she had left her home at Newport, with the belief that her Lord had called her to labour for Him at Weymouth, in Massachusetts, where her ministry was cordially received. The maid who had accompanied her on this perilous journey, to assist in taking charge of her infant, was the victim of a similar sentence; and the only protection granted the baby was that afforded by its mother's arms, who—when the executioner stayed his hands—prayed that her persecutors might be forgiven, because "they knew not what they did."

At a later date, Alice Ambrose, Mary Tomkins, and Ann Coleman (who was, apparently, young and in delicate health), were sentenced to be whipped through eleven towns, covering a distance of nearly eighty miles. Although they were themselves enabled to praise the Lord for the marvellous help He granted them, the sight of their "torn bodies and weary steps" in the third town through which they passed, excited so much pity that one of the inhabitants induced the constable to commit the prisoners and the warrant to his care, and at once set them at liberty. Taking advantage of their unlooked-for release, they went to New Quechawanah, where they had a meeting. It was for a time feared that Ann Coleman would die from the effect of other barbarous scourgings. To George Fox she writes: "Oh, the love of the Lord, who hath kept His handmaid that put her trust in Him. . . . What shall I say unto thee of the love of my Father. . . . *None can make me afraid.* . . . Much service for the Lord in this land, and it hath not been in vain; and so, let thy prayers be unto the Lord for me. . . . In that life and love which is unchangeable art thou near me." Good cause, indeed, has that patient historian, Sewel, for exclaiming, "But when should I have done, if I would describe all the whippings inflicted on the Quakers in those parts!"

Sarah Gibbons and Dorothy Waugh, soon after leaving Boston, returned to Rhode Island, where they had previously been engaged in religious service, and we now find their names associated with that of Mary Dyer. About this time Humphrey Norton was finding a short respite from persecution in the same colony. A few months earlier his ministerial labours had been interrupted by an imprisonment at Newhaven, Connecticut, where his right hand was deeply branded with the letter H, as a sign that he was a condemned heretic, and he was flogged in such a manner as to make some from the crowd, gathered by beat of drum, exclaim, "Do they mean to kill the man?" But He, who of old caused His children to receive "no hurt" in the midst of the seven-times heated furnace, wonderfully upheld him in this hour of extremest need; for he states that his "body was as if it had been covered with balm." Much did the people marvel when, at the conclusion of the infliction, he raised his voice in thanksgiving and prayer. Not long after Humphrey Norton received another scourging at New Plymouth.

His rest in Rhode Island was a short one, for he soon thought it right to go to Boston in company with a young Friend, named John Rous, who had previously been his associate in service, and sometimes in suffering, for their Lord; he was the son of Lieutenant-Colonel Rous, a wealthy sugar-planter of Barbadoes, who afterwards became a Friend, having, it is said, been much impressed by the ministry of his son. When Humphrey Norton told John Rous that sleep had fled from him because of the sorrow occasioned by a "sense of the strength of the enmity against the righteous seed" in Boston, he also felt that he must bear a part "with the prisoners of hope, which at that time stood bound for the testimony of Jesus." In order to lose no time, they travelled night and day, and on their arrival at Boston were told of the state in which William Brend then lay, from the effect of the gaoler's cruelty, and were begged by their informant to leave the town, or they would be "dead men." But they were bound on a holy mission, from which no human power could turn them aside. "Such was our load," says Humphrey Norton, "that beside Him who laid it upon us, no flesh nor place could ease us." And a few hours later we find him, at the conclusion of the usual lecture of John Norton—a minister who notoriously instigated persecution—beginning an address in these words: "Verily this is the sacrifice which the Lord God accepts not; for whilst with the same spirit that you sin—you preach, and pray, and sing; that sacrifice is an abomination."

Although a charge of blasphemy could not be proved against him, there was no doubt that his companion and himself were guilty of being Quakers, and as such they were sentenced to imprisonment and whipping.

The former, as the son of Lieutenant-Colonel Rous, who had formerly resided in the colony, was at first courteously treated by the magistrates, who hoped they might induce this young champion of the Cross to cast aside "the heresy" he was upholding. But, notwithstanding their flattery, he steadfastly stood his ground; vindicated the doctrines which he had adopted; and, as an English citizen, claimed the right of a trial in an English Court. The Governors, knowing that an alarming exposure of their conduct towards Friends would be involved by this, would not hear of such a course. "No appeal to England! No appeal to England!" was their cry. Three days later the prisoners underwent the flogging to which they had been condemned; but when this punishment was soon renewed, the public indignation, already aroused by the treatment of William Brend, became so strong that it soon led to the liberation of the prisoners.

In the midst of all afflictions the Friends were aided by the assurance that their labours and sufferings were not in vain in the Lord. In a letter to Margaret Fell, John Rous says: "A firm foundation is there laid in this land, such an one as the devil will never get broken up." He writes this letter when again in Boston prison, where, about a fortnight later, he and his companions, John Copeland and Christopher Holder, underwent the mutilation of having the right ear cut off. Shall we shrink from reading of their sufferings when we see the spirit with which they were enabled to endure them? "*In the strength of God*," is their language, "*we suffered joyfully*, having freely given up not one member, but all, if the Lord so required, for the sealing of our testimony which the Lord hath given us;" words which may recall those of Brainerd with regard to his prayers for his brother and himself: "My heart sweetly exulted in the thought of any distresses that might light on him or me, in the advancement of Christ's kingdom upon earth."

A few years later, John Rous settled in England, and married the eldest daughter of his beloved friend Margaret Fell, to whom he proved a true son. Early in 1659, and a few months after the release of John Rous and his companions, William Robinson, whose labours had been chiefly confined to Virginia, where his ministry was much blessed, arrived at Rhode Island. Here he met with Marmaduke Stevenson, who had lately come from Barbadoes, and who was a young Yorkshire agriculturist. Four years earlier, when following the plough in his native land, he was —to quote his own words—"filled with the love and presence of the living God, which did ravish my heart ... and as I stood still, with my heart and mind stayed upon the Lord, the word of the Lord came to me in a still, small voice, 'I have ordained thee a prophet unto the nations.'" He knew that he "was but a child for such a weighty matter," but he was empowered to put his trust in God, and when Barbadoes was set before him, a heavenly assurance was given him that the Lord would provide for his "dear and loving wife and tender children." Three years later he sailed for that island, where, on hearing of the law which had been passed in New England for putting to death such Friends as returned after banishment, an inward voice seemed to whisper: "Thou knowest not, but thou mayst go thither;" and after a while, finding a vessel ready for a voyage to Rhode Island, he took his passage in her. He spent a short time in religious service amongst the Friends there, but writes that "the word of the Lord came to him saying, 'Go to Boston, with thy brother, William Robinson,' and at His command I was obedient to give up to His will; . . . for He had said unto me that He had a great work for me to do."

To Robinson, also, as clear a call had been given whilst going one afternoon from Newport to the residence of one of his friends. "The word of the Lord," he says, "came expressly unto me, and commanded me to pass to the town of Boston, my life to lay down in His will, for the accomplishing of His service. . . . I was a child and obedience was demanded of me by the Lord, who filled me with living strength and power from His heavenly presence, which at that time did mightily overshadow me, and my life did say Amen to what the Lord required of me." The two young ministers arrived at Boston on one of the public fast-days, and at the conclusion of a religious service they thought it right to attempt to address the assembly, but were soon arrested. Their imprisonment was shared by a child of eleven or twelve, from Providence, named Patience Scott, who had sometimes spoken in religious meetings, and now believed herself called on to plead with the persecutors, from whose cruelty her mother had not long before severely suffered. When this little girl was examined by the magistrates we find that "she spoke so well to the purpose that she confounded her enemies," who, after due consideration of "the malice of

Satan by all means and ways to propagate error—put to his shifts to make use of such a child," decided " so far to slight her as a Quaker, as only to admonish and instruct her according to her capacity, and to discharge her."

In a letter to George Fox, from Boston gaol, William Robinson writes of how God had had compassion on him,—" seeing how willingly I was given up to do His will,"—by constraining Marmaduke Stevenson to accompany him to Boston. He thus concludes:—" Oh! my dearly beloved, thou who art endued with power from on High; who art of a quick discerning in the fear of God; oh! remember us—let thy prayers be put up unto the Lord God for us, that His power and strength may rest with us and upon us; that faithful we may be preserved to the end. Amen."*

Soon the aged Mary Dyer arrived at Boston, constrained to carry comfort and cheer to her captive fellow-believers there, and was shortly imprisoned also. When the Friends were at length brought before the governors and magistrates, Robinson endeavoured to make them comprehend that his companions and himself had come to Boston from the clear conviction that such was the will of God concerning them; and therefore, if the rulers put them to death for breaking their law, they would be guilty of shedding innocent blood. It is said—and there is no slight significance in the remark—that his words seemed to "cut them to the quick;" but the speaker was soon silenced by a hand-

---

* See *Bowden's History of the Society of Friends in America* (vol. i. p. 170), in which most of the material used in constructing this sketch has been found.

kerchief being thrust into his mouth, and was afterwards sentenced to receive twenty lashes in the streets of the city. The Friends were then liberated and ordered to leave the jurisdiction on pain of death.

William Robinson and Marmaduke Stevenson, living, as they did, under a higher and holier law than any mere human authority, felt that the Lord still had need of them to testify for Him in this colony; so on the day after their release they went to Salem, desiring to invigorate the faith of their friends in that neighbourhood. The latter, who were afraid to have meetings held in their houses, met the ministers in a wood not far from the town, where, so writes a Friend who was present, " a great flocking there was to hear. The Lord was mightily with them, and they spake of the things of God boldly, to the affecting and tendering the hearts of many." A warm welcome was given them as they went northwards to Piscattaway.

The mere fact of remaining in Massachusetts, at the peril of their lives, in order to display the banner of their Lord, naturally gave rise to inquiry concerning the doctrines they preached. A Friend who had accompanied Marmaduke Stevenson from Rhode Island, writes:—" Divers were convinced, the power of the Lord accompanying them, and with astonishment confounded their enemies before them; great was their service abroad in that jurisdiction for four weeks and upwards." When these labours were ended they were constrained by the love of Christ to visit Boston, there to be witnesses for Him. They were joined by six Friends of Salem, who, animated by a like holy motive, wished, even at the risk of their own safety, to uphold the hands of those whom they already looked on as martyrs.

As this little band of faithful men and women drew near the city they were met by the constabulary and a rough crowd, and were soon committed to prison. Robinson and Stevenson were placed in chains, and confined in a separate cell, whilst all their papers, including the journal of the former, were taken from them. A few days earlier, Mary Dyer, who had spent a little while with her family, had reappeared, and been again imprisoned. Before long the three Friends were brought before the General Court, and to Endicott's question why they had returned to the jurisdiction whence they had been banished on pain of death, they each replied that they came only in obedience to the Divine call. William Robinson asked leave to read an explanation which he had prepared, and when forbidden to do this, laid it on the table.

After describing the heavenly intimation he had received that it was God's will that he should lay down his life for the cause of Christ, he writes: "I, being a child, durst not question the Lord in the least, and as the Lord made me willing, dealing gently and kindly with me, as a tender father by a faithful child whom he tenderly loves, so the Lord did deal with me, in ministering His life unto me, which gave and gives me strength to perform what the Lord required of me. . . . Therefore all who are ignorant of the motion of the Lord in the inward parts, be not hasty in judging in this matter. . . . The presence of the Lord and His Heavenly life doth accompany me, so that I can say in truth, Blessed be the Lord God of my life, who hath counted me worthy and called me hereunto. . . . Will ye put us to death for obeying the Lord, the God of the whole earth?"

Endicott took up this document, and, after reading it, pronounced the sentence of death on its writer. A few days before his execution, in an epistle addressed "To the Lord's people," William Robinson says: "The streams of my Father's love run daily through me, from the Holy Fountain of Life to the seed throughout the whole creation. I am overcome with love, for it is my life and length of days; it is my glory and my daily strength. I am full of the quickening power of the Lord Jesus Christ. . . . I shall enter with my Beloved into eternal rest and peace, and I shall depart with everlasting joy in my heart, and praises in my mouth." After Marmaduke Stevenson had received his sentence, he solemnly addressed the magistrates, concluding with these words: "Assuredly if you put us to death, you will bring innocent blood upon your own heads, and swift destruction will come upon you." It is a remarkable fact that many of these persecutors came to an untimely end, or were visited by severe personal calamities which resulted in death. "The hand or judgment of the Lord is upon me," were the words of John Norton, who, whilst walking in his own house, leant his head against a chimney-piece, and sank down never to speak again. And Major-General Adderton, who had scoffingly said, "The judgments of the Lord God are not come upon us yet!" was overtaken by a sudden and shocking death.

During his imprisonment Stevenson wrote his "Call to the Work and Service of the Lord;" and, not losing sight of his old friends, he prepared an address to his "neighbours and the people of the town of Shipton, Weighton, and elsewhere." "My love runs out to you all in pity to your souls," he writes, "which lie in death as mine hath done, but the Lord in His eternal love hath redeemed me. . . . When I ponder it in my heart, my soul is ravished with His love, and broken into tears at His kindness towards me, who was by nature a child of wrath as well as others. Oh, the consideration of His love hath constrained me to follow Him, and to give up all for His sake, if it be the laying down of my life; for none are the disciples of Christ but they that follow Him in His cross. The Lord knows I do not forget you."

A few days before his execution, he wrote a letter, "To the Lord's People," from which the following extracts are taken:—

"You lambs of my Father's fold and sheep of His pasture, the remembrance of you is precious to me, my dearly beloved ones, . . . who are reconciled to God, and one to another, in that which sea and land cannot separate; here you may feel me knit and joined to you in the spirit of truth; and linked to you as members of His body, who is our Head and Rock of sure defence; here we are kept safe in the hour of temptation and in the day of trial shall we be preserved in the hollow of His hand; here His banner of love will be over us. . . . So, my dear friends! let us always wait at the altar of the Lord, to see the table spread, that so we may sit down and eat together, and be refreshed with the hidden manna, that comes from Him, who is our life, our peace, our strength, and our preserver night and day. Oh, my beloved ones! let us all go on in His strength, who is our Prince and Saviour. . . . If I forget you, then let the Lord forget me. Nay, verily, you cannot be forgotten by me; so long as I abide in the Vine, I am a branch of the same nature with you, which the Lord hath blessed, we grow together in His life and image, as members of His body; where we shall live together to all eternity."

After Mary Dyer had heard her sentence, she only replied by the significant words, "The will of the Lord be done." And when Endicott impatiently exclaimed, "Take her away, marshal," she added, "Yea, joyfully I go;" for her heart was filled with heavenly consolation from the love of Christ, and from the thought that she was counted worthy to suffer for His sake. She told the marshal that it was unnecessary for him to guard her to the prison. "I believe you, Mrs. Dyer," he answered; "but I must do as I am commanded." From the House of Correction she addressed "An Appeal to the Rulers of Boston," in which she asks nothing for herself, but manifests—as an anonymous writer remarks—" the courage of an apostle contending for the Truth, and the tenderness of a woman feeling for the sufferings of her people." She writes: "I have no self ends, the Lord knoweth; for if my life were freely granted by you, it would not avail me, so long as I should daily hear or see the sufferings of my dear brethren." It is said that on the day preceding that appointed for the execution, Mary Dyer's eldest son arrived at Boston, and was allowed to remain all night with his mother; he came in the vain hope of inducing her to make such concessions as might be the means of saving her life.

The erection of gallows on Boston Common for these guiltless victims awakened such strong feelings of amazement and indignation amongst the inhabitants, as to give alarm to the magistrates. On the morning of the day appointed for the execution a great number of people gathered around the prison, and gave earnest attention to William Robinson, who addressed them from the open window of an upper room. But the rulers, who always studiously endeavoured to prevent the Friends from holding intercourse with the colonists, were afraid for the crowd to listen, at this crisis, to Quaker preaching, and accordingly sent a military captain to disperse them. Finding this impracticable, he entered the gaol in a violent passion, and, hurling some of the prisoners down stairs, shut them into a low dark cell. One of this little company writes: "As we sat together waiting upon the Lord, it was a time of love; for as the world hated us and despitefully used us, so the Lord was pleased in a wonderful manner to manifest His supporting love and kindness to us in our innocent sufferings; especially to the worthies who had now near finished their course. . . . God was with them, and many sweet and heavenly sayings they gave unto us, being themselves filled with comfort. . . . While we were yet embracing each other, with full and tender hearts, the officers came in and took the two from us [Robinson and Stevenson], as sheep for the slaughter."

Boston Common was separated by the distance of a mile from the gaol, and the prisoners were escorted by two hundred men, armed with halberds, guns, swords, and pikes—in addition to many horsemen. It was thought the safest arrangement for this procession to avoid the direct thoroughfare through the city, and the drummers were ordered to walk immediately before the three captives, and to beat more loudly if they should attempt to speak: thus when William Robinson did so, the only words which were audible were, "This is your hour, and the power of darkness." Marmaduke Stevenson's voice was drowned by the same means. "Yet, they went on," as Sewel says, "with great cheerfulness, as going to an everlasting wedding"—which, indeed, they were.

In reply to a coarse taunt from the marshal, Mary Dyer said, "This is to me an hour of the greatest joy I ever had in this world. No ear can hear, no tongue can utter, no heart can understand, the sweet incomes and the refreshings of the Spirit of the Lord which I now feel." Having bade farewell to his friends, and mounted the scaffold, William Robinson addressed the assembled crowd: "We suffer not as evil-doers, but as those who have testified and manifested the Truth. This is the day of your visitation, and therefore I desire you to mind the light of Christ which is in you, to which I have borne testimony, and am now going to seal my testimony with my blood." Wilson, a minister of the city, changing the scoffing tone he had assumed whilst they were walking to the Common, now exclaimed,—"Hold thy tongue, be silent, thou art going to die with a lie in thy mouth." After the executioner had adjusted the rope, William Robinson said, "Now are ye made manifest; I suffer for Christ, *in whom I live, and for whom I die!*" Marmaduke Stevenson also spoke a few words to the spectators: "Be it known unto you all this day that we suffer not as evil-doers, but for conscience' sake. This day shall we be at rest with the Lord." We may easily imagine that Mary Dyer would now feel that much of the ordeal was over. Yet, even when witnessing the death of her young companions, we may believe, as we recur to the words she had lately uttered, that she might have said,—

> "Like to a sea-girt rock I stand,
>   Deep sunk in peace, though storms rage by,
> As calm as if on every hand,
>   Were only Thou, O God, and I."

When every preparation had been made for her execution, the awful silence maintained around the stage was broken by the piercing cry: "Stop! she is reprieved." This respite had been granted to the prolonged intercession of her son, who was waiting at the prison to welcome her. The friends of the martyrs were not allowed to provide coffins for them, nor even to enclose the pit into which the bodies were thrown. Wilson, the minister to whom allusion has already been made, composed a scoffing song on the sufferers.

But no amount of indignity which might be heaped upon them could prevent their death from being a solemn attestation to the futility of every effort of a blind bigotry to crush the conscience of those who, bearing the image and superscription of Christ, rendered unto God the things that are God's; and consequently with regard to these "things," acknowledged no ruler but Him in whose kingdom their spirits dwelt. So deep an impression was made on John Chamberlain, an inhabitant of Boston, by what he saw and heard that day, as to cause his convincement of the truth of the doctrines held by Friends; before two years were over he had been imprisoned, banished, and also cruelly whipped through three towns; yet his Saviour suffered not his faith to fail, for we learn that this persecution, "so far from beating him from the Truth, rather drove him nearer to it."

About five months after leaving Massachusetts, Mary Dyer felt that it was her duty to return to Boston once more. She had in the interval, besides visiting her home, spent some time in Long Island, and had also laboured for her Lord at Shelter Island. It was early in 1660 that she re-entered Boston, where many Friends who had arrived in the province were now imprisoned, and, after pursuing her gospel service for ten days, she was arraigned before the General Court. When the sentence of death had been passed she said: "I came in obedience to the will of God to the last General Court, praying you to repeal your unrighteous sentence of banishment upon pain of death: and that same is my work now and earnest request, although I told you that if you refused to repeal it, the Lord would send other of His servants to witness against it." Here Endicott interrupted her to ask, "Are you a prophetess?" "I spoke the words," was her reply, "which the Lord spoke to me, and now the thing is come to pass." She would have added more on what she had felt to be the Lord's call to her, had not the Governor impatiently exclaimed, "Away with her! away with her!"

At nine the following morning the marshal came to fetch her; a strong guard of soldiers were in attendance, and drummers were ordered to walk before and behind the prisoner, so soon to receive an eternal release. After she had ascended the ladder, she was told that if she would return home her life should be spared. "Nay," she answered, "I cannot; for in obedience to the will of the Lord I came, and in His will I abide, faithful unto death." To the charge of being guilty of her own blood, she replied; "Nay, I came to take blood-guiltiness from *you*, desiring you to repeal the unrighteous and unjust law; therefore my blood will be required of your hands, who wilfully do it." When asked if she wished any of the people to pray for her, she said she desired the prayers of all the people of God: and to the proposal that an Elder should do so, she answered: "Nay—first a child, then a young man, then a strong man, before [being] an Elder in Christ Jesus." When accused of having said she had been in Paradise, she replied, without hesitation, "Yea, I have been in Paradise these several days." The few more words she spoke were on the everlasting happiness now so near at hand.

A Friend who had united in her ministerial services on Shelter Island sums up his description of her by saying: "She even shined in the image of God." On the day of Mary Dyer's martyrdom, two of the imprisoned Friends, Joseph and Jane Nicholson, from Cumberland, were summoned by the rulers, in the hope that the deed that had just been enacted would shake their constancy; but, as a contemporary writer says, "The power of the Lord in them was above all, and they feared them not, nor their threats of putting them to death." These menaces were not, however, carried out: probably the manifestation of public feeling warned those in authority that there might be danger in again perpetrating an execution wholly unsanctioned by the laws of the realm. Yet some eight or nine months later, William Ledra—who is said to have been a Cornishman, though his home was in Barbadoes—was condemned to death for having returned to Boston after sentence of banishment.

When in 1658, after mutual labours for their Lord, Ledra had shared the imprisonment of his friend William Brend in an unventilated cell—the cruelty of which he had been the victim had imperilled his life: and now, notwithstanding the inclemency of a New England winter, he was kept chained in an open prison. On the day before his death he addressed a letter to "The little flock of Christ," in which he remarks that he was filled "with the joy of the Lord in the beauty of holiness, whilst his spirit was wholly swallowed up in the bosom of eternity. . . . As the flowing of the ocean [he continues] doth fill every creek and branch thereof, and then retires again towards its own being and fulness, and leaves a savour behind it: so doth the life and virtue of God flow into every one of your hearts, whom He hath made partakers of His Divine nature." In allusion to his tender yearnings for the young, he says: "Stand in the watch within in the fear of the Lord, which is the very entrance of wisdom, and the state wherein you are ready to receive the secrets of the Lord. Hunger and thirst patiently, be not weary, neither doubt; stand still, and cease from thine own workings, and in due time thou shalt enter into the rest, and thine eyes shall behold His salvation. . . . Confess Him before men. . . . Bring all things to the light, that they may be proved whether they are wrought in God. . . . Without grace possessed, there is no assurance of salvation. By grace you are saved."

The following day the fetters which had so long bound him were knocked off, and we are told that he went "forth to the slaughter in the meekness of the Spirit of Jesus." He was surrounded by soldiers, in order to prevent intercourse with his friends; but before mounting the scaffold he exhorted one of them to faithfulness, and on bidding him farewell added, "All that will be Christ's disciples must take up His cross." A visitor to the city, from England, who witnessed this scene, having asked leave to speak said; "Gentlemen, I am a stranger both to your persons and country, yet a friend of both. For the Lord's sake take not away the man's life, but remember Gamaliel's counsel to the Jews.—'if it be of men it will come to nought; but if it be of God ye cannot overthrow it;' be careful ye are not found fighters against God." This courageous stranger also told them that they had "no warrant from the word of God, nor precedent from our country, nor power from His Majesty, to hang the man." William Ledra's last words were, "I commend my righteous cause unto Thee, O God! Lord Jesus, receive my spirit."

A few weeks before his death he wrote the following testimony to the willingness of God to supply *all* the need of His faithful followers:—"I testify in the fear of the Lord God that the noise of the whip on my back, all the imprisonments, and the loud threatening of a halter, *did no more affright me, through the strength and power of God, than if they had threatened to have bound a spider's web on my finger*—which makes me say with unfeigned lips, Wait upon the Lord, O my soul!" Like Josiah Southwick, of Salem, he might have said,

"Tongue cannot express the goodness and love of God to His suffering people." "Here is my body," were the words of the latter when sentenced to a severe scourging; "if you want a further testimony to the Truth I profess, take it and tear it in pieces; *your sentence is no more terrifying to me than if you had taken a feather and blown it up in the air.*"

On the day of William Ledra's execution, Wenlock Christison, of Salem, was placed at the bar; he, too, had experienced, as Milton says of those days, that—

> "Heavy persecution shall arise
> On all, who in the worship persevere
> Of Spirit and truth."

Although exiled on pain of death, he had reappeared at Boston, and caused such consternation by entering the Court just as sentence of death was being pronounced on his friend, as to cause perfect silence for awhile. When, now, in his turn condemned to die, he said, "The will of the Lord be done. . . . If you have power to take my life from me, *the which I question—I believe you shall never more take Quakers' lives from them. Note my words.*"

Just at this crisis the rulers of Massachusetts received tidings from England which caused a sudden change in their conduct; for on the day preceding that which had been fixed on for the execution of Wenlock Christison, he and twenty-seven other Friends were set at liberty; and after two of them had been whipped through the town they were taken by a body of soldiers out of the jurisdiction.

It would be but a false refinement of feeling to be unwilling to read of the sufferings which, not young and strong men only, but tender and delicate women, were enabled to *endure* for Christ. Moreover, is there not instruction for us in this—

> "Mournful record of an earlier age,
> That pale and half-effaced lies hidden away
> Beneath the fresher writing of to-day"?

We are not called to martyrdom: yet—notwithstanding our exemption from outward suffering, our unmolested meetings, the open door set before us for sharing with others the truths committed to our trust— we are bidden to present our "bodies a *living* sacrifice wholly acceptable unto God," seeking to know His will (whether it leads in the hidden or more public path), in order that "all the good pleasure of His goodness, and the work of faith with power, may be fulfilled."

> "Thou shalt lose thy life and find it; thou shalt boldly cast it forth;
> And then back again receiving, know it in its endless worth."

JOHN GRATTON.

"WHEN I desired to speak to my Beloved, He Himself met me most joyfully. 'Behold, I am here,' He said, 'tell me now what new thing has happened; but let it not slip from thee what thou art both to do and suffer for Me.'"—THOMAS À KEMPIS.

PASSAGES IN THE LIFE OF JOHN GRATTON.

"Thrice is he armed that hath his quarrel just."

THE autobiography of John Gratton* is probably but little known in the present day. His chief end in writing it is, he tells us, "*that others may take courage to trust in God and be obedient to Him in all things.*"

He was born in Derbyshire, in 1643, and when still very young and employed in keeping his father's sheep, the voice of the Heavenly Shepherd was often heard in his soul. "Being but a child," he says, "I did not yet know the Lord, nor think it had been He that met me in my heart and conscience." The sense given him of his sinfulness often troubled his heart; but too frequently the temptation to join his playfellows in such sports and amusements as he knew to be wrong, overcame him. The "sinful foolish pastimes" were very tempting, and heavenly peace was bartered for earthly pleasure. Still did the Holy Spirit strive in his soul, at one time sharply reproving at another gently guiding him; until at length the sinfulness of his heart was shown him in such a manner as to cause him deep

---

* "Journal of the Life of that *Ancient Servant of Christ* JOHN GRATTON; giving an Account of his Exercises when Young, and how he came to the knowledge of the TRUTH and was thereby raised up to Preach the Gospel; as also his *Labours, Travels, and Sufferings* for the same. Printed by J. Sowle, at the Bible in George Yard in Lombard Street. 1720." Reprinted by Thomas Claye: Stockport. 1823. Pp. 123.

distress; but a secret hope sustained him and encouraged him to pray, though he knew not how. "Still," he writes, "I found not power to forsake the sins I was so prone to, because I received not Him to whom all is given, nor yet knew Him. . . . And though he appeared to me wonderfully by His Spirit I still rejected His counsel, . . . though He had long waited to be gracious to me." He read much and conferred with many on religious subjects, going from one place to another to hear the great preachers of Oliver Cromwell's time. After a while he joined the Presbyterian Church, and opened his heart a little to some whom he hoped would help him.

"But, alas! alas!" he writes, "they could not aid me, but would tell me it was a good condition, and I must be troubled with my sins as long as I lived, . . . and all this to persuade me to sit down contented, before I was cleansed and washed from my sins. I dared not join in the singing of psalms, feeling I could not sing them truly as *my* song. I prayed much in private, in the stable, in barns, and in bed, and on the high moor. One day, being on the top of a hill in the snow, I cried aloud with strong cries to the Lord, being all alone, and desired Him to show me my own heart, and the Lord was pleased to hear and answer my prayer at that time; so that He gave me so to see my own heart, that I knew it was the Lord did show it to me to my satisfaction, for I plainly saw it to be deceitful, and not a good, humble, pure heart." With touching simplicity he adds:—"I was pleased that I saw it and knew what it was; but sorry that it was so very bad."

Now, for the first time, he was sure that the Lord had answered his prayer, but the fear and trouble which followed were "undeclarable." Not long afterwards, the Act of Uniformity caused the Presbyterian ministers to desert their flocks, which made him weep, for he "saw clearly by the Holy Scriptures that they ought not to be silent at man's command if the Lord had sent and commanded them to preach. . . . The Presbyterian," he quaintly adds, "was not only removed out of the pulpit, but out of my heart also." One form of religion after another was tried, but he found that nothing could satisfy him short of the enjoyment of God in his own soul; for he "saw that a little measure of the Spirit of God was more precious than all this vain world." Concerning this period he writes:—

"I was mightily afraid of sinning against the Lord. . . . Sometimes I felt something that was very precious and sweet to me, yet I did not clearly understand what it was; but if at any time I did or said anything amiss, I soon lost the sight or feeling of it; oh! it hath been gone in a moment. . . . Whatsoever was tinctured with evil was against it, and it let me see it and condemned it, and me to, so far as I joined with it. Oh! this to enjoy, is a comfort beyond utterance to that heart and mind which loves righteousness and hungers after it."

About this time he met at a private house with two or three Friends, and some words uttered by one of them reached his inmost soul. Whilst wending his way home through a dark wood his mind was exceedingly distressed, but as he walked onwards he had a remarkable vision, during which the thought arose in his heart " that *they* were the Lord's people." "I was as one amazed and in great trouble," he says, "for these were the people of all others that endured the greatest sufferings, and were by all the rest hated, reviled, and scorned." He sat down on a stile and felt assured that if he would follow Him who had graciously heard his prayers, he must forsake the world, and that much which was dear to him he must let go for the Lord. He adds, "At this I was much troubled, for I was very loth to lose either, and would gladly have had both, but could not!" Conflict followed conflict; those to whom he appealed for comfort could not give it, and he had not yet fully complied with Christ's invitation, "Come unto *Me*." Once, when joining in the worship of the Anabaptists, he says that a "mighty power and weight" came over him, under the influence of which he addressed the congregation; but when he found that for fear of fines their meetings would not be held as usual, he was greatly troubled—considering such conduct a denial of Christ before men—and again he felt himself alone. On one occasion an Independent (whom he rather vaguely describes as "a man of London!") held a meeting which was attended by John Gratton, whom the preacher asked to pray; this, he says, "I declined doing, feeling that it was a service which only belonged to God to require and move men to. But before he had done preaching I was so pressed in my spirit to pray, that it was a great exercise to forbear till he was done; and then I prayed, but with such power that the people were amazed, and truly so was I too."

Next we read of much sorrow in secret:—

"I saw the baptism with the Holy Ghost and fire; and my pride and empty knowledge, yea, my faith that I had got by the wisdom of man, were burned up, . . . and it began to be much in my mind that what I had felt in me was really the Spirit of the Lord. . . . The appearance of it was mild, meek, low, and gentle, and full of good counsel, but stood firm always and condemned evil. . . . I had no power to live as I desired to do. I wanted the Lord's presence, for without that my poor soul could not find true rest; though my life and conversation were such that most loved me that knew me."

About this time he married, and his wife was very anxious that he should accompany her to church; but thinking that he could not now conscientiously do this, he tells us that great sorrow fell on them, and that they disputed oft till both wept. But the hour was at hand when this weary pilgrim's burden was to fall from him at the foot of the cross. During the corn harvest he was one day riding alone in sore sorrow of soul, when,—

"It pleased the Lord," he writes, "that whilst I was judging and condemning myself, on a sudden, unexpectedly and unlooked-for, the Day-Star arose in my heart, and the Sun of Righteousness with healing on His wings, . . . so that I was in my inward man full of the power and presence of Almighty God; . . . and I believed, and could not do otherwise. Oh, then was I glad, and my soul was filled with joy, because I had met with the Lord, who I knew was sufficient to teach me all things, and gave me to see that my sins would be remitted and forgiven in and through Jesus Christ! And Christ Jesus was now become my light, and my salvation, and living faith sprung in me. I then saw and felt what true faith was, and also saw that I never had true living faith before then; this was *the free gift of God*. . . . The Scriptures now became more sweet, comfortable and precious to me, till I wondered that I had never seen them so before, having read them so much night and day."

Again were his thoughts directed to the persecuted Quakers with a strong persuasion that with them he should be able to worship; which conviction he frankly confesses made him sorry; for if, he says,

"it had been any other people, I might have been more at liberty to have pleased the world, and not to have been so hated by it; . . . for others could flee from suffering and conform a little sometimes; but these abode and stood, though the winds blew, and the rains fell, and the floods beat upon them; for the Lord enabled them to stand and outstand it."

There were no meetings of Friends in the Peak country where he then lived, but hearing of a gathering at "one Widow Farnay's house," he attended it. Little was said, yet he writes of "A sweet melody . . . the presence of the Lord," and of "more true comfort, refreshment and satisfaction from the Lord," than any other meeting had ever afforded him.

> "Gales of Heaven, if so He will
> Sweeter melodies can wake
> On the lonely mountain rill
> Than the meeting waters make."

His affection now freely flowed towards the Friends with "such a love as none know but they that have it." Even the petty persecutions he at once met with in his own town only filled him with joy; nor need we wonder at this from one who could thus describe God's dealings with him:—

"He hath made glad my soul, and satisfied the breathings of my spirit; He hath opened to me the mysteries of His kingdom, and given me a measure of His grace. . . . He hath given to me the true bread of life, and made my heart glad with the wine of the kingdom; He is become my teacher Himself, and hath gathered me into His arm of power, and covered me with the banner of His love."

At the third meeting which he attended he felt himself called on by his Lord to make known His goodness; he could not disobey, and what he said was "to the great joy of Friends and reaching of the people." Very naturally John Gratton's wife was, as he writes, "sore grieved" at what she considered her husband's fanaticism; and though they still loved each other dearly, she was in much sorrow for him, and he for her. But during a walk one evening, when his mind was greatly tried on her account, he was made glad by the belief that the language of the Lord to his soul was, "I will give thee thy wife." Then he relates how at the next meeting a Friend named William Yardley came, and afterwards had a long conversation with her; before the interview ended he said, "Ann, God's love is to thee;" "which," her husband says, "she feeling, was given up to obey it, and was glad." Their happiness greatly increased, and for thirty-five years longer she was a very comfortable wife to him, and never hindered him from going abroad to visit Friends."

Much of his time was now spent in holding meetings in his own neighbourhood and in the surrounding counties. Very striking occasions were most of these, and in some places Friends' meetings were established, The truths on which he dwelt made a deep and lasting impression on many of his own kindred—his grandfather, ninety years old, saying, "This is that I have been seeking for all my days." During one meeting held in a barn, whilst he was praying, some officers entered "railing and raging," until they came to the spot where he knelt, "when," he says, "the power of the Lord increased, and my voice rose strongly, and they all stopped and turned back like men smitten, and went quite away. . . . We had a precious meeting, and were comforted." At another time, when disturbed in the same way whilst preaching, strength was given him to go on speaking, and the rough intruders becoming conscious of the holy atmosphere around them, and solemnised and silenced by it, quietly left the place. After his return home a meeting held in his own house was attended by John Gratton's father, whose object in visiting his son was to chide him for his long absence from his wife. But whilst he was preaching, the father's heart, like that of some of "the chiefest of the town" who were present, was deeply moved, and as soon as his son was silent, he folded him in his arms and kissed him. His varied faithful labours were followed by the peace which passeth all understanding. "Now," says he, "I was come to know what the city of God is which I had read of in the Revelation; ... the glory of God doth lighten it, and the Lamb is the light thereof." In the Peak country his ministry seemed to have been particularly blessed to the people, so many of whom flocked to hear him that the house would not hold them all; so one day, at Bradow, he went to the market-place, and, standing on the wall under a tree, addressed the assembled company. Here stones were flung at him, and two Friends who had joined him were violently pulled down; but John Gratton, going to that part of the wall opposite which the greatest crowd was gathered, knelt down, "all fear of men and stones was gone"—and as he prayed a solemn stillness came over the stormy assembly, who afterwards quietly listened to one of the other Friends, and the meeting ended in great sweetness. Nor were these the only times when the promise was fulfilled, "No weapon that is formed against thee shall prosper."

"Now, before these things happened," he writes, "I was in great exercise of mind, notwithstanding which I was willingly given up to serve the Lord. . . . I was brought very low until, at a meeting in my house, it pleased the Lord in mercy mightily to break in upon me, greatly tendering my spirit to the gladding of my soul. Thanksgivings be to Him who supported and bore me up in these days of great tribulation."

The Friends were now suffering severely from fines and imprisonments, but in the midst of these troublous times he went to the Yearly Meeting in London, and was greatly cheered by the sight of "those brave meetings." On his homeward journey he spent a night at Longclawson, and was asked by the Friends living there to have a meeting with them. Although a strong impression rested on his mind that this would bring him into danger and difficulty, he did not decline, whilst warning his friends that they might be fined on his account; but their answer was, "If thou wilt venture, we will." The meeting was interrupted; the hearers were fined five shillings each, and the preacher twenty pounds; a distraint was made on his goods for this sum, but as no one would buy them, they were given him again. Alluding to this event, he says, "Oh! the Lord's mercies were great to me. . . . So that sometimes I have been ready to say that, if I had had a houseful of goods to lose, I could freely part with it for the sake of truth."

When at Wirksworth Market on business, he was greatly grieved at the fearful oaths he heard, and saw that, if faithfully following the path of duty, it would be his place to address the people from the market cross; but being almost afraid that they might "pull him to pieces," he mounted his horse and rode home. Deep distress followed, but the next time he went to Wirksworth the call to warn the people was heard again. Without waiting "to consult any more" it was obeyed; the hearers wept aloud, none "had power to hurt" him, and one Justice Loe, who would have imprisoned him, arrived too late. Amidst much opposition the meetings became greater and greater, and John Gratton felt that he must be "abroad" as much as might be. His family he says grew "bigger and bigger, and he did not neglect his trade, for his care was great to owe no man anything; and the Lord blessed him every way." Once he was cited to the Bishop's Court, where a dignitary of the Church was called on to admonish him. Describing this, he writes:—

"Seeing nothing came but, 'I admonish, I admonish, I admonish thee,' three times, to make way for their wicked court to go on to persecute me and get money, said I to him, 'Prithee, whether dost thou admonish me, for the good of my soul, or the love of my money?' Said the registrar, 'I for the love of thy money, and he for the good of thy soul.' With that the people made a noise with laughing, for they saw it was money more than the good of souls that they aimed at. A brave convincement there was in those days. . . . Also in many other places where the Lord ordered me and went with me, and by His own right arm did unutterable things; many were convinced, yea, hundreds, I believe, and came to meetings, at which the devil was angry, and I was cast into prison."

Whilst still away from home a sense had come over him of suffering in store, so deep that he told one of his friends that he could not see to the bottom of it. Nor was it needful that he should in anticipation; wide as were the waters which lay before him, he had not to pass through them alone; the Everlasting arms were underneath, and he knew it. Soon he was arrested and sent to Derby Gaol; his bade his wife rather rejoice than weep that they were accounted worthy thus to suffer, and when she saw *his* cheerfulness, with a true woman's heart she bravely bore the trial. Having refused to pay the gaoler for leave to remain in his house, John Gratton was still determined to have "a free prison" which the law allowed, though many Friends had not long before been confined in a dungeon amongst thieves, whilst hardly provided with clean straw. Although his wife was very dangerously ill, he was not given leave to go to her.

"So," he says, "I gave up wife and children and all I had into the Lord's hand, and was contented, saying in my heart after this manner: ' Life or death, poverty or riches, come what will come, the will of the Lord be done.' But it pleased the Lord that my wife mended again ; and oh ! how easy I was after I had given up all ; and my gaol was made a pleasant place to me, for the Lord's mercy was with me, so that I even sang a living song of praise. . . . Towards the spring, my eldest son, John, died ; I obtained liberty to go to him, but he died that night after he had seen me. Some of his last words were, that he hoped we should meet where they (meaning bad men) should not part us any more. And the day after he was buried I left my wife and went to prison again."

During his captivity he sometimes addressed the people below from the window, and his faithful words sank deeply into the hearts of some young men. The word of God, as he remarks, was not bound; many persons came to the prison, and good meetings were held there. For five years and a half his imprisonment lasted, but occasional leave of absence was granted him. Throughout this time his wife carried on their business. On his release, after staying at home for a while, he travelled through most parts of the United Kingdom. The visit to Scotland seems to have been especially satisfactory and comforting to him ; after coming home he sent an epistle to the Friends there, in which he writes :—

"I tenderly salute you with pure love unfeigned, which springs from the endearing Fountain thereof. . . . Oh, the goodness of God to us is undeclarable! and we see as much need as ever to keep looking unto Him for help every moment, for all our time is a time of need, and if the Lord were not with us we could not bear up against the enemy."

In the year 1707 his faithful wife died. Of her illness their daughter thus writes :—

"I being pretty much taken up in attending her, she would often say, 'Dost thou take care of thy father?' For as their love and sympathy had been great in all times of trial of what sort soever, so it continued to the last. . . . My dear father was then very weakly, and the loss of my dear mother was a near trial and exercise to him, she having been, as he himself said, a sweet help to him in the Lord. He was deeply bowed in mind and spirit for the loss of her, yet freely gave her up to the Lord. Few who saw him thought he would continue long after her. But it pleased the Lord to raise him up in some measure. . . . The last winter he sensibly decayed. . . . Being attended with sore sickness and pain, he said, 'Lord, I pray thee give me ease if it be Thy holy will, and remove me soon out of this body. . . . It is through Jesus Christ our advocate who is gone before us that we are enabled to come to Thee.' . . . He departed this life in the sixty-ninth year of his age, on First Month 9th, 1711-12, and is, I hope, at rest with the Lord, 'where the wicked cease from troubling, and the weary are at rest.' He was buried beside my dear mother."

Such was the life and such the death of this valiant servant of the Lord. May we not add, concerning his chequered life, that, as recorded of the patriarch Joseph, "the archers sorely grieved him, and shot at him, and hated him; but his bow abode in strength, and the arms of his hands were made strong by the hands of the mighty God of Jacob"!

JAMES DICKENSON AND HIS FRIENDS.

" Hath the Lord spoken unto thee apart,
   A sudden light out-flashing from His word,
   A hope snatched from thee, or a boon confer'd?
   Or, in thy converse with a kindred heart,
   Hast thou not felt the presence of a third,
   An unseen influence, and thy spirit stirr'd?

" That which thou hearest in the secret place
   That which thou learnest in the silent hour,
   Is not for thee alone; ascend thy tower,
   And tell thy message in the open face
   Of men and day; e'en as a summer shower,
   Thy words shall fall with fertilising power."

R. H. Cooke

JAMES DICKENSON AND HIS FRIENDS.

"The business we were sent about was to labour to turn people's minds from darkness to this true light (Christ—John i. 9), and from Satan's power to the power of God; that people might come to receive remission of sins, by faith in Christ Jesus."—JAMES DICKENSON.

"OH that I had a cave in the ground, that I might mourn out my days, that in the end I might find peace with Thee!" was often James Dickenson's cry to the Lord in his early youth. For, although

> "His Soul was for the truth inquiring,
> For God, and nothing less,"

he had not yet learnt for himself that "Christ suffered for sins, the just for the unjust, that He might bring us to God."

He was born in 1659, at Lowmoor, in Cumberland, and even as a little child felt at times a secret joy in drawing near to God with a broken and contrite heart. His father and mother, who had become Friends, rejoiced over these evidences of the work of the Holy Spirit in the heart of their little son. They knew the blessedness of a holy life themselves, and longed that their children should follow them in the paths of peace. Although James Dickenson was only seven years of age when he lost his mother, and but three years older when his father died, their loving counsel and the tearful earnestness of their appeals were clearly remembered by him. He confesses, however, that for a time he disregarded his father's advice, and did not give heed to the "still, small voice" of Christ.

"Yet the Lord," he writes, "by His power did many times reach my heart, and by the Spirit of His dear Son, the Lord Jesus Christ, reproved me for my vain conversation; many times calling me to return unto Him from whom I had gone astray. But I, not minding to turn, went on in rebellion against His blessed Spirit, and ran into wildness and vanity; until the Lord, in His mercy, did visit my soul by His righteous judgments. Being warned to repent and turn to the Lord, a godly sorrow was begun, which I experienced to lead to true repentance. Then my familiars became my enemies, and I was a taunt and a by-word to them, yet still as I loved the Lord in the way of His judgments and waited upon Him, I found Him give victory. . . . In those deep afflictions and exercises the Lord was very near, so that my soul began to delight to wait upon Him in the way of His judgment. I felt the love of God to increase in my soul, which greatly affected me; and a hunger was increased in my heart after the enjoyment of the Lord's power and the operation of it, whether it was in mercy or judgment; so I knew my faith to be increased in the sufficiency of the power of God, and the Lord did often overshadow me with His love: and a sight of glorious things I had at that time."

But still sorrow and conflict were often his portion; for he was, as he says, "unskilful and not grown in strength to resist the evil one." Yet a vision which he had about this time was verified in his actual experience. He thought that he saw a sheep feeding in a green pasture by a pleasant river-side. A wicked man, however, envying its happiness, tried to drown it in the river; when it was at the point of sinking the good shepherd came with availing aid, and after bringing back the rescued sheep to the quiet meadow, he strove with the cruel adversary and, prevailing, smote him and cast him into the river, the strong current of which carried him away. "And when I had almost lost the hope of deliverance," James Dickenson says, "then the Lord appeared by His mighty power, and rebuked the enemy, and delivered my soul from him that was too strong for me. He drew me out of the troubled waters, and brought my mind into true stillness, and to the proper place of right waiting upon Him, where I found my strength to be renewed. And the overshadowing of His power I often felt to my great comfort, so that I was made to admire His goodness."

At the age of eighteen James Dickenson first spoke in meetings. He had been unwilling to obey his Saviour's intimations on this subject, seeing, as he says, "the work to be very weighty, and looking out at my own weakness;" but his loving Lord filled his soul with all needful strength for this service, and afterwards his heart was humbled by the abundance of peace which flowed into it. In the midst of his meditations one morning these words reached his spiritual ear: "Be bold and courageous for My name's sake, and I will raise thee up." They were, he says, as a fire in his bones; for he felt that God was calling him to go to the meeting of the Presbyterians at Talentire.

Thither, accordingly, he went, and found that the Lord was with him and showed him what he had to do; yet it was with much fear that he entered the room where they were assembled. Nor were his apprehensions groundless, for no sooner was the presence of a Friend discovered than there were cries of "Put him forth!" from some of the company. But though roughly turned out, he stood at a window, and there delivered the message with which he was commissioned. "This is the day of the visitation and the revelation of the power and Spirit of Christ in your hearts; therefore resist it not; for, if you do, it will rise up in judgment against you." This so aroused the wrath of his hearers that they threw him down and dragged his head over the stones; but this treatment did not trouble him much, apparently, for he writes of "great peace, the over-shadowing of the love of God," and of his soul being filled with praise.

A somewhat similar visit was paid to the Baptists at Broughton, when a deep impression was made on the hearts of several who, ere long, became Friends; John Ribton, who afterwards became a minister, being one of the number.

When about twenty-one, James Dickenson visited the Friends residing in the neighbouring counties. Persecution was raging at this time, and he was truly grateful for the protection mercifully granted him during his journey; for no informer came to any of the meetings which he held. Two years later he paid a religious visit to Ireland. In Wexford he met with Thomas Wilson, who was a few years older than himself, and also came from Cumberland. He had been travelling as a minister; but, for some time before James Dickenson's arrival, having felt the restraining influence of the Holy Spirit for a season, he had employed himself in harvest-work instead of continuing his journey. Now he joined James Dickenson, and the rich blessing of God rested on them and their united labours. "So," writes Thomas Wilson, "I saw it was good to wait the Lord's time in all things." He was an exceedingly powerful minister: it was said of him that "the heavenly love and life his heart was filled with, streamed forth to the comfort of many; for he was a cloud the Lord often filled and caused to be emptied, to the refreshing of His heritage." And James Dickenson in after years wrote: "I know there was not anything more delightful to my dear companion than to be under the influence of God's Holy Spirit wherewith he was often filled, not only for his own good, but the good of others; and though he had a large gift beyond many, yet was glad of the least child who spake from the motion of God's Spirit." *

In the following year, after visiting Scotland, James Dickenson held some meetings in the North of England, and at Kendal again met with Thomas Wilson. Here a remarkable meeting took place: some persons who were sent to disperse the congregation dragged the two ministers out of the meeting-house, but after a while allowed them to re-enter it, and we read that "the holy power of the Lord came mightily over the hearts of Friends." Even their rough opposers were

---

* In the latter part of his life Thomas Wilson was one day present at a very large meeting in London. Two gentlemen of high rank were of the company, and listened with attentive interest to the address of another minister. But when Thomas Wilson, who was of very unimposing appearance, rose up to speak, one of these gentlemen said to his companion:—"Come, my lord, let us go; for what can this old fool say?" "Nay," was the reply, "let us stay, for this is Jeremiah the prophet; let us hear him." With such heavenly power were Thomas Wilson's words accompanied that the soul of one of his scoffing hearers was affected in a very striking manner. He at first tried to hide his freely-flowing tears; but, when the preacher had resumed his seat, he stood up and expressed his hope that he might be forgiven by him, and by the Almighty "for despising the greatest of His instruments under heaven, or in His creation."

awed by it, and seemed unable to carry out their intention of again forcing James Dickenson out of the house when he knelt in prayer. After spending some time at home engaged at his trade, of fellmonger (a dealer in hides), he went to Wales in company with Thomas Wilson. They travelled in the depth of winter, and found the Friends whom they visited suffering exceedingly from persecution; yet James Dickenson says: "All things were made pleasant unto us in the love of God." A justice of the peace and an informer came to the meeting of Haverfordwest; but Thomas Wilson's ministry was so manifestly prompted by the Holy Spirit that the justice said,—"If these be the Quakers I never heard the like. Let them alone."

From Holyhead Dickenson went to Ireland, and the vessel in which he sailed was wonderfully preserved from shipwreck on the bar of Dublin in a tremendous storm. He felt himself commissioned to warn the Friends of that country that a time of trial was approaching which none would have strength to endure but "those that should be settled upon the rock, Christ Jesus, and gathered under His peaceable government; those would know a dwelling safely and a being quiet from fear of evil." This prediction was strikingly fulfilled by the war which broke out in Ireland at the time of the Revolution of 1688. During James Dickenson's first visit to that nation, also, a strong impression had rested on his mind of the sufferings in store for its inhabitants, whom he "beheld as if they were encompassed with weapons of war."

During a visit to the south of England, he attended a

meeting at Bristol, consisting chiefly of women and children whose male relatives were in prison; it was held in the yard, as the Friends were not allowed to enter their meeting-house; but the shadow of God's wing was their canopy. "As my eye was kept single," he writes, "every day waiting for the motion of the Word of Life, I found the Lord to fit and qualify me for every day's service." At Crediton, in Devon, he met with very rough treatment, but holy courage was given him for the performance of his work. God gave an abundant increase, and a meeting was afterwards established in that town.

Whilst holding a meeting in this neighbourhood, he was seized by a constable and taken before a justice of the peace, who, however, spoke kindly to him, and with his family appeared to be much affected with what James Dickenson was constrained to say to them Then he set him at liberty, desiring that God might go with him wherever he went. A meeting which he had in the Isle of Portland was held out of doors, and whilst he was engaged in prayer a constable dragged him from his knees, with the intention of casting him into a deep pool of water, but was prevented from doing so by the people who were present. But whilst he was preaching he forced him out of the assembly, flung him on the stones, beat him on the breast, and then ordered some drunken men to drag him along the ground with his head against the stones, so that the blood flowed freely; again the constable struck him repeatedly, and many people wept, thinking that such treatment would surely cost him his life. "But," writes James Dickenson, "the Lord made it very easy to me by the sweetness of His love, with which my heart was filled to the inhabitants of the island: so that I heartily desired the Lord would forgive those that had done me most harm!" No marvel that he adds, "Many hearts were reached that day by the power of God." Well has it been said—"Patience, meekness, self-abnegation, these are the miracles of the New Covenant."

When Dickenson re-visited Portland seven years later, he held a meeting on the same spot, and, in spite of menaces, was enabled powerfully to declare the way of salvation to its inhabitants. Whilst he was speaking, a man came to him with a drawn sword in his hand, but had no power to hurt him. Not long after his first visit to Portland, he attended the London Yearly Meeting, which he thus describes :—" The glory of the Lord was richly manifested amongst us, and opened our hearts unto Him and one unto another. Many living testimonies were borne to His great name; so that I may say it was like the time of Pentecost, for we were met with one accord, and our hearts were truly tendered in the love of God."

When, not long after, James Dickenson visited Holland with a Friend named Peter Fearon, the ship in which they sailed was pursued by a Turkish pirate vessel. They had nearly reached their destination, but the captain made for a point of land that was in sight, saying that he would rather run any risk of shipwreck than suffer the vessel to fall into the hands of the Turks. James Dickenson, who, on leaving Harwich, had had a presentiment of peril awaiting them on the Dutch coast, now felt, whilst his heart was uplifted to God, that He would save them from their dangerous enemies; accordingly he begged the captain to alter his hazardous course and steer for the harbour, which, after much entreaty, he did; the pirates sailed in another direction, and the English vessel safely entered the port of Brill. Before leaving home, James Dickenson had felt especially attracted to Horn, although apparently he knew nothing about its inhabitants. It therefore gave him pleasure when the interpreter told him of a people dwelling there, who desired a more perfect knowledge of the way of God. So, after many blessed seasons during the Yearly Meeting at Amsterdam, a remarkable meeting was held at Horn, when several hearts were opened to receive the message of the strange minister.

After visiting Friesland, etc., they returned safely to England, notwithstanding a very dangerous storm. "The Lord," writes James Dickenson, "is large in His love, and of great kindness to them that are truly given up to follow Him."

During the Revolution of 1688, James Dickenson, in company with another Friend, held meetings in many parts of England, striving to turn the hearts of the people to the Prince of Peace. Afterwards he again went to the western counties, having Thomas Wilson for his fellow-labourer. The latter writes, "We had a precious journey. Meetings were now very large; many people came in to seek after the Lord's truth, and much desired to hear the word, the strong wind of persecution being ceased, so that there was a great calm. We had glorious meetings: the Lord's tendering, heart-melting power, greatly breaking through them."

Whilst engaged in holding meetings in Scotland

in 1690, James Dickenson was joined by Robert Barclay, the Author of "The Apology," whom he afterwards visited at his residence at Ury, where a General Meeting was held. Just at this time Robert Barclay became ill of a violent fever, which soon terminated his life. As James Dickenson sat by his bedside, they felt their hearts to be closely drawn together in a powerful sense of the presence of their Lord; and Robert Barclay spoke with tears of his love to all faithful brethren in England, especially mentioning George Fox. But James Dickenson was probably unable to deliver this message of love, as soon after his return from Scotland he heard of George Fox's death. These tidings gave him deep sorrow, yet he writes: "When I turned my mind to the Lord, I found he had done the work of his day and was gone to rest; and we must be content: and they would be happy that followed his footsteps."

In the spring of 1691 James Dickenson and Thomas Wilson sailed for America, where each felt himself called to labour; the former was then about thirty-two years of age. Before leaving England they attended the Yearly Meeting, and met with much loving sympathy. It was a perilous time for voyaging in consequence of war with France, and it was rumoured that the French Fleet lay some thirty leagues from the Land's End. Very fervent were the prayers of the young ministers, that if it were in accordance with God's will, no evil might betide them: and strong faith was given them to commit themselves to His keeping. Whilst still in London Thomas Wilson joyfully told his friend that the Lord had made it plain to him that they should be preserved from harm. James Dickenson's reply was that God had shown him that the French Fleet would almost encompass them, but that He would send a great mist and darkness between them and their enemies, in which they should be able to make their escape. This was literally the case, which was, says Thomas Wilson, "cause of great gladness to me, who had been under a deep travail of spirit with fasting and prayer." To all on board this deliverance appeared to be a miraculous one, and in the time of trouble the two Friends were wonderfully upheld by an unusually clear consciousness of "the Lord's living presence with them." On the following Sunday a remarkable meeting was held on the quarter-deck.

When drawing near Barbadoes a man-of-war, supposed by the English captain to be a French privateer, bore down upon his vessel, and he made preparations for fighting her. When assigning posts to those on board, he said to the Friends: "As for you I know it is contrary to your principles to fight; Lord forbid I should compel any man contrary to his conscience! Take your quarters with the doctor." James Dickenson observing that the other passengers were very angry at this, and wishing to show that the conduct of his companion and himself was influenced by conscience and not by cowardice, told the captain that, since he kindly gave them leave to choose their places, they would stay on the quarter-deck with him. This announcement caused much astonishment to those who had been saying that the Quakers deserved to be shot, and effectually silenced them. The alarm proved to be a false one.

James Dickenson and his friend spent more than

two months in Barbadoes, undaunted by a very infectious malady, from which some hundreds had already died. The meetings were thronged by both the white and black inhabitants, who were deeply affected as the ministers, with hearts filled with the love of God, proclaimed the Gospel amongst them. At that which was first held, the negroes, with tears flowing freely down their faces, heard the truths which were declared in silent amazement. The voyage thence to New York was of a month's duration, and the captain was much afraid lest they should perish in a great storm which lasted for ten days; but Thomas Wilson told him not to fear, for—as he says—he *saw* that the ship would not be lost. It was the depth of winter by the time the travellers reached Pennsylvania, yet, as the meeting-houses were too small to hold the numbers who flocked to them, the meetings were held out of doors, sometimes in deep snow. Then they pursued their journey through woods and wildernesses, and over most dangerously frozen rivers, to Maryland.

Whilst crossing Chesapeake Bay a thick fog came on, and, the boat being cast on an island, they spent the winter night lying on the ground. So great were the floods in Carolina that it was unsafe to travel on horseback; they therefore waded barefoot through the swamps, giving but little heed to the wolves and other wild animals which infested this district. Through all hardships they were upheld by the right hand of Him whose they were and whom they served. A warm welcome was given them by Friends and others, for a visit from a strange minister was a rare event, and blessed meetings were held.

At Black Creek, whilst Dickenson was preaching, a sheriff, who came with some officers to disperse the congregation, asked him from whom he had his commission. He replied, "From the great God unto whom thou and I must give an account." When the intruders had left, a "heavenly meeting" was held; several of those present afterwards became Friends, and soon a meeting-house was built, and a meeting established. When returning through the wilderness to Maryland, on the first night of their journey, they slept in the woods, kindling a fire as a safeguard from the cold and from the wild beasts. While eating their bread and cheese in the twilight, Thomas Wilson found that his horse had discovered some water, and he unconsciously gives a glimpse of his peaceful state of mind when he says, " I think I never drank any wine more sweet and pleasant to me than that water was." Another night they spent in the house of a poor man who could not offer them a bed, but entertained them as they sat by his fire with an account of George Fox and John Burnyeat's visit to that part of the country.

At the Yearly Meeting at Salem, in Jersey, they met with a great number of Friends. "We had many glorious meetings, writes James Dickenson, " and were livingly open to proclaim the everlasting Gospel and day of God's love." They next went to Philadelphia, where George Keith and his false doctrine had been causing great trouble. Here they were wonderfully helped in their arduous labours. It was not until the early part of 1693 that they returned to England, having previously paid a second visit to Barbadoes. They were more than once exposed to much danger on the voyage thence from Boston. During a tornado, which laid the vessel on one side like a log of wood, they were kept in such perfect peace, that all fear of death was taken away, and their hearts were filled with joy from the wells of salvation. The captain of the vessel, having an aversion to Friends, said that if she were taken by the French, it would be because there were Quakers on board. As they drew near Barbadoes a very thick dark mist came on, by means of which they were preserved from a French privateer, and afterwards landed safely at Bridgetown. The captain did not find that he fared better when he had parted with his burdensome passengers; for, on her return voyage, whilst still in sight of the island, the vessel was captured by the enemy and taken to Martinico.

When the Friends were ready to embark from Nevis, the Governor refused to allow them to leave the island, saying they were spies; but when they showed him "the broad seal" of their passport he forthwith altered his tone. Almost as soon as they set foot on deck such a remarkable sense of God's presence was granted them as to cause them to shed tears of joy. Several epistles were written by Wilson and Dickenson to Friends in different parts of America, from which the following extracts are taken:—

"Dear Friends, Truth is the same that ever it was, and the power of it as prevailing as ever; and where it is kept to and dwelt in, hath the same effect as ever, as many of you are witnesses who keep your habitation therein, with whom our souls are bound up in God's everlasting covenant of light; in which as we walk we have the fellowship one with another, and the blood of Jesus Christ His Son cleanseth us from all unrighteousness. . . . What gifts soever you have received, be careful that you be improving them to the honour of the Giver, as those who know an account must be given unto Him. . . . He is daily opening the Divine mysteries of His Kingdom to them who are kept humble and low before Him; who wait for counsel from the Lord every day, and to feel the assistance of His Spirit, and dare not move until the Lord go before and draw them forward."

In another epistle the following remarks are found:—

"May you be kept in God's holy covenant of peace, the sweetness whereof none know, as it is, but those who *dwell in it*, and keep to the conduct of the power that gathered them."

Again we read:—

"All give up your hearts to God to be kept by His power in fellowship with Him; then will your fellowship be sweet one with another; so will you know all things that offend to be cast out of the kingdom, and you will be tender one over another, the strong lending a hand to help the weak; and be of Moses' mind, who wished that all the people were prophets. . . . All your safety is and will be to keep inward to the Lord, that He may be your teacher, your own spirits being silenced; waiting with delight to hear what He speaks. Then if He be pleased to open any of your mouths for the edification one of another, it will be in His power and wisdom from above. . . . If you keep those longing desires that are already raised in you, ye shall know 'the sincere milk of the word, that you may grow thereby' from one degree of grace unto another, until you become perfect men in Christ Jesus. . . . As all keep low in their respective gifts, waiting to know the assistance of God's Spirit—still being nothing without it—you will feel the Lord to work all your works *both in you and for you*, and give power to answer what He requires of you; and then His love will be increased unto you, and you will abide in favour with Him."

A few weeks after James Dickenson's marriage, which took place in 1694, he felt that God had commissioned him with a message of warning to the inhabitants of London. When he spoke on this subject to his wife she urged him to do his Lord's bidding, saying that she only desired to enjoy what she enjoyed, in God's favour. Some time after this service had been performed, he told her that his Divine Master was again calling him to labour amongst the Friends in America. "Mind thy freedom in the Lord," was her reply, "and let no worldly affairs hinder thee; but answer His requirings." James Dickenson admits that this matter brought "deep exercise" upon his spirit, yet so full was the sense afforded him of "God's love to His heritage and people the world over," that he was quite willing to leave all and undertake this arduous work for Him. His friend, Peter Fearon, we read, accompanied him "in pure love" to London, and they held meetings in several places. Their hearts were closely bound together, and their parting was a very touching one; they separated at Woburn, where a meeting had been held, and James Dickenson went back to London alone. "Before I had travelled half a mile," he writes, "the Lord's power overshadowed my soul, by which my heart was broken and filled with joy and gladness, which made up all my wants."

It was with similar feelings that he began his voyage; two other Friends, also bound for America, were on board the vessel: the preceding Sunday two meetings had been held at Rochester, at one of which a young man engaged in prayer for the first time in public. "I was glad," says James Dickenson, "to see the Lord at work in the hearts of babes to perfect His own praise." The ship was delayed for several weeks in the Downs as the wind was unfavourable, and during this time meetings were frequently held on board. James Dickenson also gladly availed himself of an opportunity to revisit Canterbury, where a deep impression had been previously made by his ministry. Before leaving this city he received a call from a clergyman who had been at one of the meetings, and wished to have some conversation with him. He remarked that he had himself no immediate impulse to preach. "If," answered James Dickenson, " I had no immediate impulse of the Spirit to preach the Gospel, I would never have left my wife and family to do it : but there was a necessity laid upon me. Every true minister of Christ knows a necessity so to do." As they parted the clergyman admitted that this was the truth.

About this time there was a rumour that England would be invaded by the French, which caused a strict embargo to be laid on all shipping, and for five months the voyage was delayed. James Dickenson did not feel it right to return home, but patiently waited the Lord's time, and was upheld by Him in the midst of his trials. He often went on shore to hold meetings. At Deal he was interested in a young clergyman whom he met with on the beach, and who had that evening attended a meeting held by Thomas Rudd and himself. He was much depressed, and was anxious to know more about the principles of Friends, concerning whom he had been greatly misinformed. James Dickenson says that his heart was lovingly opened to give him the information he desired, for he felt that God's love abounded towards him, and their conversation was prolonged to a late hour. Some meetings held in London are thus described by James Dickenson —

"We had a very heavenly time, and found the power of the Lord at work in the hearts of several young people. Many mouths were opened to declare the Truth; for which I was glad, and to see the Lord's work to prosper. The day before we set sail we had a public meeting on board the ship we went in: many people came to it out of the country, and the Lord by His power broke in wonderfully amongst us. I was livingly open to proclaim the word of life, and many hearts were tendered. Then I had a sight that the time of our departure was near, and that we should get on our long-desired journey."

When the vessel was lying off Cowes he wrote a brief epistle to the Yearly Meeting which was about to be held. "I entreat you all, keep to the Lord's eternal power and wisdom in the exercise of all your gifts in this Yearly Meeting, that Christ, your heavenly Head, may rule and speak through all, and carry on that glorious work which He hath begun." Before losing sight of the shores of England James Dickenson was cheered by the assurance, graciously afforded him, that he should be engaged in his Lord's service that day eight weeks in America. And so it was, though many other vessels of the fleet did not arrive until more than three weeks later, having encountered a violent storm. Many of the meetings were attended by large numbers. James Dickenson writes: "We declared, in all plainness, that a profession of the truth would stand them in no stead except they lived in the life thereof, and waited to feel the power of Christ working in them to the changing of their hearts; and knew Him to be a mediator and interceder for them to the Father."

On one occasion James Dickenson had an interesting conversation with an Indian who could speak English, and who came to the house of the Friend with whom he was staying; he said that he did not know God, yet when asked whether, after he had told a lie, sworn, or done wrong to anyone, he did not feel something which showed him that he ought not to do so, he laid his hand with deep seriousness on his breast, and said, "Yes, I know it very well." After James Dickenson had made some remarks to him on this subject, the Indian asked what made Englishmen swear when they knew that God was near; and said that in his own language there were no words for swearing.

Several Meetings in Chester County were visited by James Dickenson, where he met with many persons who had left the Society of Friends and became followers of George Keith. "I was enabled," he says, "to vindicate our ancient Testimony concerning our faith in Jesus Christ; declaring to them that we believed in Him as being the only begotten Son of God; who in the fulness of time took flesh, became perfect man according to the flesh; descended and came of the seed of Abraham and David, but was miraculously conceived by the Holy Ghost and born of the Virgin Mary; yet powerfully owned to be the Son of God according to the spirit of sanctification by the resurrection from the dead. And that as man, Christ died for our sins, rose again, and was received up into glory in the heavens, having fulfilled the law and the prophets, and put an end to the first priesthood, is a priest for ever, not after the order of Aaron, but of Melchisedec; and ever lives to make intercession to His Father, not for our sins only, but for the sins of the whole world." This he spoke of as being the faith of the Friends the world over.

The Yearly Meeting at Burlington, which he afterwards attended, was a very blessed one, notwithstanding the attempts at disturbance made by the Separatists. Whilst James Dickenson was preaching they cried out that the Light he spoke of was nothing but an idol and a frozen light. To which he replied that it was no other but Christ Jesus, the true light which lighteth every man that cometh into the world.* Among many other very satisfactory meetings, those held on Long Island may be mentioned. Several who attended them were convinced of the truth of the doctrines which they heard; and a justice of the peace and a captain in the army gave up their commissions because they could no longer take an oath, or fight. The last meeting in Pennsylvania was held at Concord, and was remarkably blessed by the Lord.

During this tarriance in America, as in the previous visit, many hardships were undergone by James Dickenson, and the homeward voyage was an adventurous one; but his heart was filled with gratitude to God for His protection from inward and outward danger, and with a stronger conviction than ever that "He is worthy to be followed and obeyed in all His requirings."

A year or two after his return he wrote an epistle to the Friends in America, a few extracts from which follow :—

---

* " Believing in Christ's inward and spiritual appearance does not in the least lessen or depreciate the value of the redeeming act of universal love, the Propitiatory Sacrifice of the dear Son of God without the gates of Jerusalem, and His there bearing our sins in His own body on the tree. *On the contrary it greatly enhances the value thereof.*"—*Edw. Alexander.*

"My spirit and life are often with you in my secret retirement unto the Lord. . . . *His hand is full of blessings to be poured down upon you if you give Him not occasion to withhold them from you by letting your minds wander from Him.* . . . Stir up one another to love and good works; and that those whom God hath trusted with heavenly gifts may all improve them to His glory. *And stir up one another to visit remote parts that want help*, as Virginia, Carolina, New England, Barbadoes, Jamaica, etc., and let all be done in the love of God. So will He bless you with spiritual blessings in His Son Jesus Christ; in whom I dearly salute you all, letting you know I am well every way."

Early in 1699 Dickenson again visited Scotland, having for his companion Jonathan Burnyeat, a child not much more than twelve years old; he naturally felt much concern on behalf of his little friend, who—he need scarcely have told us—had not travelled as a minister before. But Jonathan Burnyeat seems to have been—in almost the literal sense of the word—one of the babes to whom the Lord of heaven and earth sees fit to reveal those things which are hidden from the wise and prudent; for James Dickenson says, "My companion was deeply opened into the mysteries of God's kingdom, and grew in his gift, so as to give counsel to young and old. . . . The Lord was kind to us, and bore up our spirits in all our exercises. We had many precious meetings, and were deeply bowed under a sense of the Lord's favour to us. Probably James Dickenson often recalled the time when his young companion's father, John Burnyeat, had been a tender and sympathising counsellor to himself. Five years later they again travelled together, "in sweet brotherly love," through Yorkshire and Lincolnshire; and not long afterwards united in a religious visit to Ireland. And before Jonathan Burnyeat's early death he was James Dickenson's associate on a few shorter journeys.

In 1700 James Dickenson suffered from a dangerous illness. After alluding to God's gracious dealings with Him by "His secret hand," during this time of trial, he adds: "My eye was unto the Lord Jesus, in whom my justification remained, and I found peace. . . . The sense of it at that time was very comfortable, and engaged me to be given up to follow Him faithfully unto the end." In the summer of the following year he found that the Lord had further work for him in Scotland, where he met with Samuel Bownas and another young Friend, who were also engaged in holding meetings, and for a short time they all travelled together. James Dickenson's affectionate counsel was very helpful to his young and inexperienced associates, who had many doubts and fears with regard to the right accomplishment of their mission. Samuel Bownas was exceedingly comforted when James Dickenson told them how poor and weak *he* often felt. At Dumfries he said to them: "Lads, I find a concern to go into the streets; will you go with me?" The people were very quiet whilst James Dickenson—as Samuel Bownas says— "lifted up his voice like a trumpet amongst them," most earnestly warning them to repent and turn to the Lord.

One of Dickenson's twelve visits to Ireland followed this journey in Scotland. He gives no details of his numerous Gospel labours and travels from 1704 to 1713. The peace which was granted him as he willingly obeyed the voice of the Good Shepherd was a continual encouragement to perseverance in following Him. And he says that his wife and himself truly found that godliness is profitable unto all things.

"We were encouraged," he writes, "to follow the Lord fully, and keep to His eternal power that had prevailed over us; and the more our eyes were kept to Him, the greater necessity we found of the help of His Holy Spirit to keep us in our way heavenwards, knowing that without Him we could do nothing, and seeing our infirmities to be great, we were made to magnify that arm which is strong, and as near to help His people as ever. Those who are alive to God know it. . . . He is still faithful in fulfilling His promises, and whatever they ask in His name He gives them; such are bound in duty to return to Him thanksgiving and glory."

During one of James Dickenson's Scottish missions he met with a remarkable adventure. He was travelling with another Friend named Jane Fearon (the wife of his friend Peter Fearon), when on a very rough and rainy day, as evening drew on, he observed a lonely roadside public-house, where, as they were wet and weary, they though that it would be best to spend the night. Their Gaelic guide, as well as his imperfect English would allow him, tried to dissuade them from doing this, and when he found that he could not induce them to go on to another halting-place, refused to remain with them. They had a civil and attentive reception from the people of the house, but notwithstanding this the minds of the travellers were soon disturbed by terrible fears, which they did not at once communicate to each other. Jane Fearon's courage still further failed her when she heard one of the men say, "They have good horses and bags," and another reply, "Aye, and good clothes!" As soon as James Dickenson and herself were alone together, she burst into tears, and exclaimed: "I fear these people have a design to take our lives." James Dickenson, who was walking up and down the room, whilst his heart, we may feel sure, was uplifted to God, did not at once answer her. When he spoke, he said, "They have mischief in their hearts, but I hope the Lord will preserve our lives." He tried to cheer her by other remarks: then, after being again silent for a time, he once more expressed his hope that God would deliver them, adding, "But if so, we must run." "Alas!" was Jane Fearon's disconsolate reply, how can we run, or whither can we go?"

James Dickenson took a careful survey of the room, with a candle in his hand, and found a second door, on opening which he saw a flight of stone back-stairs on the outside of the house. Leaving the candle burning in the room, after taking off their shoes, they noiselessly descended the steps, and then ran until, at a considerable distance from the public-house, they reached an outbuilding, which they entered. But soon James Dickenson said, "We are not safe here; we must run again." Jane Fearon answered that she was so weary that she did not think she could go any farther. However, as her friend thought it essential that they should quit this spot, they did so, hastening on until they came to a river, which they soon discovered was crossed by a bridge; they were about to go over it, when James Dickenson felt this would not be the right course for them to pursue, and that it would be safer to go farther up the bank. Then they sat down to rest, but soon James Dickenson said, "We are not safe here; we must wade through the river." "Alas!" replied his companion, "how can we cross it, and know not its depth? It will be better for them to take our lives than for us to drown ourselves. The swollen river was safely passed over, and soon after this had been accomplished, while the fugitives were seated on a sandbank, James Dickenson remarked that he did not yet feel easy, and believed that they ought to go farther on. "Well, I must go by thy faith," was Jane Fearon's answer.

Before long they saw another sandbank containing a cavity, and soon Dickenson said, " I am now easy, and believe that we are perfectly safe, and feel in my heart a song of thanksgiving and praise." But his companion's faith was far from being as strong; and when they heard voices on the other side of the river—fearing that her terror might cause her to make an outcry—he gently said, "Our lives depend upon our silence." It was plain that the voices were those of their pursuers, for the words, "Seek them, Keeper," were frequently heard. Apparently the dog had led them as far as the bridge—but *not* over it—as he naturally followed the scent of the footsteps along the river side until he lost it at the spot where the travellers had crossed. They now saw the people, who carried a lantern, and heard one of them suggest that they had crossed the river to which another made answer, "That's impossible unless the devil took them over, for the river is brimful." For some time they continued their search, and then left the place.

In the light of the early morning the Friends noticed a man on a high hill looking around in every direction, who, they imagined, was endeavouring to discover their hiding-place. On examination they found that the position of the hollow in which they had taken refuge was such as to prevent them from being observed from the opposite side of the river ; whilst the sandbank on which they had first sat down could be plainly seen, and would have been a most unsafe retreat. They now began to think of their horses and saddle-bags, and Jane Fearon proposed that they should go on to a town and make known their case. But James Dickenson reminded her that they could give no positive proof of the guilty intentions of the inhabitants of the public-house, and moreover, that such a course might give the magistrates an excuse for imprisoning the accusers instead of the accused. " I incline," he added, " to return to the house, fully believing our clothes and bags will be ready for us without our being asked a question, and that the people we saw last night we shall see no more."

Jane Fearon, not sharing her fellow-traveller's faith (which was, it seems, marvellously manifested at this juncture), said that she dared not go back, but consented to do so when James Dickenson added, " Thou mayst safely, for I have seen *that which never failed me.*" Doubtless he felt perfect confidence in following the " still " and " small," though well-known voice of the Heavenly Shepherd—the gentlest whispers of which, long-continued listening and constant obedience had caused him easily to recognise.* On arriving at the inn,

---

* " Assuredly the New Testament does place the Christian Church under a dispensation of spiritual influence not common to those without it, and does also make the individual's participation of such influences proportionate to the measure of his faith, and love, and obedience. . . . And assuredly there can be no logical line drawn between the special and general communications of Divine influence. . . . The experience of a Christianised soul—of a soul bared to all the influences of God's special revelations—who shall limit, and who shall define ? "—*Lectures on Great Men, by the late Frederick Myers, Incumbent of St. John's, Keswick.*

they found their clothes ready for them, and the horses in the stable with the saddle-bags on them, but the only person visible was an old woman sitting by the fire, whom they did not recollect seeing on the previous night; having paid her what they owed they continued their journey.

When James Dickenson afterwards visited that neighbourhood, he learned that, some suspicion having been awakened respecting this house, a search had been made, which resulted in the discovery of a large quantity of wearing apparel and a great number of human bones! The house was pulled down and some of its inhabitants were executed.

In the autumn of 1713, he joined Thomas Wilson at Dublin, in order to undertake his third visit to America. His deep sense of God's love made it easy to do His will, for long experience had taught him that—

> "There is no blessedness but in such bondage;
> Sure it is sweeter far than liberty."

In Carolina they were cheered by the reception given to their message by many young Friends, whom they trusted the Lord was preparing for His service; and also by meeting with those to whom their previous labours had been greatly blessed. Some of the meetings in Pennsylvania were so large that several hundreds of people were obliged to stand out of doors. A meeting, also at New Plymouth, was held under the trees, on account of the great number present.

Somewhere in that crowd was a young English girl, the depths of whose soul were stirred by the ministry of Thomas Wilson; her name was Jane Hoskens, and she had been residing in America for about two years. She had been brought up as a member of the Church of England. During a severe illness, and whilst in great mental distress, she had been ready to covenant with God that if He would prolong her life she would dedicate it to His service. Her mind was deeply impressed with the conviction that if He restored her to health it would be His will that she should go to Pennsylvania. When about eighteen she left England with a family who were about to settle in Philadelphia. After passing through many trials she went to New Plymouth, where she was employed as governess by some families of Friends. It was at first from a feeling of curiosity that she attended their meetings; but after a while she was convinced that spiritual worship was a blessed reality to many present, and this led her to consider why it was not so with herself, for she had supposed that she knew a great deal about religion. And often these words came to her memory:—"In Jesus Christ neither circumcision availeth anything, nor uncircumcision, but a new creature." Her earnest prayers that the true way of salvation might be shown her were answered, as again and again, whilst sitting in meeting, the sermons which she heard seemed as a message to tell her that the way to the Father was through Christ, the Door, and to turn her attention to the teaching of the Holy Spirit.

But it was when quite alone that a sense of God's loving forgiveness was granted her: then it was easy to give up many things at her Saviour's bidding, for she loved Him more than her own life. One day whilst in meeting these words seemed to be spoken in her heart: "I have chosen thee a vessel from thy youth to serve Me, and to preach the Gospel of salvation to many people; if thou wilt be faithful, I will be with thee unto the end of time, and make thee an heir of my kingdom." She was for some time unwilling to give heed to this call, and deep suffering ensued; but when she yielded her will to God, He was her shield and exceeding great reward. In Thomas Wilson's ministry on the day alluded to, he said much with regard to the captive maid's service to her Lord and Master (2 Kings v. 4), very powerfully dwelling on the blessedness enjoyed by those who have placed themselves under Christ's control. Jane Hoskens was urged to dine at the house where the English travellers were entertained. Thomas Wilson looking earnestly at her said, "What young woman is that? She is like the little captive maid I have been speaking of this day. May the God of my life strengthen her: she will meet with sore trials, but if she is faithful the Lord will fit her for His service. He is at work in her for good and will in His time bring her through all." Often in future years did Jane Hoskens recall these words, when she travelled extensively as a minister in her adopted land, and twice in England and Ireland.

When Dickenson and Wilson were at Burlington Yearly Meeting, the concourse of people was so great that two meetings were held at the same time, the Court-house being made use of for one of them. From Oxford, in Maryland, they sailed for Liverpool; to their great disappointment the captain of the vessel refused to allow them time to attend the meeting at Oxford, before sailing. That night there was a great storm, which lasted for several days, during which the vessel sprung a leak, and, being soon afterwards becalmed, was in great danger. The Friends poured forth earnest prayers for deliverance; and the next day a south wind arose, and the ship safely ran into Lynhaven Bay. They again went on shore, and spent many weeks in holding meetings in Virginia, Maryland, etc. When travelling through this region twenty-two years earlier, they had no guide for a hundred miles, and slept in the woods; yet faith was given them to believe that the Lord would exalt His truth there. Now they found their hopes, in part, fulfilled, and were firmly persuaded that God would carry on His work to His own glory. Many Friends rendered them what aid they could during these renewed labours, which appear to have been much blessed.

Soon after his return from America in 1715, James Dickenson attended the London Yearly Meeting, and writes of these assemblies being "crowned with the Lord's living presence," and of hearts filled with the joy of His salvation. Two years later he visited many parts of England. In allusion to Bristol, he writes:—

"My exercise was great that all might be sensible of the work of the Lord to sanctify and fit them for His kingdom. I saw the fields ripe unto harvest, which was great, and the faithful labourers therein were but few. My cries went forth unto the Lord that He would fit many and send them forth into His harvest. He was near to answer and to bow the spirits of many under the operation of His hand; of which I was glad under a sense of His great love to mankind."

When not engaged in religious journeys he diligently attended to his business. In 1722 he went to Ireland in company with John Urwen, who was a very powerful minister, and singularly useful also in other labours for the Lord, at whose disposal he had placed his great natural talents.* At Edenderry James Dickenson had the pleasure of staying at the house of his beloved friend Thomas Wilson, and says that they "were sweetly refreshed together in the enjoyment of God's love," and that they parted in much tenderness. Probably this was their last interview on earth, as Thomas Wilson died early in 1725. One evening during his last illness, when several Friends were in his room, he spoke very sweetly of the evidence God had granted him,—"That a great harvest-day was coming over the nations, and that the Lord was fitting, and would fit many, and send them into the harvest." He said he was comforted in feeling that "Friends were inward with the Lord in their spirits," and remarked on how closely their hearts had been drawn together in the beginning, trusting that such nearness and unity might continue and increase. and that they might "dwell in humility and keep low." He gave God all the glory for the blessing which had eminently crowned his labours, saying : "Although the Lord hath made use of me at times to be serviceable in His hand, what I trust in is the mercy of God in Jesus Christ."

After returning from Ireland, James Dickenson, accompanied by another Friend, travelled through the

---

* On his death-bed, when eighty-six years of age, John Urwen remarked, that if he had his life to live over again, he did not well know how to do better. At first one reads these words with surprise ; but, on deeper consideration, do they not seem to bear the stamp of a genuine humility ? The assurance that the work had been well done—being such as a trustful child might feel, notwithstanding its helplessness, from the simple consciousness that it had been implicitly carrying out the directions of a wise Father.

Western Counties, from Lancashire to Cornwall. Their labour being, he says, "to turn people to the Lord and settle them on His teachings." At the York Quarterly Meeting in 1726 he spoke of how extremely important it was that particulars should be preserved—*for the benefit of future generations*—of the persecutions and deep trials which Friends had undergone for the cause of Christ, as well as of the wonders which He had wrought for their deliverance. When he laid this matter, which had long rested on his mind, before the next Yearly Meeting in London, to his great satisfaction an arrangement was made for the carrying out of the proposition. Later in the year we find him, as usual, labouring as God enabled him " to gather people to the teachings of His Holy Spirit." He has left no record of his journeyings to the Yearly Meeting, and to many parts of England, after the year 1727.

About twelve months before his death his speech was much affected by palsy, yet he was able occasionally to tell those around him—as they might well have believed had no words been spoken—that " God, whom he had served, was still with him, and that he had the evidence of peace and future felicity sealed upon his soul."

For about *sixty-five* years he was engaged in the ministry. He died in 1741, when in his eighty-third year, at Moorside, in his native county. "There are," writes Dora Greenwell, "many gains, many losses in Christ, over and above that great, inappreciable loss of the salvation of the soul in Him. *We are made poor by what we miss as well as by what we lose.*" And why should not the least child of the household of God commit himself, as completely and confidingly as James

Dickenson did, to the discipline, the control, the care and the love of his Father in Heaven? that thus, in God's good time, he also may have the blessedness of knowing for himself that, "as the mountains are round about Jerusalem, *so the Lord is round about His people,* from henceforth even for ever."

> "For of a new Jerusalem
>   Sons are we all:
> Round us are mightier towers,
> A brighter heaven above:
>   O, be the Lord's, as He is ours,
>   In faithful love."

WILLIAM EDMUNDSON.

"But best they learn whom Thou dost teach
A wisdom all uncramp'd by rules;
And silence may say more than speech,
And more than schools."

R. H. COOKE.

WILLIAM EDMUNDSON.

"We could not be satisfied without the sure, inward, Divine knowledge of God and Christ, and the enjoyment of those comforts the Scriptures declared of, which true believers enjoyed in the primitive times."—WILLIAM EDMUNDSON.

"THE common discourse of all sorts of people was of the Quakers, and various reports were of them; the priests everywhere were angry against them, and the baser sort of people spared not to tell strange stories of them; but the more I heard of them the more I loved them." Thus writes William Edmundson, in allusion to the year 1651, when he was about the age of twenty-four, and employed as a soldier in the Parliamentary army. Although unable to become acquainted with Friends, he says that when he heard of them a fervent yearning that the Lord would show him the way of righteousness arose in his heart.

He was born in 1627, at Little Musgrove, in Westmoreland, and was left an orphan at an early age. The uncle to whose care he was confided was unjust and harsh, and he could have felt no regret when leaving him, in order to be apprenticed to a carpenter and joiner at York, where at that time there seems to have been a religious awakening. William Edmundson's heart now became sorely troubled with Calvinistic perplexities, and with the unanswered question, "What shall I do to be saved?" One day he was so overcome by his feelings whilst sitting in church, that he attracted the attention of both the clergyman and the congregation, yet no one told him of the Lamb of God which taketh away the sin of the world.

When in Scotland under Oliver Cromwell, in 1650, "The Lord," as he says, "began afresh with him: at one time he would be brought very low, feeling deep condemnation for the life he was leading, and at another his heart would be so touched by the mercies of God as to cause him to shed tears of joy. And yet, strange to say, he knew not Who it was that thus dealt with him, nor did any of the high professors of religion whom he met with in the army enlighten him on this point. Sometimes, as he lay down in his tent at night and thought of the imminent peril to which his life had been exposed, he would resolve to repent and turn over a new leaf. But too often he allowed all serious considerations to be driven away by the active service in which he was engaged; and although after the battle of Worcester he was conscience-smitten anew by the Lord's mercy in preserving his life, he not only rejected this visitation to his soul, but even made light of it. Yet that love which all the day long stretches forth its hands unto the disobedient and gainsaying, followed him still, awakening in the reckless young soldier a deep interest in the scoffed-at Friends, and an earnest desire to be shown the path of life.

In the following year he left the army and married. He had intended to settle in Derbyshire as a shopkeeper, but was persuaded by one of his brothers to take up his abode in Ireland, whither he went, promising himself "great matters and religion besides!" Much disappointment, however, awaited him on his arrival at Dublin with his wife, servant and merchandise. He had expected that some preparations for the opening of his business would have been made by his brother; but instead of realising this hope he learned that the company of soldiers to which his brother belonged had been ordered to the north of Ireland. William Edmundson was strongly urged to remain in Dublin, where it seemed probable that a very successful trade might be carried on; this proposal he declined, and afterwards believed that he was prevented from accepting it by an unseen Hand, which thus preserved him from being "laden with riches as thick clay, and thereby hindered from the Lord's service." In after years he would often express his opinion that "the too-eager pursuit of the riches and greatness of this world was the chief engine the enemy had wherewith to hurt us." And in a letter to his friend William Ellis he writes, "The love of the greatness and riches of this world, and the earnest pursuit after them, is a surfeiting weed, and surfeits those noble parts in a man which otherwise are capable of serving the Lord."

On leaving Dublin William Edmundson took a house at Antrim, where his brother was then stationed, and after selling the goods he had brought with him, returned to England for a fresh stock. Whilst with his relations in the North he heard that James Naylor was going to hold a meeting, and still retaining his loving interest in Friends, and strong desire to have some intercourse with them, he attended it, accompanied by his eldest brother and another relative. He thus describes this epoch in his life:—

"We were all three convinced of the Lord's blessed truth. Then I knew it was the Lord's hand that had been striving with me for a long time. . . . Now being turned to a measure of the Lord's Spirit manifested in my heart, I knew it was the truth that led into all truth, agreeable to the Holy Scriptures of the law and prophets, Christ and His Apostles; and I thought all that heard it declared must needs own it, it was so plain to me. A few days after the Lord's power seized upon me through His Spirit, whereby I was brought under great exercise of mind. . . . But I loved the Lord's judgments."

On the return voyage he was assailed with the temptation to land his goods without paying duty. This caused, he says, " a great contest betwixt conscience and self, and many Scriptures were opened to my understanding, and self struggled hard for mastery, yet at last was overthrown." When he arrived at home his brother came to the door to meet him, and, seeing that some great change had come over him, was so much impressed by it that, on re-entering the house, he sat down in silence. William Edmundson, whose wife no doubt was also present, tells us that he was " much broken in the power of the Lord before them," and adds that his brother " received the truth and joined with it."

On going back to Carrickfergus for his goods, he was told that they would be seized unless he would take an oath to the correctness of his bills of parcels. But though only beginning to understand the value of the Pearl of great price, he felt that it was worth selling all for; so he told the officers that he could not swear because it was contrary to the commandments of Christ, which seems to have been altogether a new idea to them. It led to a good deal of talk about Friends in general, and William Edmundson in particular; but after delay and opposition he obtained an order to bring his goods to the Custom House.

A time of deep trial, described by himself as "a great war and conflict betwixt flesh and spirit," soon followed. None of those around him could understand what ailed him, or afford him any comfort. Sleep forsook him, and in his solitude of soul he longed for the fellowship of some one who had trodden such a path before him. One day his wife told him that, whilst he had been out, a stranger from England, named Miles Bousfield, had called and said much in favour of Friends, and of his great pleasure at the prospect of becoming acquainted with William Edmundson. The latter, not foreseeing the disappointment awaiting him, took his horse and rode a distance of twelve miles to the house where Miles Bousfield was staying, and spent the night with him. Silently and heedfully William Edmundson listened to his plentiful discourse on the work of God by His Spirit, and also to his advice to be "cheerful and merry, and not look at the inward troubles that bowed him down." But such counsel could not availingly comfort him, for it was premature; according to his own confession, whilst loving the truth he would fain have had it without abandoning worldly pleasures and profits. When at the end of a week he found himself in even a worse state than before, some fresh ability was given him to apply to the Physician who "maketh sore and bindeth up." He writes:—"I was weak but the Lord's strength was perfect in weakness, and His Spirit and power increased in me through obedience to the cross of Christ, wherein I was daily exercised, and thereby grew into acquaintance with the Lord's work to make me a vessel for His purpose."

In the spring of the following year he removed with

his family to the County of Armagh, where he took a house and opened a shop. He became aware that his conduct was narrowly watched by those who wished to oppose the doctrines he upheld, and he was often sorely tried. His business at first suffered from his keeping to one price in the sale of his goods. Inward suffering was also his portion, and yet he writes:—"Sometimes, when the Lord's hand would be easy with me, I would be afraid lest He should withdraw His hand; then my desires were to the Lord not to slacken His hand, but to search me thoroughly; for His judgments were become sweet to my taste, which He many times mixed with springs of mercy, to my joy and comfort."

At this time he was twenty-seven years of age, and twice a week a meeting was held at his house, consisting of himself, his wife and brother, and, after a while, of four others; often these seasons of waiting on God were times of refreshing from His presence. In the following year a Friend named John Tiffin paid a religious visit to Ireland, and William Edmundson thought it right to travel with him. As they made their appearance at fairs, etc., there was pretty much questioning on the tenets of Friends, about whom so many false stories had been circulated, in order to arouse prejudice, that the travellers even found it difficult to obtain a lodging. John Tiffin longed, we find, "to get an entrance for Truth" in Belfast, where many of the inhabitants made a high religious profession, yet "ears, doors, and hearts" were alike closed against an uncompromising 'setting-forth of Christianity in, what a modern writer styles, its "objective reality." One day, therefore, accompanied by William Edmundson and his brother, he went to a part of the high road not far from the town, where three lanes met, and there sat down to hold a meeting. "People came about us," writes William Edmundson; "we were a wonder to them, and something was spoken to direct their minds to God's Spirit in their own hearts."

William Edmundson now found, he says, that "the Lord's power and Spirit" influenced him to express a little in meetings. "Several," he adds, "gathered to our meetings, were convinced, and received the Truth. So we got meetings in several places, there being a great openness among people."

Many were to be the seals to his ministry of fifty-seven years' duration. We are told that though "bold as a lion," he bore persecution with "a lamb-like spirit;" and whilst zealous in his care of the churches, and valiant for the cause of Christ, he was also "a confirmer of the doubtful and sympathiser with the mournful." A Friend, who had known him for thirty years, writes of him as one of the first instruments in the hands of God in that day in Ireland, turning the thoughts of the people to "the marvellous and inshining light of Jesus Christ, the glorious Sun of Righteousness." He also alludes to his great concern to "stir up those the Lord had gifted to answer their respective services;" and describes him as "a man of undaunted spirit, grave, meek, free from affectation, and fit to stand before princes." Another Friend writes of "his incessant labours and travels both by sea and land, to gather to Christ, and that the churches gathered might be rooted and grounded in Him;" and mentions one especial occasion when a deep impression was made by his ministry, and when he had himself remarked that on "that morning the word of the Lord burned in him as a fire."

About the time that Edmundson first spoke in meetings he had a strong desire to meet with George Fox, whom he had never seen. Accordingly he went to England, and met with him at Badgeley, where a large meeting of Friends from various towns was held. When it was over he went up to George Fox, and they withdrew to an orchard, where the latter knelt in prayer; he dealt tenderly with his inexperienced companion, who felt that the interview was hallowed by the presence and power of the Lord.

During the same year William Edmundson went with his brother to transact some business at a fair at Antrim, and, not being able to leave until a late hour, they proposed to spend the night at a place called Glenavy. But before arriving there William Edmundson had a strong conviction that his shop was in danger of being robbed, and consequently resolved to return home without delay. Yet a little while after they had left Glenavy, he believed that a heavenly intimation was given him, that the Lord had need of him at Clough. No wonder that in this perplexity he should feel what he terms "a fear of a wrong spirit." He earnestly prayed for guidance, and was answered by the belief afforded him that He who now drew him back would also save his shop. The night was therefore spent at Glenavy, but William Edmundson's doubts in relation to the course he was taking prevented him from obtaining much sleep. Towards the evening of the next day he arrived at Clough, and rode up to an inn where he found that two Friends, who were ministers from England, were lodging ; one of them, Anne Gould, was ill, having undergone much hardship whilst travelling on foot. She was in a despairing state of mind, being tempted to fear that God had forsaken her, but when she heard that William Edmundson—whom she knew by report—was come, her heart was cheered ; he at once saw why he had been guided to Clough, and did not hesitate to tell the Friends that he had been brought there "by the good hand of God—led as a horse by the bridle." With great thankfulness and joy they received his visit; Anne Gould was enabled to see that her trial was in reality a grievous temptation, and was delivered from it. On his return home, William Edmundson found that, during the night he had spent at Glenavy, his shop-window had been broken, but had fallen with so much noise as to awaken the inmates of the house and drive the robbers away for fear of detection.

We now frequently find Edmundson going from place to place to publish the truths which he held dear ; he often encountered harsh usage, yet some Friends' meetings were established. At Armagh he was imprisoned in a little room in the house of the gaoler, who did not find it pleasant work to hold this prisoner of the Lord ; and his wife would sometimes exclaim that William Edmundson's presence was a torment to her—though he was quite silent. During this confinement he was taken ill, but arose from his bed to have a discussion with a Presbyterian minister, some elders, and two colonels. Notwithstanding their strong opposition to him, they went quietly away when it was over, for he says his heart and tongue were "full of the word of

Life to declare the way of Truth to them." He adds that in the midst of that morning's work the Lord healed him of his illness.

One of these disputants was a Colonel Cunningham, who was Chairman of the County Sessions, and, being a ready talker, he renewed the controversy when William Edmundson was brought before him and the other justices. The prisoner would willingly have avoided this, but, being unable to do so, a close argument followed, in which his antagonist was thoroughly worsted. He was annoyed at this defeat, in the presence of a large assembly from the surrounding country, and began to threaten Edmundson; but another justice arose, and, remarking on the unfairness of such conduct, told him that if he would dispute, he must do it on equal terms and lay aside his authority. He spoke also with approval of what had been expressed by William Edmundson, and it was soon decided that he should be set free; indeed the Bench seemed to be somewhat ashamed of his commitment.

Soon afterwards William Edmundson thought it his duty to give up his shop, and take a farm, in order, he says, "to be an example in the testimony against tithes." His brother and several other Friends with their families accompanied him to the county of Cavan, where many were added to their number and new meetings were opened. Their living was hard, and their bedding straw —whilst they were vigorously persecuted for the non-payment of tithes. Yet the peace of God was their portion. "For," writes William Edmundson, "in those days the world and the things of it were not near our hearts, but the love of God and His Truth lived in our hearts. We were glad of one another's welfare in the Lord, and His love dwelt in us."

He now felt that the time was come for him to pay a religious visit to other counties, going—to quote his own words—"from place to place as the Lord's good Spirit guided." We read of two troopers being "convinced," and coming to meetings; and of a sojourn at Belturbet, where the provost of the town, bringing a rough company, broke up a solemn meeting, and sent both men and women to prison, where the latter suffered much from the extreme cold. In the morning, after liberating the other Friends, he had William Edmundson placed in the stocks in the market place, and thus unwittingly afforded him an excellent opportunity for addressing the people assembled there, who, thronging around this unusual pulpit, listened gravely and feelingly to the persecuted stranger.

Nor did they hesitate to censure the provost for his conduct; one of them—a mere boy, Robert Wardel by name—telling him to his face that he had set a better man than himself in the stocks! We cannot wonder that this speech was the cause of his soon finding himself in the stocks by William Edmundson's side. He was quickly released, as his father threatened the provost with the law; but that day was an epoch in his life, for his heart had been reached by the truths taught and exemplified by the strange preacher; he boldly joined the new sect, and in after years himself became a minister, and in that capacity travelled in Great Britain, Germany, Holland, and America.

After a while Edmundson was summoned to the Court-house, before the governor of the garrison, the officers, and some of the chief inhabitants of the town. The clerk read Cromwell's declaration that all should be protected in their religion who "owned God the Creator of all things, and Christ Jesus the Saviour of men, and the Scriptures," etc. William Edmundson was then desired to answer to the various points: after he had done so, the governor and his companions decided that the Friends and their religion were under protection. William Edmundson did not abstain from appealing to those present that they could bear witness how long his friends and himself had been illegally imprisoned, and how unjustly he had been placed in the stocks. Nor did he hesitate to remind them that the law gave amends in such cases. Several gentlemen hereupon offered to be evidence if he would go to law with the provost; and the governor arose from his seat and taking his hand spoke of his regret for the ill-treatment to which his companions and himself had been subjected, assuring him also that he had had no hand in the matter. To these remarks Edmundson replied by asking where he had been during the last two days that he did not appear with his band of soldiers to appease the uproar? "My spirit," he writes, "was borne up in the power of the Lord as upon the wings of an eagle that day. Truth's testimony was over all their heads, and my heart was filled with joy and praises to the Lord. Many were convinced that day, and several of them received the Truth and abode in it."

William Edmundson now rejoined his friends, in whose company he found a Baptist minister, named William Parker, whose wife was a Friend, and one of the prisoners of the preceding night. As she did not arrive at home her husband had set out to seek her, and although he had felt a strong opposition to William Edmundson, he was touched to the heart on seeing him in the stocks, exposed to the rigorous temperature of a keen winter morning. The governor and several of those in authority were Baptists, and William Edmundson asked William Parker what he thought of his brethren's conduct? He answered that he was ashamed that those "who had been so long professing and fighting for conscience, should now suffer conscience to be trodden in the dirt." From that day he attended the meetings of Friends, and became an earnest minister. A Captain Morris—a highly-esteemed Baptist elder, a justice of the peace and governor of the garrison—when told of what had happened at Belturbet was much troubled, and, as he did not keep his sentiments to himself, a rumour reached the Court of Dublin that Captain Morris was turned Quaker. When examined by the general and chief officers, he owned that he held the faith and principles of Friends, and was therefore discharged from his command; he, also, became a minister.

During a confinement of fourteen weeks in a close and filthy dungeon in Cavan—where he was one night nearly stifled—William Edmundson was distressed at the news of James Naylor's fall, and with the consequent reflection that if such a man were the prey of temptation how could he himself hope to withstand it? But his spirit was comforted by the conviction that "Truth is Truth, though all men forsake it." William Edmundson was often imprisoned when travelling in other parts of the North of Ireland. Here one day we find him taking the Scotch Presbyterians of Donegal by surprise as he rode from house to house asking if there were any that feared God there! And the next, standing in Londonderry market place, amidst stage-players and rope-dancers, calling all to repentance, whilst directing them to Christ and the enlightening influence of the Holy Spirit; and going on with this discourse from a prison-window, until the gaoler fettered him as a condemned felon. But—

> "Stone walls do not a prison make,
> Nor iron bars a cage,"

so he sat down very peacefully to enjoy sweet communion with his Lord.

In the tumult caused in Ireland in 1661, by the accession of Charles II., the Friends were persecuted with increased vehemence. William Edmundson, during twenty days' leave of absence from Maryborough Prison, obtained an order of release for Friends throughout the nation from the Earls of Orrery, Mountrath, Lords Justices of the Kingdom, and Sir Morris Eustace, Chancellor. The Lord's power, he says, won him a place in the Earl of Mountrath's heart, which he retained until the death of that nobleman. In 1665 the Friends of Mountmellick were shamefully oppressed by the clergyman residing at that place, who even tried to prevent the miller from grinding corn for them. This clergyman was a justice of the peace and had William Edmundson, who lived in that neighbourhood, apprehended at a meeting, and appeared against him with two indictments. Four lawyers, of whom Edmundson knew nothing, and to whom he had given no fee, pleaded most successfully for him. Much sympathy was felt by the assembled people, many of whom said, as he passed them, "The Lord help you!"

In the same year he visited Londonderry, believing that he was commissioned to warn the inhabitants of that city that, if they did not repent, God would "bring a scourge over them, and scale their walls without a ladder." This he did in the cathedral and in the streets. Twenty-four years later the people of Londonderry recalled his words, when thousands of their number perished miserably during the terrible siege of that city, from the famine and wretchedness which its high walls could not shut out, as they did King James's troops.

In 1671 William Edmundson sailed for the West Indies and America, in company with George Fox and other Friends. One moonlight night they were in great danger from pirates who were about to board their vessel, when a cloud concealed her from them, and a fresh gale of wind meanwhile carried her beyond their reach. In the West Indies they had good service in gathering the people to Christ, and in Jamaica established meetings among them. Great were the hardships borne by William Edmundson and two Friends who accompanied him, during a wilderness journey in Carolina. One dark night in a forest was spent by the former in walking backward and forward between two trees, because his clothes were so drenched with rain that he dared not lie down, notwithstanding his weariness. He writes: "I had eaten little or nothing that day, neither had I anything to refresh me but the Lord."

The following morning they reached Albemarle River,

and the home of a Friend named Henry Phillips; his wife and himself wept for joy on seeing one of their spiritual kindred, a pleasure which they had not experienced for seven years. It was a Sunday, and William Edmundson bade them give notice of a meeting to be held at mid-day, asking to be called if he slept too long. It is supposed that at this time there were only about 3,000 Europeans in Carolina, whose houses were scattered over the State, one rarely within sight of another, and usually unconnected, except by paths lying along the banks of rivers and inlets, and marked by notches in trees. A religious meeting was a great novelty, and the men who came to it thought it quite superfluous to lay aside their pipes. "But in a little time," writes William Edmundson, " the Lord's testimony arose in the authority of His power, and their hearts were tendered." A Justice of the Peace, who was present with his wife, having " received the truth with gladness," asked that a meeting might be held at his house the next day, and a blessed one it proved to be.

Bancroft states that from the commencement of the settlement, there seems to have been no minister in the colony, and " no public worship but such as burst from the hearts of the people themselves." Towards the end of the year, George Fox, and other Friends, visited Carolina and the isolated converts there were remembered by him with such deep solicitude that, before leaving America, he addressed an epistle to them, exhorting them to meet together in the name of Jesus—" There is no salvation in any other name. He is your Prophet, your Shepherd, your Bishop, your Priest in the midst of you, to sanctify you, and to feed you with life; wait in His power and light that ye may be built upon Him the true Foundation."

Whilst in Virginia Edmundson visited the governor, Sir William Barclay, to lay before him the sufferings of the Friends who dwelt there. He had by no means a courteous hearing, but afterwards learnt that he had fared better than might have been anticipated; for Major General Bennet—described as a "brave, solid, wise man, who received the Truth"—asked him if the governor had called him "dog," or "rogue," and on receiving a negative reply said, "You took him in his best humour." In Shelter Island William Edmundson had the pleasure of meeting with George Fox and other Friends, from whom he parted, after two or three days, "in the sweet love of God." His homeward voyage was a swift one. From Jamaica he addressed an epistle to Friends, from which a brief extract follows:—

"Stand fast and firm in the freedom and liberty of the blessed Truth. . . . Take heed of being linked and married to your shops and trades and merchandise, whereby you are hindered from coming to meeting, serving the Lord and doing His work, as though your work and business must be done first, and the Lord's last. . . . If any be linked and married to the world, and have their delights therein—how then are they God's freemen and Christ's spouse? . . . Be ye therefore good merchantmen. Prize the love of God who, as a tender Father, gave His Son for us."

In 1675 William Edmundson again visited the West Indies and America; he landed in Barbadoes, where a great blessing seems to have rested on his labours in public meetings for worship, "Men and women's meetings for Church affairs, and negroes' meetings in families." When the governor told him that he had heard that he was making the negroes Christians, and thus leading them to rebellion and murder, William Edmundson owned that that he had endeavoured to bring them to "the knowledge of God and Christ Jesus, and to believe in Him who died for them, and for all men;" such teaching, he remarked, would be likely to deter them from insurrection, and if they did rebel it would be the result of the state of brutal ignorance and oppression in which they were kept.

In New England he felt that he was travelling with his life in his hand, on account of the war with the Indians. One day, accompanied by five or six other Friends, he called on an aged man, whose house was fortified for fear of the natives. When the gates had been unlocked, William Edmundson, observing that an elderly man was engaged in prayer, delayed entering the room until he had arisen. William Edmundson then told those who had assembled that he did not come to disturb them, for he loved religion and was seeking religious people. Then he relates how, as he sat among them, his "heart being full of the power and spirit of the Lord, the love of God ran through him to the people," and he begged leave to address them. After speaking, he says, of the mysteries of God's kingdom, he "touched a little upon the priests," whereupon the old man stood up, laid his hand on his shoulder, and said, "I must stop you, for you have spoken against our ministers." William Edmundson was silent for a while, and remarks that he was tender of them, for he felt they were "a tender people." But he soon told them he had much "to declare unto them of the things of God," yet could not do so without the sanction of the master of the house. This was again granted, and utterance was given him to make known the mystery of the Gospel. Many hearts were touched, whilst tears flowed freely, and he ended the meeting with fervent prayer; then his host rose up and embraced him, and said he wished to know what was the difference between their own ministers and Friends. To this William Edmundson replied: "Your ministers are satisfied with the *talk* of Christ and the Scriptures; and we cannot be satisfied without the sure, inward, Divine knowledge of God and Christ, and the enjoyment of those comforts the Scriptures declare of, which true believers enjoyed in the primitive times." The old man answered, with tears, "Those are the things I want;" and, dear as provisions then were, he would not allow the Friends to leave until they had taken a meal with him. He wept as he folded William Edmundson in his arms as they were about to part, saying, "I doubt I shall never see you again."

The latter had also an interesting interview with some Baptists in the neighbourhood of New London, who thought it right to keep the old Jewish Sabbath on the last day of the week. He told them that Christ had ended the law of the Old Covenant and was the Rest of His people, and that all must know rest, quietness, and peace in Him. In reply to their questions on Baptism, he quoted Matt. iii. 11, and John iii. 30, and said that it was a "material question to such as held water-baptism to be in force, to show how far it was decreased, and when it would be at an end, and Christ's baptism increased to perfection, and established according to John's testimony; but as for himself he believed that John's water-baptism was ended long ago, and Christ's established; and there was one faith, and one baptism." On the following evening Edmundson went on board a sloop bound for New York, although he had been strongly impressed with the belief that his Lord had work for Him at New Hertford, in Connecticut; but as the fifty-mile journey through the wilderness was a most perilous one, on account of the Indian warfare, he was unwilling to undertake it. When the vessel was a few leagues from land a storm came on, which made the captain take shelter in a harbour, where she lay for some days on account of the strong head-wind. William Edmundson did not doubt that by this detention God was mercifully preventing him from directing his own steps, and that, be the consequences what they might, he must go to New Hertford. When he told those on board how it had been with him, the captain wept, and the hearts of others were also touched.

In 1667, after an absence of two years, he returned to his home, meeting his family, he says, " in the same love of God that had made them willing to part with one another, for a season, for the Lord's service." In 1682 William Edmundson and another Friend were confined for twenty weeks in a dungeon, with thieves and murderers, at the instigation of a clergyman, on account of their refusal to pay tithes. They were liberated by means of the mediation of their landlord, the Lord of Ely, with the Bishop, who ordered them to come before the Court at Kildare. In reply to his questions, William Edmundson told him of his conviction that "the Law was ended that gave tithes, and the Priesthood changed that received them, by the coming and suffering of Christ, who had settled a ministry on better terms." A dean who was present spoke in a very kind manner, and said that had he known William Edmundson as well before he should not have thus suffered. William Edmundson was enabled also to answer fully the queries put to him with regard to Faith, to the Gospel ministry, and the true worship of God. This conversation lasted for three hours, and a Friend (John Burnyeat) who was a listener, remarked that he had never been better satisfied with a day's work in his life. From that hour the bishop and officers of the Court dealt kindly with Friends.

In the following year William Edmundson again visited the West Indies. In 1685 he had some unusual service in different parts of Ireland, for he was made deeply sensible that a time of great calamity was not far distant, when the dead bodies of men would be spread over the ground; and, as an ambassador for Christ, often and faithfully did he warn those whom he addressed, " to lessen their concerns in the world, and be ready to receive the Lord in His judgments that were at hand, and to flee unto Him for succour, that they might have safety." This season of grievous trial began when, on the accession of James II., the Earl of Tyrconnel, Lord Deputy of Ireland, disarmed most of the Protestants and placed arms at the disposal of the Catholics. Several of the former were thus caused to leave the country, or take refuge in garrisons : but in the war which soon broke out many were wholly unprotected from the Catholic soldiers and from the plundering bands of Rapparees.* One day a party of

---

* Those who carried on war on a small scale ; (*ee* is an Irish diminutive). This merciless banditti, belonging to neither army, spread terror through the land.

horsemen arrived at Mountmellick, and violently abused the Protestants who resided in that neighbourhood. William Edmundson they dragged by the hair among the feet of their horses, swearing they would kill him. The following morning he went to Mountmellick, and had an interview with Justice Warnford and another English gentleman, who told him they thought this outbreak was the harbinger of a massacre. In reply he gave them his opinion that it was more probably a plan for making the English flee from the country, and he strongly advised that a full investigation should be made of the abuses which had been perpetrated, and that some one should be sent to Dublin to lay the matter before the Government. The justice and his friend highly approved of this suggestion, but said that no one would dare to take this step unless it were himself. Although he well knew that a journey to Dublin at this time would be with the hazard of his life, he consented to run the risk for the good of his countrymen. In consequence of the appeal made by himself and two gentlemen from Mountmellick some of the troopers were disarmed and sent to Maryborough gaol.

During these years of trial Edmundson often visited Dublin, and gained material aid from the Government for the distressed Protestants, and especially for Friends, as being altogether unarmed. Occasionally he spoke to King James himself, who gave him a patient hearing. After the battle of the Boyne, in 1689, some of the defeated Irish army plundered many houses, including that of William Edmundson. He told the most influential Irishmen who lived near him that if they would do all that lay in their power to keep their fellow-countrymen from spoiling the English of the little that was left to them, he and his friends would strive to do as much for them when the advancing English army should arrive. The proposal was fully accepted, but the sworn promises of protection were but ill kept. Yet William Edmundson felt that no failure of duty in others could exempt him from its performance.

William III. had issued a proclamation to the effect that all the Irish who would remain quietly in their homes should be unmolested, but nevertheless a body of 300 soldiers, under two captains, came to Mountmellick, and seized some of the Irish residents and 500 head of cattle. Amongst their prisoners was an old gentleman of the name of William Dunn, who had been a captain in the army, and his two sons; one of the latter they stripped, saying they should hang him on suspicion of being one of the banditti. The Dunns managed to acquaint William Edmundson with their perilous situation, and with all possible haste he rode after them and their captors, followed by some of his Irish neighbours, who hoped that he might help them to the restoration of their friends and cattle. When the two captains saw him they made a halt. He urged them to release all the prisoners, and reminded them of the king's promise. They said they were willing to act on his advice if the soldiers could be led to do so. The latter meanwhile were on the verge of attacking the men that had followed William Edmundson, who now dismounted, and, at the risk of his life, went amongst the excited soldiers, and succeeded, with the assistance of their captains, in persuading them to restore most of the cattle. He next sought out the young man whose life had been threatened, and having thrown his own riding-coat around him, told his captors how unmanly their conduct towards him had been; adding that he, who had himself been a soldier, would have scorned so base an action. Not only were young Dunn's clothes given back to him, but he was liberated, as were also his father and brother, and most of the other prisoners.

Although, during this time of misery towns were burned and Protestants murdered, the Friends held their meetings regularly, and "enjoyed them peaceably." In the latter part of 1690 some hundreds of Rapparees one night surrounded William Edmundson's home, and, after discharging several shots through the windows, set fire to the house. They robbed him of his cattle and goods, and carried off his two sons and himself as prisoners. With hardly any clothing on, and barefoot, they suffered much, for their path that winter night led them over rough ground, amidst bushes, and through mire and knee-deep water. The next morning their captors held a sham council in a wood, and determined to shoot the father and hang the sons. The former told the banditti that many of them knew him and his family, and challenged them to prove that his sons or himself had ever wronged them of a farthing; on the contrary—so he reminded them—he had imperilled his life on behalf of their fellow-countrymen. To this appeal several made answer that they knew he was an honest man. "If I die," he then said, "you are my witnesses that I am innocent. God will avenge my blood." They were astonished at the fearlessness he manifested—having two firelocks ready with which to shoot him. After having blindfolded his sons, they were about to perform the same office for him. "You need not," he said; "for I can look you in the face, and am not afraid to die." At this critical moment Lieutenant William Dunn, whose father and brother had been so effectually aided by Edmundson, came up, saying that he would take the three captives to Athlone.

Yet this young officer's conduct was not influenced by gratitude, but by the hope of preferment. Although Athlone was only twenty miles off, he kept them for three nights without food or fire. When some of the Rapparees expressed their wonder at William Edmundson's power of withstanding such hardship, he said that whilst thus deprived of provisions, the Lord had taken away his appetite, so he was well fitted for his condition. He knew, however, that his sons were very hungry, and noticing an expression of pity on the face of an old Irishman whose door they were passing, he asked for a little bread for them. The old man answered that he would give him a piece of bread, even were it bought with gold, for he did not look like one who was used to beg. When, on the following day, the Edmundsons were led through the chief street of Athlone, they were in danger of being stabbed with the bayonets of the crowd of soldiers who filled it, and who called them traitors and rebels. In this behaviour they were encouraged by the high sheriff of the county. But just then an Irish gentleman, Lieutenant Valentine Toole, pressed through the crowd, and courteously greeting the persecuted prisoner as "Master Edmundson," said to the sheriff, "I have known him above twenty years to be an honest man, say you all what you will of him." This quieted the angry rabble, and after a little while William Edmundson and his sons were brought before the governor, who knew the former well, and had occasionally been at his house. When he now saw him, wrapped in an old blanket, he expressed his sympathy, whilst tears stood in his eyes. He also blamed Lieutenant Dunn for the false accusations he had been making; yet he was afraid to release the prisoners, for he knew that many suspicious eyes were fixed on him because of his consideration for the English.

After committing them to custody he sent them some beef, bread, drink, and money, but they had nothing to lie on except the floor. William Edmundson was greatly exhausted, and was so much distressed at the language of some of his fellow-prisoners that he asked the governor to remove him to the dungeon, for he thought he would rather die there than be amidst such depraved companions. The governor said he had not the heart to grant such a request, but gave him leave to go to the house of a Friend, who lived six miles from Athlone, and who had promised to "engage his body and all that he had" for William Edmundson's "true imprisonment." The latter was now able to send a few lines to relieve the suspense of his poor wife. The governor soon liberated the young Edmundsons, and with the aid of an Irish colonel released their father a few days later.

During his absence William Edmundson's wife had one day gone with some of her English neighbours to the farmyard of one of her sons, in order to fetch his stock of hides and leather. Whilst they were loading the cars they were attacked by another basely ungrateful son of old Captain Dunn, with a party of Rapparees. Notwithstanding the cold winter weather they stripped William Edmundson's wife of all her clothing, which exposure brought on an illness that caused her death seven months later.

The most conspicuous events of William Edmundson's life have now been recorded, and the patient diligent labours of his latter years, the result of which it is impossible to estimate, must be hastily passed over. They were often performed under much bodily infirmity, but—to quote his own words—"The Lord who had carried him through many exercises and perils was his strength and song;" and again and again we meet with such acknowledgments as the following, "The Lord's power healed me and carried me over." Once, when ill at Leominster, a physician, who had been at the meeting which he had held in that town, offered to attend him by day and night, and with skilful kindness ministered to his need gratuitously.

In 1697 he attended a meeting for eight counties at Bristol, which lasted for four days. He writes: "The Lord's eminent power went over all, whereby many hearts were made glad and thankful to the Lord for that visit and service." In the summer of 1700, whilst visiting Connaught, we find that he was placed in the stocks at Ayrescourt, to the grief of the people of that place, some of whom, he says, wept "to see an ancient man set in the stocks for worshipping God, having never seen the like before." They might have spared their tears had they known what consolation was granted to him and his companions. He tells us that, after they were liberated, "a brave, heavenly meeting was held."

In 1704 his strength was so much reduced that he thought his end was near. "I was not afraid," he writes, "of death or the grave, but could say, through the tender mercy of God, O death, where is thy sting? O grave, where is thy victory? Through steadfast faith and hope in my Lord and Saviour Jesus Christ, who suffered for me, and whom death or the grave could not hold, but rose again and appears before the Father for me as Advocate, Mediator and Interceder."

Three months before his death, and when in his eighty-fifth year, William Edmundson attended the half-year's meeting at Dublin, and took leave of his friends. A few hours before the attack which terminated his life came on, he finished arranging his journal and other writings. He told his friends that it gave him pleasure to consider how he had spent his time since the Lord called him to the ministry; and said to George Rooke, "We have had many good meetings together, I believe we shall meet in heaven." To Thomas Wilson he remarked that "The Lord had a great work to do in the earth, though many did not see it, and that His glorious day which had broken forth would rise higher and higher upon His people."

William Edmundson died in the summer of 1712. Very varied are the ways in which the Lord's children are called to serve Him, perhaps as varied as are their characters and mental and physical capabilities. For each one, who is willing to be shown it, is there not a path often lying parallel with the daily ordinary routine of life, in which he can glorify God better than in any other? For some it may be a similar one to that of the old cripple who could not even turn in bed, but was wont, as he lay there in his poverty and pain, to pray, "Lord Jesus Christ, have mercy upon me and every one; not upon one only, but upon EVERY ONE, Lord Jesus Christ." May each keep that which is *committed to his trust*, whatever it be! and as we take leave of William Edmundson, let us unite in these words of one of his friends, "May it please the Lord of the Harvest to raise up other labourers therein; for the harvest is great and such labourers but a few."

WILLIAM ELLIS AND HIS FRIENDS.

"No tongue of mortal can express,
No pen can write the blessedness,
He only who hath proved it knows
What bliss from love of Jesus flows."

WILLIAM ELLIS AND HIS FRIENDS.

"Blessed be the Lord that hath made His arm bare in our time, to bring us to the discovery of a most excellent situation, the glory of which cannot be told with the tongue of men; and it is intended by Him that we should grow steadfast in the faith which gives victory."—WILLIAM ELLIS.

Two remarkable ministers in the early days of the Society of Friends were the brothers John and Roger Haydock. The elder became a Friend at the age of twenty-seven, and soon after found himself a prisoner for conscience' sake in Lancaster Gaol. Thus began the "much persecution both of tongues and hands," borne with invincible patience, though often his lot, during fifty years of apostolic labour in Great Britain, Ireland and America. It was said of his ministry that it "tended to the building up in the most holy faith in our Lord and Saviour Jesus Christ, which gives victory over sin." He died a prisoner in Lancaster Castle; his friends, in a brief "testimony" about him, state that they "could not stand acquitted before God or man to have buried the corpse with a few short sighs, and to let his name go with him to the grave. We have raised no monument over his sepulchre [they add] but there is one due to his worth. His life was a sweet savour and ought not to go under foot."

After he had become a Friend his mother one day induced his younger, but learned and talented brother, Roger, to reason with him on the course which he had taken; but as John Haydock proved the good ground he had for pursuing it, his brother soon became silent, much to the mother's disappointment and displeasure. But in reply to her words of blame young Roger said, "It is truth, I dare not speak against it;" ere long he publicly professed the same views, and, undeterred by persecution and delicate health, spent much time in ministerial journeys. Roger Haydock died of fever at the age of fifty-three; his wife—to whom in her early life he had been a faithful instructor in righteousness—remarks on his readiness to leave her, when needful for the service of their Lord. She adds, "I was made a blessing to him more comfortable every day than other; he would often express it; and truly so was he to me every day, every way, and in every respect. No tongue nor pen can relate the full of that comfort and joy we had in God and one in another. . . . His name and memory is blessed, and will live and be of a sweet savour in the hearts of the righteous through ages."

When he was about thirty-three, on a winter day early in 1667, Roger Haydock had held a meeting at Lower Bradley, in the West Riding of Yorkshire. Eleanor Lowe—who afterwards became his wife—and her cousin, Elizabeth Hodson, both of whom were ministers, were also present. Amongst the assembled company was a youth of eighteen, named William Ellis, who two years earlier had left his home at Calton and engaged himself to a Friend at Skipton, a linen-weaver, named John Stott. He had heard that a Friends' meeting was to be held at Bradley, and he asked leave from his "master and dame" to attend it, which was readily granted. Probably he was impelled by curiosity, but he had cause ever after for gratitude to God for guiding his steps to Bradley that day. Many years later he thus writes of Roger Haydock:—

"Though I have had many instructors in Christ, yet I have not many fathers; for in Christ Jesus was I begotten, by him through the Gospel and the operation of the Holy Spirit, which did effectually open a door of entrance in my heart, as it opened a door of utterance unto him. . . ."

He goes on to say how his soul now became "in love" with righteousness and with those who exemplified it, most of all with Roger Haydock himself, with whom after a while he had the satisfaction of becoming more closely acquainted, and found that it was the chief aim of his life to labour for the spreading of Christ's Kingdom amongst men. William Ellis's own history of the change wrought in him, by means of the ministry of Roger Haydock, is fully endorsed by his mistress, Abigail Stott, who felt sure, on his return from Bradley meeting, that some great change had passed over him— an opinion amply confirmed by three years of daily intercourse. She did not doubt that he had realised the prophet's words: "The Lord whom ye seek shall suddenly come to His temple; . . . and He shall sit as a refiner and purifier of silver, and He shall purify the sons of Levi, and purge them as gold and silver, that they may offer unto the Lord an offering in righteousness."

Although he had been very frivolous in his tastes and pursuits, he now became remarkable for the watchfulness which regulated his words and actions; and his influence over the children and servants of the household was of great value. The steadfastness of his faith was, moreover, not unfrequently put to the test of persecution, of which however only one instance seems to be recorded; it is of his being violently laid hands on, when on his way to a meeting, and confined in the Skipton tolbooth.

At the age of twenty-one William Ellis took up his residence in the village of Airton, and soon afterwards found that the Lord was calling him to advocate His cause as a Gospel minister. At this time he found a wise, faithful, and tender counsellor in John Wynn, a Friend, whose ministry had been greatly blessed to him at an early period of his renewed life. His young heart—suddenly awakened to the truth that the things that are seen are temporal, whilst the things that are unseen are eternal—was just in a state to be deeply impressed by a simple illustration from Job, made use of by John Wynn; and the more so that his own employment would both show him its force and keep it in his memory. "All should prize their time," said the minister, "for it is as swift as a weaver's shuttle."

After an interval of nineteen years, in a letter to this Friend, William Ellis says that this figure dwelt in his mind as much as ever. "I plainly see," he writes, "that there must be devout faithfulness when time is truly prized; and oft I say if I had it to spend over again I could spend it to better advantage. However, the Lord is a God of great kindness and tender mercy, and delights to see judgment work out into victory, and that the hearts of His people should be freely willing to venture all for His name, even soul, body and substance. In all the good that is come upon me every way I do not give the honour to that which some call good luck, but only to that great Name that is over all powers."

John Wynn left the army and became a Friend when about six-and-twenty, having received deep religious impressions in a meeting at Pall Mall; and, literally laying down his arms whilst standing in the ranks at a review, he afterwards had his discharge and settled at Bradford as a clothier. A soldier now, under the Captain who goes forth conquering and to conquer, he sought with unwearied zeal to fulfil the ministry which he had received, and though suffering deeply from persecution, visited most of the counties of England and Wales. His wife, Deborah Wynn, was also a minister, and, as meetings were regularly held at their house, they were the especially chosen victims of informers, and three times all their property of any worth was seized.

On one of these occasions John Wynn, when returning from market, had his horse, goods and overcoat taken from him; on arriving at home he found his shop cleared of its stock and his house of its furniture, with the exception of the bed occupied by his wife and newborn infant, and which would have been also taken but for the interference of humane neighbours. Some of these, when they heard him speak of laying out the little money left him in goods for his shop, begged him not to take such a course, saying it was manifest that his persecutors we bent on ruining him. He answered that he was not at all disheartened, they could take no more than all, and he believed "they would be limited in the Lord's time;" and so it proved. His wife had been early inured to similar trials: an only child, at the age of fifteen she carried on her parents' business whilst they were prisoners for conscience' sake at York, whither she walked—a distance of twenty-two miles—once a fortnight to visit them and give them the amount she had earned. Two or three years later her ministry, which was to be of sixty-four years' duration, had commenced. She long out-lived her husband, beloved and respected in her own neighbourhood; her "heart and house" were ever open to entertain those who were travelling in the service of the Lord, and many of the early ministers of the Society she numbered amongst her friends. In her old age she spoke of the great cause she had for praising God who had upheld her in all her troubles. John Wynn died in 1699, after a short illness, during which he earnestly exhorted those who visited him to "stand faithful unto the Lord."

How highly Ellis had valued his friendship we may learn from allusions in letters received by him, as well as from his own pen. John Tomkins writes:—" I cannot blame thee for mourning the loss of a good man. Good men are too few everywhere. God complained in old time that the righteous were taken away, and no man regarded it or laid it to heart. The Lord help thee in thy service for Him, and stand by thee if He takes away thy outward helps."

Another correspondent acknowledges the receipt of two letters "about thy sorrowful exercises on parting with thy ancient friend, counsellor and comforter;" whilst William Ellis himself writes of how his heart was made willing to receive John Wynn's reproofs and kind counsel; and, describing a visit paid shortly before his death to the neighbourhood of Airton, adds:—

"Oh, what strength, power, and zeal were upon him. . . .

Oh ! the unutterable joy that has filled my heart when I have remembered him, with many others whom I am satisfied did delight to serve God in their day, and followed Him truly, like the worthies of old. And the sense of this reward and crown of life being laid up for the faithful, makes my soul the more earnestly to travel forward. . . . So that at the last upshot of all, through Him that loved me and washed me from my sins in His own most precious blood, I may receive a sentence of Well done ! "

When about the age of thirty, William Ellis married a Friend named Alice Davie, who became a Minister, and in this capacity, in company with other Friends, not unfrequently visited various parts of England. No record it seems was kept of the early itinerant labours to which her husband felt himself called. Whilst absent on one of these journeys his spiritual interest was awakened for the eldest son of his former mistress, Abigail Stott; and therefore on his return he paid a visit to the family. He found Jacob Stott seriously ill, and thought it right to pray vocally for him; during that prayer the young man—who had often confided to his mother the fear that he was unprepared for death—felt a blessed hope arise in his soul which, strengthened by a heavenly earnest, remained unclouded until his death, a fortnight afterwards.

One of Ellis's friends remarks that, in meetings, he often "hit the mark" by addressing those altogether unknown to him as if he had been acquainted with their spiritual condition. In 1669, two years after his marriage, William Ellis paid a visit to Cornwall, to which a Friend of Launceston thus alludes, on the following New Year's Day:—" Oh, my dear and well-beloved friend ! I cannot forget the many heavenly opportunities wherein we have been comforted and refreshed together." A letter from another Cornish correspondent, Thomas Gwin, of Falmouth, congratulates William Ellis on the birth of his little son, Jonathan, who was apparently an only child, a treasure which, after a few months' possession, his parents were called on to resign. In the same letter Thomas Gwin states that he has been " exceedingly exercised " by the death of a little daughter, and adds :—

"I have a true unity with thee in thy concern on account of Friends' children, and a jealousy sometimes on my mind lest the ensuing generation—receiving the profession of truth in a traditional way, and being unacquainted with the wonders which the Lord has wrought for His exercised people,—may be ready to sit as those that are at ease in Zion, and trust in a formal profession."*

In the winter of 1694-5, William Ellis went on a gospel mission to Ireland, crossing safely to Dublin, though two Whitehaven ships were taken by a privateer during the same night. After expressing his belief that his service would be acceptable to the Lord, for which his " soul had much travailed," he reminds his wife to take care of herself; " first for thy mind, that thou do not overbow it; and that thou take care of thy body that thou do not overwork thyself. . . . It is great ease to my mind that thou parted so freely with me." A month later he writes an epistle to Settle Monthly

---

* From Thomas Gwin's MS. Journal we find that a special meeting for children, in which he was much interested, was held at Falmouth on Saturdays. In the summer of 1704 he writes :— " I was with the children, and was drawne forth in testimony plaine and demonstrative, telling them how much more helps they had as outwardly, to stirre them up than some of us had, and how they, by waiting and retiring, might obtain the same inward help we enjoyed."

Meeting, to which he belonged. In this he advises his friends to

"meet often together; and when met, labour to be rightly exercised towards God in your particular gifts, and that none give way to an indifferent mind or a conceited spirit. . . . Those who walk in the Truth do receive the goodness of God when met together; it is such that take delight to come together on God's account, and cannot cry, 'My business, my business;' neither will they be hindered by it, for they know the great business is to increase their strength in the Truth."

When his Irish labours are nearly ended he writes to his wife of how wonderfully the Lord had upheld him, "even as through deep and rough waters," so that he could exceedingly rejoice. In the following summer William Ellis received a letter from William Edmundson, which afforded him timely aid; for, in allusion to its arrival, he writes (when answering it three days after) of being "much better in mind since," and of his gratitude to the Lord for still putting it into the hearts of His servants to animate and advise others. He also states that for nearly three years, even "before my son died"—so the infant's death was an epoch in his life—he had at times felt "a flowing of kindness" to the inhabitants of the West Indies. And this constraining power of the love of Christ was lasting still, though he admits that he had not yielded to it as he ought, and that consequently the chastening hand of the Lord had been so laid on him as to cause the fervent cry to arise that He would once more allow him to "stand in His delightful presence, and he would be willing to run His errands by sea or land." The following passage from William Edmundson's letter is probably one of those which came to his correspondent as a word in season:—

"The Lord's labourers that He hath called into His vineyard and gifted with His Holy Spirit for the work of the ministry, are to follow His work and business close, and finish their work in the daytime. There is need of good workmen, for the old enemy is hard at work; and his old engine is this world and the things and kingdom of it, to twist and draw men from the Lord's business."

On the day that he received William Ellis's answer to it, William Edmundson, who was his correspondent's senior by five-and-twenty years, wrote again, reminding him that Christ's will and mind are cleared up in His own time to His servants' understanding that are devoted to His will; also telling him of the great need of faithful and skilful labourers on the other side of the Atlantic, and bidding him "write at large" to him: no doubt he was deeply interested in the idea that his younger brother would visit lands on behalf of whose inhabitants his own heart had been deeply stirred. William Ellis now replies that God's goodness to him makes him long to serve Him fully; and remarks—paradoxically—"I shall forbear to tell thee the benefit thy letters are to me." It was about two years after this time that William Ellis sailed for America. Before leaving home he had the pleasure of renewed personal intercourse with William Edmundson, who spent two nights at his house, and had good service in the neighbourhood." *

---

* Probably William Edmundson held a meeting in the meeting-house which William Ellis had lately erected at Airton at his own expense. It is built of stone, and will contain about one hundred and fifty persons; above the door are the initials W.A E. and the date of its perfect completion (1700). It stands with its back to the village street, on the other side of which William Ellis built his own

The people who resided near the village sometimes came with eagerness to the meeting now held there, which was visited by many ministers. "So I am in great hopes," writes William Ellis, "great part of our valley will be convinced; and if they will not be converted the fault will be their own."

Up to this time he seems to have attended the meeting held at Rilston. It was in the early part of the winter of 1697 that he sailed for America, in company with Aaron Atkinson, a remarkable minister, then about thirty-two. Just before leaving England they received a letter from John Tomkins, the compiler of the three first parts of "Piety Promoted," asking them to visit some relatives of his in West Jersey, and encouraging them to put their whole trust in Him on whose errand they were going: "I believe you have tried the name of the Lord, and found it to be shot-proof," he writes; "it is the whole armour of God."

At this time John Tomkins was about thirty-four, and in the following year began to speak as a minister; he had lost his father in early childhood, but was very carefully brought up by his mother. As he grew older he delighted in searching the Scriptures; and one of his publications, in after years, was on "The Harmony of the Old and New Testaments." His affectionate and sympathising disposition found a field of action in aiding his step-father and half-brothers and sisters,

---

substantial dwelling in farm-house fashion : in the front, above a doorway, now walled up, is the date 1690, and the initials, W.A.E.; the same letters are to be seen over the wide arch around the fire-place, in the comfortable room which no doubt answered many purposes besides that of kitchen. A little further up the street William Ellis mounted a sun-dial on a pillar.

who were in very reduced circumstances, as well as in visiting and relieving others who might be afflicted in mind, body, or estate. His heart had early responded to the alluring influence of a Saviour's love; even when a boy he felt a warm affection for the ministers with whom he came in contact, and in after life could say that he had dedicated his whole strength and time to the honour and service of God. When on his death-bed, at the age of forty-three, he said, "I have seen great things since my sickness, things which I think not lawful to be spoken." And after referring to the sweet peace granted him by his Saviour, he added, "Oh, the love of the Lord Jesus Christ is great to mankind!"

Before leaving London for Deal, William Ellis and Aaron Atkinson had, we learn, "a fine time" in that city, where they were also encouraged by the sympathy of their friends and the prayers of the Church; so that William Ellis wondered at the entire willingness he felt to leave what was nearest and dearest to him, though he knew that this ready compliance was "God's work" and not his own. Before his long absence he wrote to a friend of his at Skipton on behalf of his "old dame," Abigail Stott, now a widow, and in pecuniary difficulties. His generous and kindly disposition, yielded to the guidance of his Lord, made him an effectual helper to those who were in outward want, whilst it also enabled him to sympathise with the hungry and thirsty in spirit. To himself, his wife says, it was "as meat and drink to serve the Lord and His people." The scant details to be found of William Ellis's life are chiefly those recorded in his correspondence, but a few brief memoranda were made by him during his outward voyage. He thus writes:—

"*Eleventh Month 9th*, 1697-8.—We had a meeting, and through deep travail of mind the Lord answered, and filled my heart with the sense of the good things of His kingdom. . . . Now I see it is easy to drink the cup of sweetness and comfort, and many will be thankful to retain it; but to drink a bitter cup of exercise at the Lord's hand many are unwilling; yet it is good to labour to take it thankfully at the hand of the Lord: for those that do so in patience may be sure that the Lord will give them to drink of the cup of consolation."

The voyage was a perilous one, and the vessel narrowly escaped being wrecked when only two miles from Virginia. Very soon after landing the ministers set to work, and William Ellis's heart overflowed with gratitude and joy for opportunities granted and ability given to declare the tidings of salvation. And this blessed beginning to his labours confirms his trust that God will still afford him the aid of "His good presence, which has been," he writes, "my chiefest pleasure for many years. I often think in my heart that all is too little that I can do for the worthy name of God." Whilst surrounded by fresh scenes and interests the members of his own meeting are by no means lost sight of.

Only three days after writing his first American letter to his wife, he begins an epistle to the Monthly Meeting at Settle, in a postscript to which he asks his friends, when gathered together and feeling the Lord's power, to pray that he may be kept from dangers of every kind. In Virginia the travellers found many in a state of indifference, owing, William Ellis believed, to their own unwatchfulness, and to the absence of religious visits: indeed their hearts began to warm under the genial influence of the ministry of Aaron Atkinson and himself.

Whilst in Virginia his life was in great danger, from a sudden squall whilst out in a boat. After telling Alice Ellis of this adventure, he adds: "Here is much travel by water, but I will take what care I can, and the rest must be committed to God." Meanwhile she cheers him by the invigorating tone of her letters, never doubting that the Lord, who had hitherto helped them, would still be their 'all-sufficient strength. "So, my dear love," she writes, "though we be far distant in body, yet, as we keep in the universal love of God, we are present in spirit and as near as ever. I cannot word the nearness I feel in remembrance of thee, which many times causes my soul to rejoice." And then she wins one's heart by the unselfish expression of her fear lest he should be "drawn homeward over soon," and of her earnest hope that he will be "very careful to mind the drawing of the Father's love. When in sleep," she continues, "methought I had been talking with thee, and saying, 'Take thy time, and perform thy service fully. Take no care of me as for outward things.'" Another of her letters is thus ended: "I daily feel the shedding abroad of the love of God to fill my soul and to overcome my spirit, so that He makes up all wants, on all hands, on every account: such are His doings to those that serve Him with a willing mind. . . . So, my dear love, let not the care thou hast for me lie over hard upon thee; only remember me in that bond which cannot be broken. And in this inexpressible love do I remain thy true and loving wife." We cannot wonder when her husband reminds her that he has ever found her true in his greatest trials.

Whilst the travellers were in North Carolina, some negroes were deeply impressed by their ministry. Amongst the numerous letters which followed Ellis to the New World—so much further off in those days than in our own, excepting only the numeration of miles—were two or three from a Friend of Airton named Adam Squire. He was probably several years younger than William Ellis, who reminds him in a letter that he has told him of things for his good, as if "thou hadst been my son. And still," he adds, "my counsel is to thee, to hold on in every good work, and let everybody have the benefit of thy love to the Truth." To his wife William Ellis writes: "I cannot express the good I had by Adam Squire's letter; tell him I say not much, but my deep desires are that he may be kept safe from the hurtful things of this world." Adam Squire wrote, it would seem, with the twofold aim of animating his friend by the manifestation of his deep spiritual sympathy, and of appealing to him for his prayerful aid.

"My friend, whom I dearly love," he says, "in the everlasting Truth, I beg it of thee to pray unto the Lord in the secret of thy heart, that I may be preserved out of the snares of death. . . . O that thou would call to mind when thou wast beset, as it were, with enemies within and without! and as thou patiently waited upon the Lord how He in His due time wrought thy deliverance every way; so that now thou art become free to the commonwealth of Israel; and then thou mayst remember me before the great Lord. . . . I cannot word my desires in this respect, but believe thou hast a feeling sense of my condition, and that to thy private supplications the Lord will say, Amen."

Before attending the General Yearly Meeting for Pennsylvania, William Ellis and Aaron Atkinson were present at a meeting of Ministers and Elders, of a week's duration.*

Two other English Friends attended this meeting, Mary Rogers and Elizabeth Webb. The latter had been brought up as a member of the Church of England, and went to a school kept by a clergyman, who was very kind to her, and whom she greatly loved and respected; indeed, in her childhood, she thought that ministers of religion "resembled angels bringing glad tidings to the children of men." She was, therefore, perplexed when, at the age of fourteen, she noticed the frivolous conversation of the chaplain of a knight, in whose family she then resided. At this time she was earnestly longing for an assurance of salvation: she thought of the promises made at her baptism, that she should renounce the devil and all his works, and the pomps and vanities of this wicked world —which had many attractions for her young heart— and felt her utter powerlessness to keep such vows. Whilst seeking for aid from the Scriptures, she was struck by Christ's injunction, "Freely ye have received, freely give," as well as by the declaration that those

---

* In William Ellis's memoranda of this meeting, the following passages occur:—"Friends being met together, and the Lord's power and presence eminently attending the meeting, divers testimonies and cautions were delivered. . . . Whereas it was the way of the world to forget God, yet the Lord had gathered us to Himself, that we could not forget Him; for though we came poor and empty together, the Lord met us with a full hand. . . . The wisdom of God was to be waited for, therefore Friends were cautioned to wait for it in silence. . . . None should go before or stay behind the power of that which had called them."

who run when the Lord has not sent them should not profit the people at all. Child as she was, she pondered these things, and when reading Ezekiel xxiv. found much comfort in her soul-weariness from the promise that God will "bind up that which was broken, and will strengthen that which was sick." She thought of how gladly she would have followed the Redeemer had she lived in the days when He was personally on earth; not knowing, at this early period of life, the present and far greater privilege, open to the true follower of Christ, of union with his risen Lord. The views which she had learnt from the Bible with regard to ministry led her to the belief that she ought to give up her attendance at church; yet, perhaps, from a fear of the surprise or displeasure of her friends, she did not act on this conviction, until driven to do so by her dread of what might be the consequence of a persistent disobedience to what she now felt was the will of God concerning her. Perhaps the unusual course she took was passed lightly over as a girlish whim; at all events, we are not told that it brought her into trouble. It was, we may believe, a hard trial, also, to give heed to the heavenly voice, which called her to forsake vain habits and worldly society, until she realised that a Saviour's love could far more than make up for all she might abandon at His bidding. "O Lord," was her frequent prayer, "preserve me in Thy fear and in Thy truth; show me Thy way, and make known Thy mind and will unto me. O Lord, where dost Thou feed Thy flock?"

It is easy to imagine that in those days, as she herself says, "she walked alone." Three or four years earlier she had once or twice attended a Friends' meeting, and now some of the words of a minister to whom she then listened came freshly to her remembrance. The mental development during this interval—for she was now about sixteen—and above all the teaching of the Holy Spirit, of which she had availed herself, led her to recognise the agreement between the teaching of the New Testament, and the leading views of Friends, which she more clearly understood after reading a little book on the subject. But the false pleasures with which the subtle enemy once more endeavoured to allure her from a steadfast adherence to Christ, had not yet lost their power to charm, and she tried to persuade herself that she might retain them a little longer, and yield a whole-hearted allegiance to God when she grew older.

This change in her feelings was, no doubt, in the first place, the result, and in the second, the continuing cause, of the relinquishment of her recent serious habits; for she writes, "I let go my exercise of watching and praying, and left off retirement. Pride and vanity grew up again; the Divine, sweet, meek, loving Spirit withdrew, and I could not find it again when I pleased although I did seek it sometimes; for I could have been pleased with the sweet comforts of His love, yet I did not like to bear the daily cross." She believed that the Friends frequently tasted the sweetness of the love of God in their meetings, and sometimes went a considerable distance in order to attend one, yet could not find the comfort she yearned for. By bitter experience she learnt that no man can serve two masters, and her distress was often great; but when about nineteen she took the blessed resolution to give herself up into the hands of God: "O Lord, if I perish it shall be at the gate of Thy mercy. I will give up my soul, my life, and all into Thy holy hand; do Thy pleasure by me. Thy judgments are just, for I have slighted Thy sweet love."

Such an abandonment of her all to Infinite Love, Infinite Power, and Infinite Wisdom, could not be in vain; the heart, which to herself had seemed so hard, was broken, and once more she rejoiced in a Saviour's mercy. But, for the fulfiment of the purposes of His own good pleasure concerning her, and, it may be for the sake of those whom she should influence in future years, the Lord saw good to try her faith yet further and more deeply.

"'Twas hard the unbroken dark to bear,
But harder still re-gathering night."

As in countless instances before her day, and since, "The Lord was near, *but she knew it not.*" Her anguish was intensified by the temptation to question the truths recorded in the sacred Scriptures, because she could not understand them, forgetting *the impossibility of the Infinite being clearly comprehended by the finite.* "The world by wisdom knew not God," and how many, even of powerful intellect have been well content to say—

"I am not skilled to understand
What God has willed, what God has planned,
I only know at His right hand
    Stands One who is my Saviour,

"'I take God at His word' and deed,
Christ died to save me—thus I read,
And in my heart I find a need
    Of Him to be My Saviour."

But, as one who trod a similar path fifty years earlier

has said—" A storm lasteth but for a time, and winter is but for a season, and the night remains not always." After a while a wonderful measure of heavenly love, life, and light, was granted her. She saw clearly that, "purifying, saving faith, is the gift of God, and the very spring and vital principle of it Divine love." And such was her sense of this love that she could covenant with her Lord to lay down her life for Him, if such were His will; yet even now the enemy would fain have caused her to stumble in the path of daily self-denial. But grace was granted her to bear each cross imposed by One who knows how to adapt His discipline to the varied wants of His children, who are no more skilled in choosing crosses for themselves than in directing their steps aright, but whose aim should be to yield themselves wholly to the transforming hand of the Lord who died for them.

When she reviewed this portion of her life, whilst never in the least questioning that the love of the world and the indwelling of the love of the Father are incompatible, and believing that every son and daughter whom He receives He chastens, tries, and proves—she yet does not hesitate to say: " If it please the Almighty to accept of souls without leading them through such fiery trials as He brought me through, or without requiring such things of them as He required of me, far be it from me to judge that such have not known the Lord, or the indwellings of His love, if the fruits of the spirit of Jesus be plain upon them."

And now the time was come when she did indeed, to use her own forcible expression, "*reap the benefit of the end of the coming of Christ,* . . . who said, ' I am come that they might have life, and that they might have it more abundantly.'" Constrained by this love, she found it to be her duty to kneel in the congregation of His people to acknowledge His great goodness, and to ask for its continuance, and afterwards felt as if her soul were in a better world, so "enlightened and enlivened" was it by the love of God. Even the "fragrant herbs and beautiful innocent flowers had a speaking voice" to her; the judgments of God had become sweet, and she was led to bid others "prove the Lord by an obedient, humble, innocent walking before Him, that they might see that He would pour out of His spiritual blessings in so plentiful a manner that the overflowings would return to Him who is the Fountain." Although the sweet consciousness of her Lord's presence might for a while be withdrawn, when the light of His countenance again shone on her, He seemed to be nearer than before; and her soul, she says, loved to dwell with Him, although He is a consuming fire to the corrupt nature of the old man; words which may recall Whittier's lines:—

> "Thou judgest us: Thy purity
> Doth all our lusts condemn:
> The love that draws us nearer Thee
> Is hot with wrath to them."

She was also learning that "the finite yearning after the Infinite heart" need never be in vain, and that the soul that is born of God may be daily brought into a closer communion with Him, "breathing to Him as constantly by prayer as the sucking child when it is born into the world doth draw in and breathe out the common air. . . . It is a certain sign to me," she continues, "of the Divine life and health of a soul if I find it sweetly breathing unto the Lord, and hungering and thirsting after His righteousness."

As Elizabeth Webb was one day sitting in a meeting for worship, waiting on the Lord for the renewal of spiritual strength, a passage of Scripture afresh applied to her soul by the Holy Spirit afforded her extreme consolation. And from that hour there was granted her, she says, "a more abundant entrance into the heavenly kingdom." Nor need we regard this as a mere mystical phrase, for is it not easy to imagine that problems, unsolved by the wise and prudent, as to whether "the heavenly places" (Eph. ii. 6)—to quote Dean Alford's words—"are to be taken as present or future, actual or potential, literal or spiritual, will be easily disposed of by those who have apprehended the truth of the believer's union in and with Christ"?

Her first ministerial journey was to the North of England, and spiritual conflicts were often her portion, although the guidance of her steps by her gracious Lord seemed to be as clear as the pointing of the needle of a compass. In the summer of 1697, whilst in the meeting at Gloucester, where she then resided, her heart was, in a time of stillness, remarkably drawn out towards the inhabitants of America, and overcome by the love of God under the influence of which she knelt to offer prayer on their behalf. By night and day the subject rested on her mind, peace or sorrow following her in turn, as she either mentally gave herself up to cross the ocean at the bidding of her Lord, or yielded to fears of her unfitness for the mission. Her husband was at first unwilling that she should visit such a distant land, and she told him she would not do so without his free consent; but when she became ill of a violent fever he granted the longed-for permission, saying it would be easier to part with her for seven years than to have her taken from him for ever; and a few months later she sailed from Bristol, with a Friend named Mary Rogers. It was in the following year that William Ellis met with them, at the Philadelphia Yearly Meeting, as already stated. Ten years later John and Elizabeth Webb settled in Pennsylvania; but in 1712 she returned to Great Britain for awhile, on a Gospel mission.

William Ellis and Aaron Atkinson next visited New England, where the former, in the midst of much physical weakness, found the Lord to be his strength, though sometimes greatly troubled by the thought of what his wife's distress would be should he not live to return to her. His heart must have been gladdened, twelve months afterwards, to learn from a letter signed by fourteen New England Friends that a great blessing had rested on the labours of his companions and himself. To John Wynn he writes, from Philadelphia: "The Lord had grafted that care on my heart to supplicate Him daily for new supplies. I see little to boast of, unless it be weakness: and, as I have travelled in a sense of these things, the Lord hath wonderfully assisted my spirit." Before leaving that city for his return voyage, in a letter to a friend who had shown him kind hospitality, he says: "I believe the love of God is much towards thee, and if thou mind the Word that is ingrafted in thy heart it will open thy understanding in things pertaining to thy salvation; and, let men say of it what they will, I do know that it is the leaven of the kingdom."

Whilst rejoicing to be homeward-bound, William Ellis must have felt that he was leaving behind him not a few from whom his spirit could never be separated; for, doubtless, the thoughts expressed by them were mutual. "I shall have that spiritual enjoyment of thee," writes Phineas Pemberton (at one time a member of Council and Speaker of the Assembly of Pennsylvania), "of which the saints in fellowship are made partakers, and wherein we are often comforted in those dear remembrances." Whilst another says: "I could not well omit to signify my true love to thee, and unity with that measure of the blessed, holy power, which I have had a sense of as attending thy ministry; and thy plain doctrine; and of thy promoting true spiritual and inward worship to God." An extract from one more farewell note must suffice: "Dear heart, our spirits go along with thee, and love follows, and melts and runs towards thee; but it is for His sake who sets the fountain open: for His love's sake we love thee."

At a later date, Nathan Newby, of Nancemund, remarks, in a letter in which he tells William Ellis that for the two preceding years he had felt it his duty to testify publicly for God: "O, that I could have a time with thee, if it cost me the travelling some hundreds of miles!" William Ellis's deep interest in the welfare of the cause of Christ in the New World is manifested in letters to his brethren there, one of whom he thus counsels:—

"Stir about now and then, and see how Friends meet on week-days; and when thy spirit is full of life and sweetness, if thou drop a word or two amongst Friends, I do think it will be to profit. . . . Put Friends in mind to visit John Lewis's meeting now and then. . . . My soul—O, my soul within me is in a deep travail for your growth in the most precious truth!"

He afterwards expresses his desire " that all who feel God's word like a fire in their hearts may run to and fro to spread the truth." Again, his concern for some, probably, small meetings is evinced by his advice that those to whom he was writing should " now and then step down to Potomac, and sit amongst the poor people there," whose hearts would thus, he believes, be comforted, even if no word were spoken among them; and also suggests that " sometimes one and sometimes another should run over to the Bay," taking some ministers with them. To such service as this, he believed, the Lord would say, " Well done!"

Aaron Atkinson did not return to England until the early part of 1700. William Ellis and himself had frequently parted from each other whilst in America, for the better accomplishment of their mission; and also in consequence of the severe illness of the latter, who tells William Ellis, in a note written soon after landing in England, that he could not forget the sad expression of his face at the time of this trial, and that he believed the prayers he then offered had availed before God. He adds: " I came over in the same ship thou camest in, and lay in the same cabin thou lay in; and I loved it the better for thy sake."

In 1702, William Ellis had some property left him by a Friend named Jennet Stow, whose home was not far from Airton. She became a minister in early life, and visited many parts of Great Britain and Ireland.

At the age of thirty she died of consumption, at Dronfield, in Derbyshire, and was attended in her last illness by a physician named Gilbert Heathcot, who much esteemed his young patient, and remarked that she was helpful to him in her life and death. As her end drew nigh she spoke of the blessedness of living near the Lord, and of how her heart was warmed by His goodness: "Lord, Thou hast turned me every way; Thou hast made me what Thou wouldst have me to be. Praised be Thy holy name!" She said that God had indeed fulfilled the promise which she believed was made her when, in her weakness, she had been ready to shrink from the mission set before her: "Be not afraid; for, though thou art weak, yet I am strong; and I will make thee a trumpet in my hand which shall give a certain sound."

In 1705, Ellis writes to tell William Edmundson of the death of a young Friend, to whom they were both attached. "I am touched with sorrow at my very heart," William Edmundson replies, " for the loss of dear Isaac Alexander.... The Lord's mighty power accompanied his testimony. We travelled together in sweet unity, and parted in that love and life *that death and the grave cannot overcome.*" Isaac Alexander had sent several letters to his aged friend, and had asked him to bequeath him some written counsel, not foreseeing that his own pilgrimage would be ended first. At his earliest visit to the home of William and Alice Ellis he had found his " very soul knit and united to them;" and in a letter to the former he expresses his hope for the life-long increase of " the living, feeling enjoyment of this hearty, spiritual nearness, and heavenly gospel fellowship." His ministry began in his seventeenth year, and in the course of his short life he travelled extensively, visiting all the meetings of Friends in Scotland and Ireland, and most of those in England and Wales. He died at the age of twenty-five, and during his last illness, often alluded to the Lord's abounding mercy to him. " Oh! what an excellent thing it is," he said, " to keep in the truth and visit one another in the life of it. . . . Love God; love God; you can never love God too much. Oh! what hath He done for my soul. I have seen glorious things, yea, such things as I never saw before. I beheld a Friend, lately deceased, in a glorious place, and that I was to be with him; and I said, it is enough to be there; oh! such salvation." His prayer for " an easy passage out of the world," was granted, his dying words being, " Now I will fall upon my sleep."

After William Ellis's return from America his missions were chiefly confined to his own county and those immediately around it, although he often attended the London Yearly Meeting. During the last few years, especially, of his life he suffered acutely from the malady which terminated his life in 1709, when in his fifty-first year. Yet not many weeks before his death he took advantage of a slight improvement in health to attend a Yearly Meeting at Lancaster; at its close a remarkable meeting was held, when the Almighty Head of the Church manifestly reigned over those assembled, constraining many of His children to speak well of His name. A Friend from Wales, who was present, says:—

" A sweet, pure current of life largely flowed through the meeting. . . . William Ellis had a blessed opportunity, and was carried on in the power and life of truth, even beyond a usual manner. Oh! methinks it affects my heart to remember the glorious presence of the Lord that appeared with him, he being full of love, full of zeal, full of courage, and as one triumphant over the devil and the powers of darkness, and in the divine region of light and life. This was indeed a glorious season."

It is traditionally stated that Alice Ellis was absent from home at the time of her husband's death, having gone to a distant place to attend a meeting; and that after they had parted, he took his stand on some rising ground that he might keep her in view as long as possible, having a presentiment that they should not meet again in this world. On his death-bed, when speaking to one of his friends of the time of his conversion, he said, "It was a glorious day for me and I have large tokens that the day of my death will be so also."

A few years earlier, Ellis had conveyed to trustees his house and certain lands, directing that after the death of his wife and himself, they should "farm the said premises a pennyworth unto Friends, by way of scorn called Quakers, who should willingly entertain such teachers as might be called of God, and by Him commissioned and sent abroad to preach the Gospel in the free dispensation thereof." After needful deductions the rents accruing were to be employed for putting out as apprentices the poor children belonging to York Quarterly Meeting, and also the children of the poor "of what profession soever," residing in Airton and two neighbouring villages.

William Ellis had had many apprentices to linen-weaving under his care, and his wife and himself were deeply interested in the welfare of youths of this class. Alice Ellis also conveyed to trustees a close; called

Welldales, a portion of the rents of which was to be used in paying the future tenant of the house in which she still lived for the board and lodging of travelling ministers of the Society of Friends. She arranged that the great bedsteads and such other things as were nail-fast and heirlooms, should remain for the use of the tenants, that they might the better entertain travelling Friends.

The house, now inhabited by George Cartwright and family, is kept hospitably open, but the "six men's coats and six women's hoods," which Alice Ellis provided for the use of visitors in rough weather, it has long been thought needless to renew.

In her sympathetic kindheartedness we find that the poor widows of Friends are especially borne in mind in another benefaction. She lived until the year 1720. Her loss appears to have been widely as well as deeply felt, for she delighted in showing hospitality, and was a true friend to the poor, freely dispensing what had been acquired by patient industry. She was a very regular attendant of meetings, and earnestly longed for the advancement of the kingdom of her Lord.

To men and women, such as those who form this faintly-sketched group, the following quotation seems applicable whilst revealing the secret of their lives: "The crowning excellence of their ministry, and that of every man and woman who faithfully received their message—and followed, in their measure, where their leaders guided—was the entire consecration of their lives, as knowing no aim but the glory of Christ; and no happiness which interfered with a constant and abiding communion with Him."

RICHARD CLARIDGE AND HIS FRIENDS.

"I thought on Pain and straightway answered Peace;
On Death, but Life immortal made reply;
The tears of sorrow gathered in mine eye,
Only to feel sweet comfort bid them cease;
Evermore Faith would thoughts of Love increase
Through every cloud still gleamed cerulean sky."

J. E. A. BROWN.

RICHARD CLARIDGE AND HIS FRIENDS.

> " Travellers at night, by fleeing
> Cannot run into the day;
> God can lead the blind and seeing;
> On Him wait, and for Him stay:
> Be not fearful, be not fearful,
> They who cannot sing can pray!"—T. T. LYNCH.

EARLY in the year 1698, good Richard Baxter preached one day in Charter-House-yard, whilst keeping his seat in the pulpit on account of the feebleness caused rather by ill-health than old age. Amongst his hearers was a very talented and highly-educated clergyman, who had come to London from his Worcestershire rectory with the hope that the ministry of some celebrated preacher might afford him the enlightenment, comfort, and help which his soul had in vain craved for. Baxter gave out his text: "But the sons of Belial shall be all of them as thorns thrust away, because they cannot be taken with hands," etc. (2 Sam. xxiii. 6, 7)—and as these words fell on the ears of Richard Claridge he feared that they were applicable to himself and was so weighed down with mental anguish that he was ready to sink under it; but, unknown to himself, the everlasting arms were underneath.

He was the son of a Warwickshire yeoman, and was now about forty years of age. At St. Mary's Hall, Oxford, he had gained a high standing in philosophy, and as an orator and Greek scholar,—at the age of twenty-one taking his degree as a Bachelor of Arts.

Three years later he become rector of Peopleton, where he kept a grammar school, and prepared pupils for the Universities. He describes this portion of his life as being a mixture of vice and virtue. He prepared his sermons with studious diligence and delivered them with eloquence, preaching repentence and regeneration although practically unacquainted with either. Meanwhile, notwithstanding an uneasy conscience, he again and again yielded to temptation, ignoring the injunction, "Quench not the Spirit;" until at length his sins were so plainly set before him that he became overwhelmed with fear, and Baxter's sermon, as we have seen, instead of alleviating, increased his distress.

Nor did he fare better under the teaching of several clergymen whose churches he attended whilst in London. One day, indeed, he did expect comfort and cheer, when the following text was given out, "Lord, Thou wilt ordain peace for us, for Thou hast wrought all our works in us," but was bitterly disappointed at only hearing a long disquisition on the advantages which the nation had derived from the advent of the Prince of Orange. One cannot, however, be surprised to learn that he found some consolation from a sermon by an Independent minister on the text, "In whom we have redemption through His blood," etc., although much of the address struck him as being unsatisfactory and irrelevant.

On his return to his parish he prayerfully strove to lead a godly life, and at the same time began to test the doctrines and ceremonies of the Church of England by the standard of the Scriptures,—an examination which resulted in the conviction that, great as was the cost, he must renounce the Church of which for nearly twenty years he had been a highly-esteemed minister. His prayers for Heavenly guidance and support were granted, and in the summer of 1691 he resigned the rectory of Peopleton, his last sermon being on the text, "But in vain do they worship Me, teaching for doctrines the commandments of men." He comprised what he had to say in one proposition—"That all that faith and worship which men taught for doctrines, and could not be found in the Scriptures, were the commandments of men, and was vain worship, and unacceptable before God;" pressing his hearers "not to receive things upon the authority of any, whether kings, parliaments, convocations, or bishops; but in every article of faith, and in every part of worship, and every rite, usage, or ceremony enjoined, to examine it by the Scriptures, which are the only revealed rule of faith and practice." He believed that Divine help was afforded him, and finished the service with an earnest prayer that his auditory might be taught of God.

After leaving the Established Church his character was violently assailed by some who now viewed him as an enemy. "I stand amazed," he writes, "to think how the scene is so soon changed, and that I, whilst of their communion, should pass for a very honest man, and now should be such a knave as they endeavour to paint me." He then joined himself to the Baptists, hoping he says, to find their "doctrine, worship, and ordinances in all things conformable unto the primitive pattern of our Lord Jesus Christ and His holy apostles." But on the day on which he was baptised, as he was removing his wet garments, he was shocked when some one who entered the room said, whilst taking off his hat with sham politeness, "You are welcome, sir, out of one form into another!" These words sank deeply into his heart, from which secretly arose the bitter cry, "Lord! what a condition am I in! Is this all the advance I have made?" Yet for a time his doubts were allayed by some of his Baptist friends, and about twelve months later he was installed as minister of one of their London chapels. Talented scholar and eloquent speaker though he might be, he was already beginning to entertain new views of the ministry, for about this date he writes, "It is blessed preaching of the Gospel when Christ inspires the preachers, and the sermon is His not theirs. . . . We may talk an hour or two, but if Christ be not with us by His Spirit, it is but an useless, empty sound."

In the spring of the following year Richard Claridge was married to a lady named Mary Tomkins, who was his third wife. After a while, a longing arose in his heart for an experimental acquaintance with the baptism of the Spirit, of which he was now convinced that baptism with water was but a type, a temporary dispensation belonging to the ministry of John:* for his mind had been gradually impressed with the belief that the *dispensation of the Gospel is a ministration of the Spirit,* though at first it was merely "a kind of glimmering of a higher state and a more spiritual worship." His distress and bewilderment were great, and were increased

---

* "By the true Baptism of the New Testament we do actually put on Christ, and are made one with Christ; and this is not done by water-washing, but by the Spirit. . . . The Spirit carrying us into Christ, and bringing Christ into us, and being one and the same Spirit in both; and this is to be baptised into Christ."—*The Doctrine of Baptisms.* By William Dell, Minister of the Gospel, and Master of Gonvil and Caius College, in Cambridge. 1652.

even in proportion to the further light which broke on his soul, and showed him that the question was not one only of the right way of worshipping, but also of the qualification of the heart for its right performance; that (to quote his own words) "It was not the name of Christian without the nature, nor the profession of religion without the possession, that would do; all must be parted with that was contrary to the holy will of God, which is our sanctification; and that not in part, but wholly, as the Apostle's prayer was." (1 Thess. v. 23.)

Yet this season of perplexity was also one of blessing, in which William Law's wise words—addressed to Wesley in his young days—might have been applied to him: "You are troubled because you do not understand how God is dealing with you. Perhaps if you did, it would not so well answer His design. He is teaching you to *trust Him further than you can see Him*." He sought for solitude, but found that the Lord was near, and whilst waiting in lowliness of heart upon Him " the light of the knowledge of the glory of God in the face of Jesus Christ " was graciously granted, and with heart-tendering power. And now the idea, which had so strongly impressed his mind, that the dispensation of the Gospel is a ministration of the Spirit, was made plain to him as his Saviour enlightened the eyes of his understanding. " I came to see," he writes, an end of all former dispensations, as of Moses, the prophets, or John, which had their time; or such as men had shaped and fashioned in their own wisdom. I saw also what God had to be and remain as the highest dispensation, *the immediate teachings of Christ by the Holy Spirit.*"

Richard Claridge now gradually withdrew from the Baptist community, by many of whose members he was much beloved, and began to frequent the meetings of Friends, to which he soon regularly resorted, finding, as his biographer Besse states, "their ministry to be lively and edifying, and their meetings attended with the gracious presence of God, ministering abundant consolation and refreshment to weary and waiting souls." Several leading men amongst the Baptists retained a personal regard for him after he became a Friend, and freely discussed doctrinal points with him. In the course of a conversation with the pastor of a country Baptist congregation, who had come to London to visit Richard Claridge, the latter observed that the Apostle Paul grounds his prayer for perfect sanctification upon the faithfulness of God : "*God is faithful who also will do it.*" "To walk with God is to walk in the light, as God is in the light. And he that walketh in the light, the blood of Jesus Christ cleanseth him from all sin. The question is not whether good men are not liable to commit sin, which I do not deny, but whether good men have not been freed from sin?"

A few days later we find him at the meeting held at the house of Sarah Sawyer, in Aldersgate Street, during which he bore witness to the grace of God in his own experience; thus for the first time speaking in a meeting of Friends. He was soon afterwards much cheered by a visit from an aged minister named Francis Camfield, who spoke of how those who knew something of the work of the Lord should be instrumental in His hand to edify one another in their most holy faith, and counselled him "to wait in the strength of the Lord, and to take heed of making haste." Richard Claridge was greatly comforted by his interview with this venerable Friend, who spoke also of how the Lord taught all true Christians to overcome. They did not part until eight p.m., when Richard Claridge accompanied him to his house in Bartholomew Close. He was likewise much helped by visits made him from time to time by a large number of other Friends. George Whitehead, after hearing from his own lips many details of the Lord's dealings with him, cordially encouraged him to press forward in the path of the just. A week later, Thomas Story, Gilbert Molleson, and Aaron Atkinson spent some hours with him. It is recorded by some of Aaron Atkinson's contemporaries that the Lord anointed him "for the ministry in early life in a very extraordinary manner;" and as he was now on the eve of embarking for America, in company with William Ellis, a fervent prayer arose in Richard Claridge's heart that he might have a favourable voyage, and that his Transatlantic labours might be crowned with the blessing of the Lord.

About this time, when writing of the ministry, Claridge remarks:—" The apostles of Christ did not preach in their own wills. . . . When they preached, they spake as the oracles of God, according to the measure and ability He gave. . . . We must be still and silent before the Lord, and wait for the drawings and influences of the Holy Spirit, and feel the constrainings of His power."

Towards the end of the following year, Richard Claridge went one day to Newington to attend the first Friends' meeting held there, and thus missed a visit from Mary Gulson, of Coventry, who spent some time in prayer with his wife and a few other Friends. He had already reaped great advantage from the counsel of this experienced Christian, and on the following evening he went to Lawrence Lane, to call at the house where she was staying. The interview was a blessed one, their heavenly converse being sweetened by the clear consciousness that their Lord hearkened and heard. Richard Claridge, whilst unable to control his deep emotion, told his faithful friend of his spiritual trials and perplexities, and she replied, that before coming to London on this religious mission she had apprehended his condition, and had believed that it was the Lord's will that she should especially visit him and one other Friend. She encouraged him to believe that God was leading him on in the right way, and would make him a minister of His everlasting Gospel. He asked her to pray for him, to wrestle with the Lord that he might be kept by His mighty power, through faith, unto salvation. They parted, we read, " in the great love of God, and in a deep sense of His wonderful power." On the same day he writes :—" Blessed be the God of my life, His succours and refreshments have been greater than my exercises and temptations. Sometimes the thoughts of death have awakened me; ' What! be idle and do nothing for God ! I will put a spirit of life into thee, and put My words into thy mouth, and thou shalt be my instrument to turn many from darkness to light !' But then it would open in me again, ' The time is not yet come. God is faithful who hath promised, and will perform His promise; yet the times and seasons He hath put in His own power.' "

A year or two later he sent Mary Gulson some copies of his recently-published work, "Mercy Covering the Judgment Seat," apparently a record of the Lord's gracious dealings with himself. He wished to have these books distributed amongst the Baptists residing at Coventry. The parcel was accompanied by a letter in which he remarks: "It is a very precious and comfortable thing to walk in the light as God is in the light. ... In this Divine light wherein we have been enabled to believe, we see and enjoy the pure living presence of the Lord our God; and therein our fellowship stands; ... though we are many members, and may be bodily absent from one another, yet we are spiritually present in the Divine light and life of Jesus, who hath baptised us by one Spirit into the one body. ... What I have enjoyed of His presence in times past is not sufficient food for my soul now; and therefore *my soul waits in humility before Him to feel the rising of His living power to tender my heart before Him, and to make and keep me alive unto Him.* ... A glorious and lasting dispensation hath commenced and taken place, which is Christ in us the hope of glory. And I testify that neither Christ Himself in the flesh, barely, nor the Holy Scriptures, though given by inspiration of God, nor any outward ordinances whatsoever, are the true rest of the people of God: but Christ Jesus in His inward, spiritual appearance in our hearts to be our light, life, and hope of glory."*

---

* Fletcher of Madeley, writes in a somewhat similar strain in reply to a letter from Lady Mary Fitzgerald: "'Not a text,' say you, ' came to me, only I knew none perished at His feet;' then you remembered Christ, the sum and substance of all the Scriptures; then you believed on Him in whom all the sweetest texts and all the promises are Yea and Amen."

In this year, 1700, Claridge removed to Barking, Essex, and there opened a boarding-school, and was soon occupied in visiting some of the meetings in the south-eastern counties. He was accompanied in part of this service by Christopher Meidel, a Norwegian, who had come to England as chaplain to Prince George of Denmark, but had about two years earlier united himself to Friends; a long practical acquaintance with the work of God in the soul of man seems to have remarkably qualified him to minister to the needs of others.*
Throughout their ministry they were aided and upheld by the power and presence of their Lord.

At Watford they were most heartily and hospitably entertained at the house of Alice Hayes, where they

---

* In the unpublished journal of Thomas Gwinn, of Falmouth, there are interesting allusions to Christopher Meidel. In 1707, Thomas Gwinn met with him at Liskeard, where a meeting was held for the Friends of Devon and Cornwall, and records that Christopher Meidel spoke in the streets. A few weeks later he writes: " I rid to Truro with some other Friends to visit Christopher Meidel, who was brought from prison there to the Quarter Sessions ; he had been fined £20 by the Sessions before on pretence of disturbing the priest at Liskeard, and while we were with him was called from us to attend the Sessions at Truro, where he was ordered to subscribe the Declaration of Fidelity, but he answered them nothing, so was convicted to suffer as a popish recusant convert. He preached through the streets immediately as he came forth of the Court, as he did sundry times whilst there. I left with him a paper which I thought might be of service to him to give in to the justices." In the latter part of the same year Thomas Gwinn and another Friend visited Christopher Meidel in Launceston prison. His trials appear at this time to have caused a morbid state of mind, for T. G. says : " We used both arguments and persuasion in much tendernesse and plaine dealing against his working on First-days (as judging it a means to prejudice people against the reception of our testimony), as also to diswade him from some other imaginary scruples he seemed to labour under, as that he must not write or walk out though he had liberty granted, nor eat some sort of victuals or drinks, nor receive what's needful for his nourishment." In reference to the Yearly Meeting of 1708, T. G. writes : " I was at the Meeting for Sufferings, and got an order for reimbursing our charge on Christopher Meidel."

lodged for three nights. Like themselves, she had become a Friend from deep religious conviction. She had been brought up as a member of the Church of England; in early childhood, when supposed to be almost dying, her mother fervently besought the Lord to take her own life instead of her child's—a prayer which He answered, as Alice Hayes remarks, " for what end was best known to Himself." At the age of sixteen the harshness of her step-mother led her to leave her home, and seek a new one in a family whose affection she won, whilst gladly and conscientiously yielding them her services. Her fondness for frivolous pursuits, for which she had often felt herself chidden by a secret voice, although she knew not whence the warning came, had now greatly lessened; she enjoyed reading the Holy Scriptures, and frequently sought opportunities for private prayer, besides diligently attending public worship. The quietness of her situation was very congenial to her, and her heart was soothed as she steadily pursued what she believed to be the right course.

She had on one occasion a remarkable visitation of Divine love, when she felt that no words were needed, but that her soul was led into a deep sweet silence before the Lord. Probably she was not wholly unprepared for the worship usual amongst Friends, when for the first time she attended one of their meetings, at the solicitation of some of her acquaintance, whose curiosity had been awakened by the rumour that a lady greatly esteemed as a preacher in that Society was to be present. She was affected by her sense of the worship silently ascending to God from many hearts, as well as by the ministry she heard, which so sank into her soul that she could not keep back her tears. But much of the hallowed influence of this season was soon swept away by the strong and subtle enemy. She went soon afterwards to live in the family of a justice of the peace, and her new mistress would often say, "This Alice will be a Quaker;" but no such thought dwelt in her own mind.

About two years later her health suffered severely from the effect of a terrible sprain in the ankle, and more serious evil befell her from intercourse with an irreligious family with whom she had found a temporary situation, whilst her master and mistress spent the winter in London. As her lameness increased she had to return to her father's house, and soon found that sorrow of soul was harder to bear than bodily pain. She felt that if Christ did not rescue her she was undone for ever, and earnestly sought to enter into covenant with Him. Whilst still a cripple supported on crutches, she was married to "a comely, handsome, honest man," whose faithfulness and constancy she does not forget to record, for they had become engaged in the time of her health and vigour. These blessings were, however, in a few months' time restored to her; her walking powers returned, and she seemed to have all that heart could wish for.

But prosperity, instead of making her strive with a grateful heart to live closer to the Almighty Giver of every good gift, led her to forget Him, until illness brought her almost face to face with death. Then from her agonized soul was wrung the cry, "Spare me a little longer; try me once more, and I will become a new creature." *I will become a new creature!* We see that she had much yet to learn; yet doubtless her importunate cry—like every true prayer which ever has been, or ever will be, offered to God — "came before Him, even into His ears." Holiness she now saw was what her Redeemer called for from her, and she set herself the task of diligently cultivating it. But she learnt that this must be the Lord's work, and not hers. She found also, that during the twenty years she had kept Him waiting at the door of her heart, "much fuel" had accumulated for the Refiner's fire. "Oh! happy man and happy woman," she writes, "that doth thus abide the day of His coming; for sure I am His fan is in His hand, and if men will but submit when He appears, He will thoroughly do that for them which no other can do. This is the baptism that doth people good." Looking back on this portion of her life she saw that a Saviour's secret hand alone had kept her from despair; for she was uncheered by any counsellor such as, "blessed be God," she writes, "many now have." Week after week she sorrowfully entered and sorrowfully quitted the parish church, finding nothing that would satisfy the hunger, and allay the thirst of her soul. It was no marvel that she was sad, for she thought of God only as dwelling far away in the heavens.

After a while her mind was powerfully impressed with the belief that it would be right for her to go to a Friends' meeting, but the idea of doing so was very distasteful, and for long she tried to persuade herself that, as no angel directed her steps, it was needless to give heed to an inward voice. At last, without telling anyone of her design, she went to a small meeting, where the ministry of a Friend, named Elizabeth Stamper, came as a heavenly message to her soul answering its deep need; as if the speaker, whom she had never seen until that day, had been well aware of her spiritual state. She returned home with a joyful heart, and from that time gave heed to the manifested will of her Lord, and found that no day passed by without some consciousness of His presence. She could now do no other than continue to join in the worship of Friends, and this led her into much trouble; even her husband, being urged to oppose her, treated her with scorn and hatred, threatening to sell his farm and leave her; but nothing could make her swerve from the path appointed her by Him in whom she had found the joy of salvation. Her loyalty to her Saviour was not long allowed to alienate her husband from her; his affection returned, and after a while he manifested some appreciation of the views which were so dear to his wife.

Alice Hayes became a minister, and, besides visiting many parts of England, had much valuable service in Holland and Germany. Her ministry is described as being very plain and powerful, satisfying the sorrowful soul, yet applicable to most conditions. Once, after her husband's death, on account of her conscientious objection to the payment of tithes, she was taken from her farm and five fatherless children and imprisoned for thirteen weeks in St. Alban's Gaol: she was also deprived of corn and cattle to the amount of "several score pounds." Yet from her inmost soul she could bless God for counting her worthy to suffer for His name's sake, and could bear witness that to "as many as *trust* in Him, He will give *life for the soul and bread for the body.*"

"The Son of God," she writes, "is come indeed that we may have life, and it is in obedience that the aboundings of it are known. . . . Through His precious blood we have all these great benefits. Oh! who would not be a follower of the Lord? Remember that you are soldiers under the banner of the unconquered Captain, Christ Jesus, who always stood by His own in every age; follow Him in all perseverance through good report and bad report, and keep to the standard—the Spirit of Truth. If you do this you may pray for what you stand in need of, let it be bread for soul or for body, or for faith or hope, or courage, or the armour of light, or whatever else your wants may be. Take courage and ask; . . . and *for the life which you have lost, which you had in vanity and evil, you shall find a life a hundredfold exceeding in peace and inward joy.* Oh! faithful soldiers! come on. . . . The effect of the grace and coming of Jesus is indeed to save people from their sins, and to them that will be His and believe that He has all power committed to Him in heaven and earth,—He can and doth give power. *More powerful is Jesus to save than the devil to compel men to sin.* . . . *Oh! happy souls, that can thus believe on His name;* these shall be baptised with Christ's own baptism."

About a month after this visit of Richard Claridge to Watford, he again went there to attend the funeral of a relative of Alice Hayes, whose friendship he much valued. The following extract is from one of his letters to her:—

"Esteemed Friend, Alice Hayes,—Yesterday my heart was broken and melted before the Lord, both in silent waiting and testimony, at a little meeting in Barking; . . . panting and thirsting after Him, He was pleased to appear in power and glory. When I felt myself to be nothing without Him He filled my soul with treasure. . . . My soul dearly salutes thee, and cries to the God of my life for thee, that as He hath enabled thee to bear a noble testimony to His blessed truth by word, doing, and suffering, so He would keep thee faithful unto death. . . . Oh! sweet and comfortable communion! when distant in person we are present in spirit. Life often flows and circulates after a secret and invisible, yet sensible, sympathizing manner. . . . I desire I may neither run before nor stay behind my Guide. My dear Friend, travail with me and for me. Blessed are they who live by faith."

In a long reply to two letters received from an entire stranger, Claridge writes:—

"Loving Friend, Hugh Kirk, . . . Though thou art unknown to me outwardly and by face, yet I have an inward sensible perception of thee in the light and life of Jesus. . . . These hungering and thirsting ones that cannot be satisfied with anything short of God, and the enjoyment of His living presence, shall, as they continue so travailing, hungering, and thirsting, be satisfied; for the Lord never said to the seed of Jacob, 'Seek ye Me in vain.' . . . It is a matter of rejoicing to my soul that the Lord hath been pleased to make my book, 'Mercy Covering the Judgment Seat,' helpful unto thee, as I hear He hath also done to many more."

Claridge had become an author whilst a clergyman, and his pen had not been idle during his sojourn amongst Baptists. The books he afterwards wrote were chiefly in reference to the principles held by Friends; his *Lux Evangelica Attesta*, like the work Hugh Kirk mentioned, is said to have been made a blessing to numerous readers.

In 1702, Richard Claridge went to the Yearly Meeting at Colchester, in company with Samuel Waldenfield and William Hornold. The home of the latter was near Ratcliff Highway, but he spent much time in diligent, itinerant, ministerial labours, especially endeavouring to have meetings in places where they had never or rarely been held. The former was also a minister, residing in Middlesex whose unwearied zeal and powerful preaching in Great Britain, Holland, and Germany, were greatly blessed. Most exemplary in his daily life, ready to every good work, courteous as well as charitable, he was beloved by rich and poor; and many who had been prejudiced against Friends viewed them in a very different light after becoming acquainted with him. "What a brave thing it is," was his characteristic remark on his death-bed, "for Friends to dwell in unity; here we can sit together as the children of God, the church of the first-born, whose names are written in heaven."

On their way the three ministers held a meeting at the Spread Eagle at Ingatestone; and whilst at Colchester, in conjunction with another Friend, they had meetings on two successive days, which were very large and satisfactory: it was supposed that one of them was attended by at least 1,500 persons. In the autumn of 1703 Richard Claridge gave up his school, and spent a good deal of time in preaching and writing. When John Love, Jun., was at Barking he held an evening meeting, and on the following day preached in the streets and market-place, accompanied by Richard Claridge. On the morrow, Barking Three-Weeks' Meeting had an influx of visitors, on whom John Love's striking ministry appeared to make a deep impression. He was probably the son of the Friend who bore the same name, and who died, or was put to death, in the Inquisition in 1660.

Amongst other meetings at which Richard Claridge was present were two held in the barn of a Friend named Roger Palmer, who lived at Navestock, near Harold's Wood, in Essex. As no meeting of this kind had ever been held in the parish, Roger Palmer was anxious to have an opportunity of bidding his neighbours to one, and about one hundred and fifty of them responded to this invitation. They were very powerfully addressed by Richard Claridge and Samuel Waldenfield, both of whom also engaged in prayer. At the eager request of the people, a second meeting was held, in which Richard Claridge spoke at great length. "I entreated them," he writes, "to turn their minds to Christ, the inward Teacher—the Teacher sent of God to teach them the way of life and salvation; and then signified to them that our directing them to turn their minds inwardly to Christ was not to take them off from the Holy Scriptures, or faith in Christ crucified as outwardly. Though we press men to believe in the light and to walk in the light, yet we do not declare that, as though they could do it of their own will or power, but that they ought to look to and wait upon Christ for ability so to do. . . . God hath provided a means sufficient for the salvation of men, and this means is Christ Jesus, the One Mediator between God and men, the great and alone Sacrifice of propitiation."

Early in 1707 Richard Claridge removed to Tottenham, where he opened a boarding and day school. This proceeding gave great offence to the vicar of the parish, his curate, and the master of the Free School, and led them to appeal for aid to Lord Coleraine and Hugh Smithson, Esq., justices of the peace, who threatened Claridge with persecution; the only reason they could allege for this menace being the evil that might ensue if he infused his pupils' minds with erroneous views. When Richard Claridge was told of this, he said his purpose was to do good in the position in which God's providence had placed him, and that he could not abandon the performance of his duty. The two clergymen next went from house to house endeavouring to induce the parents of the children to withdraw them from the teaching of one whom they stigmatised as an apostate, an impostor, a heretic, and a Jesuit. The vicar even vilified him from his pulpit, which shocked several members of his congregation, who strongly expressed their disapproval of such uncharitableness. Many of his hearers afterwards went to the Friends' Meeting, and listened with grave attention to Richard Claridge's ministry; and the next evening a large number of the inhabitants of the town came to a meeting held at his house, at which three or four other ministers of the Society were also present.

A few weeks later, whilst sitting one day at dinner, Claridge was arrested with a writ of *qui tam*, etc. The officer who did so, civilly handed him the warrant that he might obtain legal advice. His adversaries having been foiled when prosecuting him in Doctors' Commons, now attacked him upon a statute passed in the reign of James I. against Roman Catholic recusants, the penalty being forty shillings a day for keeping school without a license. The damages demanded of Richard Claridge were £600; but his opponents were once more unable to carry their point; and the Lord Chief Justice, in summing up the evidence to the jury, referred to the violent manner in which the prosecution had been conducted.*

---

* The reasons assigned by a modern writer [Julia Wedgwood] for the bitter opposition of the clergy of the eighteenth century to the Methodists seem—in addition to more palpable causes—to apply also to that encountered by the early Friends one hundred years before:—" The Articles which every clergyman had signed, the

In the summer of the following year, Richard Claridge wrote a long letter to a gentleman who had at one time been a Baptist minister, but who, like himself, had adopted the views of Friends. In reference to his own experience, he alludes to the time when, although believing the whole history of Christ, he was still ignorant of Him as a personal Saviour. "To remove this darkness," he writes, "there was first light (not natural, but divine): and that showed me my sin . . . and directed me to Christ, the alone Saviour. . . . And as I was enabled by the grace of God—for without *that* I could do nothing—to believe in Christ and repent of my sin . . . so I came by the powerful and effectual working of the same grace, to pass through the ministration of condemnation, and to witness, gradually, the ministration of life and peace. I say gradually, for so it was with me. The work was not instantaneous, but by degrees; not but that the Almighty could have done it in a moment. . . And as this purging work went forward, so I became in love with it, and earnestly cried unto the Lord that He would take away all iniquity, and make me perfectly clean and fit for communion with Himself. I am fully persuaded that *then* the work of the Lord goes

---

Liturgy which he habitually read, had been emptied of meaning; he declared the Holy Ghost had called him to the office of a deacon, and he meant only that he saw no reason why he should not enter on it; he prayed that he and his congregation might receive the inspiration of God's Holy Spirit, and He meant only that they might go to Heaven when they died. He signed the Articles which were drawn up to secure the doctrine of justification by faith, and he meant only that God would overlook the sins of those who acknowledged a certain historical person to be His Son. Hence, when a set of men arose, not only believing these doctrines with all their soul, but regarding them as the medicine for a diseased world, the clergy started back with horror."

rightly on, when we are in love with His righteous judgments."

In the latter part of 1713 Claridge gave up his school and removed to London, spending much time in visiting the meetings in and around the city. Three years afterwards a heavy trial befell him, in the death of his daughter and only child. Amongst his MS. there was found some serious counsel written for her use. One sentence is as follows:—"Walk in the light of the Lamb continually; so thou shalt be a witness of His work, which is to take away the sin of the world." About this time he wrote to a relative who had recently lost a son, whose conduct had been marked by disobedience and dissipation. After expressing sympathy, he says:—

"I would not have thee sorrow as one without hope, for the mercies of God are boundless and His judgments are unsearchable. It behoveth us to be still and to exercise hope and charity: the mercy extended to the penitent thief ought to caution us against judging of the everlasting state of any, for who knows what faith and repentance the Lord in His abundant compassion might be pleased to give thy poor son before his exit out of the body! Comfort thyself, therefore, in the Lord alone, to whom secret things belong, and whose mercy rejoiceth against judgment."

When a cousin of Richard Claridge sent him a genealogical table of their family, recently obtained from the Heralds' Office, he copied a part of it, but, when returning it with thanks, writes of "The Christian pedigree, which is noble indeed, and worthy of our most diligent search."

A few weeks before his death Richard Claridge received a letter from the wife of an intimate friend, who was in a state of deep despondency. Brief extracts from his long and kind reply must suffice :—

"Dearly beloved Friend,— . . . Oh, be not faithless; but believe that Jesus Christ will, in His own appointed time, deliver thee, as thou abidest in faith and patience, bearing the indignation of the Lord because thou hast sinned against Him. . . . The times and seasons of the Lord's delivering of His people are in His own hands, and when the set time is fully come He will appear, and bring salvation with Him. Satan labours to possess thee with fears, doubts, and questionings concerning the loving-kindness of God to thy soul. But, my dear Friend, I have waited on the Lord on thy behalf, and am persuaded that this is one of Satan's wiles. . . . I also find an openness in my heart, not only to sympathise with thee, but also to put up my fervent supplications to the Lord for thee; and I believe He will answer my cries for the sake of His beloved Son Jesus Christ, in whom alone is my trust. . . . The reason thou givest for desiring a few lines from me, and not a personal visit, is somewhat strange; for thou sayest, 'I do not desire to see the face of any honest Friend;' and thy allegation for that is still more strange—'I am an afflicted, disconsolate, poor woman, not worthy that any honest Friend should come under my roof.' For the greater thy affliction, the more need, in my judgment, thou hast of an honest Friend to visit, advise, and comfort thee. Heavenly conversation is often blest to the disconsolate person, and by being too much alone the recluse party often becomes very dull, heavy, and melancholic, and lies open to various assaults and impressions of Satan. . . . Solitude, in a proper time and season, is an excellent thing; but in a time of such deep exercises as thine are, it will be convenient for thee to admit the conversation of some friend or friends, who have passed through the fires and the waters, and felt Satan's buffetings, and known the Lord's preservations. It is a Christian duty to entertain very low and humble thoughts of thyself; but I tenderly caution thee, in the wisdom of God, to *take heed of a Satanical wile here, for Christ is an all-sufficient and all benevolent Saviour.*

"Thy truly sympathising friend and brother,
"Richard Claridge."

The health of Richard Claridge had been declining for some years. The last MS. which occupied him was a memorial sketch of his venerated friend George Whitehead, who had lately died, after spending between sixty and seventy years of his long life in the service of his Lord. But, before he could complete this, he had to lay down the pen, of which he had long made a conscientious use. After a few days of increased illness, during which he spoke to those who visited him of the peace which was his happy portion, he expired in the early part of 1723, in the seventy-fourth year of his age.

His loss was a great one—to the Church, where it had been his wont to urge all to single-hearted holiness; to the friends to whom his sweetness endeared him, whilst adding a charm to his conversation; to the poor, who would miss his visits no less than his open-handed charity: and to his own household, on whose behalf his fervent prayers had often ascended to heaven, and to whom he had been a standing witness of the blessed result of a life lived "by the faith of the Son of God." For he had not only applied to Christ for healing, but had also placed himself passively in His hands, to effect the restoration in His own way and time; and had found—as Richard Baxter writes—that "He is not such a physician as to perform but a supposed or reputative cure. He came not to persuade His Father to judge us to be well because He Himself is well, or to leave us uncured. . . . This is the work of our blessed Redeemer—to make man fit for God's approbation and delight. He regenerateth us, that He may sanctify us and make us fit for our Master's use."

THOMAS STORY.

"Do not think that your earthly circumstances make a holy life to God's glory impossible. . . . Only cultivate large expectations of what the Lord will do for you. Let it be your sole desire to attain an entire union with Him. It is impossible to say what the Lord Jesus would do for a soul who is truly willing to live through Him as He through the Father" (John vi. 57).—ANDREW MURRAY'S "LIKE CHRIST."

THOMAS STORY.

"God called for my life, and I offered it at His footstool; but He gave it me, as a prey, with unspeakable addition. He called for my will, and I resigned it at His call; but He returned me His own in token of His love.... I begged HIMSELF and He gave me all."—T. STORY.

THE life of this remarkable man seems to be well worthy the attention of those—especially—who are members of that religious body which he did not join until (after carefully studying the doctrines of many other sects) he had become fully convinced that the principles held by Friends are in accordance with those laid down in the New Testament. For about half a century he preached the Gospel, his field of labour including the British Isles, the Netherlands, the United States of America, and the West Indies. Very skilful in religious argument, which he conducted in a truly Christian spirit—he was courteously and attentively heard by archbishops, dukes, earls, and countesses. During a residence of fourteen years in America he was the coadjutor of William Penn in the arrangement of the affairs of Pennsylvania; and in addition to being one of the Governor's Council, he filled the offices of Keeper of the Great Seal, Master of the Rolls, etc., and was also appointed Recorder for Philadelphia; the mayorality of this city was offered him in 1706, but he did not accept it.

Thomas Story was born about 1663, and was brought up as a member of the Church of England. Having chosen the law as his profession, he practised it in

Carlisle, and afterwards in London. From a very early age his heart was inclined to serious thoughtfulness, and when alone he often read the Bible, which even then he loved above all other books. As soon as he began to adopt some of the rude habits and words of the school-boys with whom he was associated, he says he felt something within him suddenly surprising him with a sense of sin, and thereby powerfully influencing his conduct. As he grew older the necessity of the great work of regeneration strongly impressed his heart; and, conscious of the uncertainty of life, he felt that "a secret stain rested upon the world and all its glory."

When he was about five-and-twenty, he was one day riding to a country church when his horse fell and broke its neck, whilst he himself was quite uninjured. Standing by the side of the prostrate animal he could but feel in how great peril his own life had been, and his heart was sorely troubled with the remembrance that, "Except a man be born again he cannot see the kingdom of God." He remarks that

"by the grace of God I had been enabled in measure to shun all words and acts which I felt to be evil." "And yet," he writes, "I did not know the Divine grace in its own nature, as it is in Christ; nor as a word of faith, sanctification, justification, consolation, and redemption. But my mind being truly earnest with God, thirsting unto death for the knowledge of the way of life, He was pleased to hear the voice of my necessity; for I wanted present salvation, and the Lord knew my case could not admit of further delay. And therefore being moved by His own free mercy and goodness—even in the same love in which He sent His Son, the Beloved, into the world to seek and to save the lost—on the first day of the second month, in the evening, in the year 1689, being alone in my chamber, the Lord brake in upon me unexpectedly; quick as lightning from the heavens, and as a righteous, all-powerful, all-knowing, sin-condemning, judge, before whom my soul, as in the deepest agony, trembled, was confounded and amazed, and filled with such awful dread as no words can declare. . . . But in the midst of this a voice was formed and uttered in me :—' Thy will, O God! be done ; if this be Thy act alone, and not my own, *I yield my soul to Thee.*' From the conceiving of these words from the Word of life, I quickly found relief. There was all-healing virtue in them, and the effect so swift and powerful that, even in a moment, all my fears vanished as if they had never been ; and my mind became calm, still and simple as a little child. The day of the Lord dawned, and the Sun of Righteousness arose in me with Divine healing and restoring virtue in His countenance, and He became the centre of my mind. . . . I had a taste and view of the agony of the Son of God, and of His death upon the cross, when the weight of the sins of all human kind were upon Him. Now all my past sins were pardoned and done away, and my carnal reasonings and conceivings about the knowledge of God and the mysteries of religion were over. . . . I now found the true Sabbath, a holy, heavenly, divine, and free rest, and most sweet repose."

Refreshing sleep, to which he had long been a stranger, followed this blessed visitation, and the next day he felt as free from care as a little child. As evening again returned, he says that his "whole nature and being were filled with the Divine presence in a manner he had never known before." He beautifully and forcibly compares his assurance of the reality of this experience, to the certainty felt by man—without any train of reasoning—of the fact that he beholds the sun, although that glorious orb can only be seen *through the medium of his own light.* In God's own presence Thomas Story learnt that He is love, and that perfect love casts out fear; no marvel that he should add, "I was filled with perfect consolation." Henceforth he hungered only for the bread of life, with which his Lord did not fail to supply him, whilst gradually leading him onwards in the path of the just, where the snares of the enemy, revealing to him his own weakness, taught him also the exceeding greatness of God's power.

Although he spoke to no one of what was passing within his soul, his friends must have seen that some great change had occurred: his sword and other ornamental articles of attire were laid aside, his instruments of music burnt, and he felt it right to discontinue his attendance at church, with a belief that one day it would be his duty to oppose the world with regard to matters of religion. Meanwhile Christ was his teacher, and "mysteries," it has been said, "are revealed to the meek." "As the nature and virtue," he writes, "of the Divine essential Truth increased in my mind, it wrought in me daily a greater conformity to its own power; reducing my mind to a solid quietude and silence as a state most fit for attending to the speech of the Divine word; being daily fed with the fruit of the tree of life I desired no other knowledge."

Whilst thus withdrawn for a while from outward religious fellowship, his heart was filled with love and compassion to all his fellow-creatures, whether "Protestants, Romans, Jews, Turks, or Heathens." His desire was to worship God in spirit and in truth, but he did not know that any others held views on this subject similar to those which Christ had taught him. One day, as he was finishing a long poem in blank verse "To the Saints in Zion," the Quakers, to his surprise, were suddenly brought to his mind, in such a manner as to awaken a strong desire to know what their principles were.

Early in the summer of 1691, having some business in the west of Cumberland, he lodged at an inn which was kept by a Friend, with whom he had some religious conversation; and on the following day accompanied him to the Friends' meeting at Broughton. This good man had, no doubt, become much interested in his young companion, and as they journeyed together was inclined to give him further details of the views held by the sect of which he was a member; but he no longer found an eager listener, for Thomas Story says that his mind was composed, and its attention directed towards God, who knew that he "wanted only to see the truth and not be deceived." So they rode together for some miles in perfect silence, in which Thomas Story enjoyed a blessed consciousness of the presence of God. In this state of mind he took his seat in the meeting, giving no great heed to the words of a minister who was contrasting some of the views of Friends with those of the Presbyterians, etc.; for he did not doubt that in common with other denominations they could speak in favour of their own principles, "and my concern," he writes, "was much rather to know whether they were a people gathered under a sense of the enjoyment of the presence of God in their meetings; or, in other words, whether they worshipped the true and living God in the life and nature of Christ, the Son of God, the true and only Saviour: and the Lord answered my desire according to the integrity of my heart. For not long after I had sat down among them, that heavenly and watery cloud overshadowing my mind, brake into a sweet abounding shower of celestial rain, and the greatest part of the meeting was broken together, and comforted in the same

Divine presence and influence of the holy and heavenly Lord, which was divers times repeated before the meeting was ended."

He had been no stranger to similar feelings when alone with God, but now he learnt that "as many small streams by forming a river become more deep and weighty," even so in a company that with one accord draw nigh to God, through Jesus Christ, there may be a stronger realisation of the fulness of joy to be found in His presence. And in this solemn hour he learnt also that, like the prophet of old, he had been wrong in supposing that there was "scarce any true and living faith in the world."

Greatly did the Friends who formed Broughton Meeting rejoice in spirit over the young stranger in their midst, who they imagined had now for the first time been brought to the true knowledge of God. He accepted an invitation to the house of an aged widow; the peace of God, "inexpressible by any language but itself alone, remaining as a canopy" over his mind. No marvel that on such a day as this he should resolve henceforth, at any cost, to count all things but loss for the excellency of the knowledge of Christ; to abandon whatever would hinder his communion with his Lord, or mar any service for Him to which he might be called.

Soon his sincerity was severely tested. An acquaintance came to him one evening to ask him to appear the next day, as a witness in his favour, at a trial concerning some houses which formed the greater part of his property. As Story had made the deed of conveyance, the young man thought that his evidence would prove the justness of his claim. Whilst his friend was talking to him Thomas Story saw that he must now either take up the cross of Christ, or forsake Him for ever. His Saviour did not desert him in this time of need; he said, " I am concerned it should fall out so ; I will appear if it please God, and testify what I know in the matter, and do what I can for you that way, but I cannot swear." Passionately, and with an oath, his astonished friend made reply, " What, you are not a Quaker, sure !" For a few moments Story scarcely knew what would be a true answer to this question, but as " the power of that life of Him who forbiddeth all oaths and swearing arose," as he says, yet more clearly and fully in him, he replied, " I must confess the truth ; I am a Quaker." His angry acquaintance heaped him with reproaches, threatened to have him fined by the Court, and dealt with according to the utmost rigour of the law. No sooner had he left the house than Thomas Story withdrew to his own room, for in that hour of sore temptation and trial he felt that he must be alone with God. A gentleman by birth, education, and association—life, with fair prospects, opening before him—his young spirit was, he knew, in danger of quailing before Satan's suggestions of what might be the consequences of the course he had taken ; fines, imprisonment, the displeasure of his father, loss of friends, scoffing, and scorn.

His account of the victory won by *faith* is too remarkable to be given in any words but his own :—

" From about eight in the evening till midnight the eye of my mind was fixed on the love of God, which still remained sensible in me, my soul cleaving thereto in great simplicity, humility, and trust therein, without any yielding to Satan and his reasonings on those subjects where flesh and blood in its own strength is easily overcome. But about twelve at night the Lord put him to utter silence with all his temptations for that season, and the life of the Son of God alone remained in my soul. And then, from a sense of His wonderful work and redeeming arm, this saying of the Apostle arose in me with power—'The law of the spirit of life in Christ Jesus hath made me free from the law of sin and death.'"

Perfect love had cast out fear, and calmly and with undaunted confidence he committed his cause to his Saviour's keeping. The following morning, whilst on his way to the Hall where the judges sat, his acquaintance met him with the information that the opponent had yielded the cause, and that the case was now satisfactorily settled. On hearing this, Thomas Story "stood still in the street," for he knew that it was the Lord's doing.

This circumstance made him the common topic of conversation : a few looked sorrowful and wept, whilst others scoffed and sneered. But none of these things moved him, for the love of God was to his soul as "a rampart of invincible patience." Some gentlemen whom he knew, wishing to reclaim him from what they hoped was but a temporary fit of fanaticism, asked him to meet them at a tavern. This invitation he thought it right to accept, and the secret presence of his Saviour accompanying him, affected them in a way they had little looked for. A health to King William was being drunk, but when the glass was handed to Story he told his companions that, whilst wishing well to both the king and themselves, he must refuse it, having given up the habit of health-drinking. The glass did not go round ; a solemnity pervaded the assembly, causing silence and weeping; then some of Thomas Story's friends spoke of their conviction that every man should be allowed to do what he thinks right in the sight of God, and they parted, we read, "in solid friendship."

Although at this time Thomas Story had but little intercourse with Friends, he constantly attended their meetings, where, he says, in a state of silence his heart was frequently broken and tendered by the Divine influence of the powerful truth: a holy pleasure which the world could never afford.

He now became convinced that, in his own case, the practice of the law would be a hindrance to his growth in grace, and to his fulfiment of the ministry for which he felt that God was preparing him. The abandonment of all hope of worldly preferment was probably a far lighter trial than the displeasure which his father manifested when he became aware of this resolution. About this time, whilst attending a meeting at Sunderland, Thomas Story's heart was much affected, as was often the case, by a powerful sense of the presence and love of his Saviour; he noticed that at the same time many others shared in his blessedness, and this, he remarks, made it clear to him that "there is a communication of Divine love through the one Spirit, and that unspeakable, among the sanctified in Christ at this day as well as in time past, and that in a state of holy silence."

When travelling in Scotland, as companion to a minister named John Bowstead, Story for the first time spoke a few words in public in a street at Coupar, after which the people in a very loving manner directed them on their way. He was then about thirty years of age. Not long afterwards he attended the London Yearly Meeting, in company with John Banks, whom he describes as "that good, old valiant warrior for Truth on earth." At Edmonton he first met with William Penn, and their hearts were closely drawn together by those holy ties which can never be broken. He also formed a similar friendship with Thomas Wilson, who seemed to him to be the most able and powerful minister of the age.

Whilst accompanying this Friend on a religious visit to the west of England, Thomas Story, as he sat by his side in meetings, often enjoyed unspeakable blessedness and satisfaction. But before his return to his father's house, his state of mind was a very different one, for he saw that he had done wrong in not giving expression to a few words which had been powerfully impressed on his mind in several meetings. Deep as was his distress it was not of long duration; the presence of the Lord had become his "all, and too dear to part with," and when in a meeting at Kirklington his Saviour once more comforted his sorely stricken heart, he resolved to give good heed to the next intimation to duty. Having done this by uttering the words, "It is a good day to all those who obey the voice of the Lord," his soul was filled with joy which found vent in tears. At the same time most of the assembled company were affected in a like manner, and for a while all were silent under the canopy of the most High. Afterwards John Bowstead, who had that day felt particularly attracted to Kirklington Meeting, spoke at some length on the subject which his young friend had introduced.

In 1695 Thomas Story removed to London, where, through the influence of William Penn and others, he obtained employment in conveyancing. In the following year he paid a general visit to the meetings in the north of England and Scotland. Whilst at West Allandale, amongst others who had come to see him was Cuthbert Featherstone, "an ancient and honourable friend." Whilst they communed together, they so realised the loving presence of their Lord that the tears flowed down the old man's face to his long white beard, and Thomas Story's heart was deeply moved with love towards him, and with the conviction that if he also faithfully followed his Saviour, God would be as near him in his old age as when He first revealed Himself in his soul. The encouragement thus graciously granted him at an early stage of his pilgrimage should, he thought, be kept in lasting remembrance to the praise of the Lord.

In 1697 we find Thomas Story and Gilbert Mollison calling at the residence of Peter the Great, who was in London *incognito*, where they wished to leave the Latin edition of "Barclay's Apology," hoping that it might fall under the notice of the Czar. They had an opportunity of conversing with him on some of the views held by Friends. The following Sunday morning as Thomas Story was sitting in Gracechurch Street Meeting he saw two gentlemen enter; they were dressed in the usual costume of Englishmen of that period, but this did not prevent him from recognising the Emperor and his interpreter. A minister named Robert Haydock was preaching about the cure of Naaman, and—entirely unaware of the high rank of one of his hearers—he said,

"Now if thou wert the greatest king, emperor, or potentate upon earth, thou art not too great to make use of the means offered by the Almighty for thy healing and restoration, if ever thou expect to enter His Kingdom, into which no unclean thing can come."

Fifteen years later, when Peter the Great's troops had taken possession of the Friends' Meeting-house at Frederickstadt, he not only ordered them out of it, but gave notice that he would attend a meeting in it, if the few Friends residing there were inclined to hold one. As his Generals did not understand German, the Emperor, with much seriousness, acted as interpreter in this meeting, remarking that whoever would live in accordance with such doctrine would be happy.

In 1698 Thomas Story accompanied William Penn to Ireland, where, in the intervals of meetings, the latter accomplished much good by interviews with the Lord Justices of Ireland, and the chief members of the Government of that country; directing their attention to subjects connected with the spread of religion, and the welfare of the Society of Friends. At Clonmel, Thomas Story met with his brother, the Dean of Limerick, who was the author of a history of the late war, during which he had filled the post of chaplain to a regiment commanded by his relative, Sir Thomas Gower. On returning to London, Story found his friend, Roger Gill, waiting at his lodgings, to converse with him on the subject of a religious visit to America.

About five years before this time, as Thomas Story was riding alone one autumn evening, his heart was exceedingly moved by the power of the Lord, and greatly comforted by the conviction given him that a visitation of God was "coming over the western parts of the world, towards the sunsetting." From this memorable hour, his soul was often deeply stirred by a sense of God's love and compassion to a people whom he had never seen. And two years later, when at the house of John Whiting, in Somerset, as he was one day looking at a map of the world, "the power of the Lord," he writes, "suddenly seized my soul, and His love melted me into a flood of tender tears; but hitherto I knew not the call of the Lord was to me to visit those parts, though from henceforth I began to be afraid of it."

The belief that his gracious Master had work for him to do in America became still stronger when, during the Yearly Meeting, a Friend was led to pray that God would send forth His ministers to "the western countries and places beyond the seas." Before going to Ireland, Thomas Story had, on a winter day, attended a meeting held at the Park Meeting-house, at Southwark, where Roger Gill had also been engaged in the ministry. As they returned together to the city, Story, finding his mind very open towards his companion, told him of his feelings with regard to America, and asked him if he knew of any Friend who felt constrained to visit that land. Roger Gill's reply was: "It is now long since I was concerned that way, and the last night in my sleep was as if making all things ready for my voyage." "Is it not more than a dream yet?" said Thomas Story. Before the latter left for Ireland, however, Robert Gill told him that he would accompany him to America, although he should not be ready for some time, as he had to make arrangements for "his wife and children, not knowing whether ever he might see them any more."

It is no wonder that after-events should cause these words of his friend to return vividly to Thomas Story's memory. When they visited the vessel in which they thought of taking their passage, Thomas Story says that his heart was "sweetly comforted by the Divine love and life of the Lord Jesus in the centre of his soul, so that for that time all loads and weights were removed."

On the day of their departure many of their friends accompanied them on board the ship. Story thus describes this parting hour: "Being together in the great cabin, the good presence of the Lord commanded deep and inward silence before Him, and the Comforter of the just broke in upon us by His irresistible power, and greatly tendered us together in His heavenly love, whereby we were melted into many tears. Glorious was this appearance, to the humbling of us all and admiration of some there, who did not understand it. Then William Penn was concerned in prayer. . . . And when he had finished, the Lord repeated His own embraces of Divine soul-melting love upon the silent weeping assembly; to the full confirmation of us more immediately concerned, and further evidence to the truth of our calling. When the time for separation had arrived, the voyagers looked after their friends as long as they remained in sight, but with no yearnings to turn back with them, for they were comforted, Thomas Story says, with "that Divine love, which neither place nor number of years shall ever be able to obstruct or deface, as we keep true to the Lord in ourselves."

The passage was an exceedingly stormy one, the first tempest they encountered being the most violent. Story was enabled to wrestle in an agony of prayer for their deliverance, at which, as he remarks, some stout hearts were broken, and the Lord's power was glorified; afterwards he told his companions "in full assurance," that the storm was over—and so it proved to be. When in the midst of the succeeding tempests he was at one time tempted to think that God was dealing hardly, he was comforted by a clear conviction of His holy presence, giving strength in proportion to the need, and manifesting His power most fully in the hour of greatest extremity.

Cold as was the New World's winter welcome, the strangers had a very hospitable reception at the house of a Friend, at Queen's Creek, who had of late apprehended that such visitors from England would arrive, although he did not know who they might be. One meeting, held about this time, seems to have been especially satisfactory to Thomas Story; many hearts being moved whilst the ministers spoke of "the free and universal grace of God, through Christ, for life and salvation—endeavouring to turn them thereunto; that through faith therein they might come to know the full end of the sacrifice of the blood of Christ shed at Jerusalem of old."

Soon we find the travellers on their way to North Carolina, passing through a wilderness, in the midst of which they kindle a fire, and rest whilst eating their bread and cheese and drinking water from a brook, and are "well refreshed and content." On another occasion, after describing the circumstances of exceeding discomfort amidst which he had passed a night, Thomas Story adds that he "slept very well, for where the Lord subjects the mind and makes it content, all things are easy." His American travels afforded him ample opportunity for verifying this statement.

Some negroes attended the meetings held in Carolina, and Thomas Story's heart was cheered at finding " the poor blacks so near the truth and reachable." One of them told him that a Friend who had previously visited that part had assured them—although they had been taught the contrary—that the grace of God, through Christ was as free to them as to the white people. A satisfactory interview was also had with the Chickahomine Indians, and, before attending the Yearly Meeting for the western shore, visits were paid to the families of Friends. About this time tidings reached Thomas Story and his companions of the terrible yellow fever which was raging in Philadelphia, and Roger Gill felt that he must immediately go to the distressed Friends there, saying that if he had wings he would fly to their aid. Soon Story joined him, and was made deeply sensible, as he visited the sick and dying, of the Lord's presence with His people in this day of sore affliction.

The time for the Yearly Meeting in this city was now at hand, and the Ministers and Elders were not sure whether it would be best to suspend it, or to hold it as usual. As they waited on the Lord for counsel they saw that it would not be desirable to give up holding the meetings, which were remarkably blessed; those held on the first, second, and third days being for worship, and that on the fourth for business. Violent as the pestilence had been during the preceding week, it was believed that no fresh case occurred during these four days; and soon afterwards the plague was stayed. The two English Friends continued their visits to the sufferers, and Thomas Story writes: "O the immortal sweetness I enjoyed with several as they lay under the exercise of the devouring evil (though unspeakably comforted in the Lord). Let my soul remember it, and wait low before the Lord to the end of my days! Great was the majesty and hand of the Lord! Great was the fear that fell upon all flesh. . . . But the just appeared with open face, and walked upright in the streets, *and rejoiced in secret in that perfect love that casteth out all fear.* . . . Nor love of the world, nor fear of death could hinder their resignation, abridge their confidence, or cloud their enjoyments in the Lord."

Soon Roger Gill showed symptoms of illness, and, when his companion talked to him of their plans for the future, only answered that he did not see his way any further. As some meetings had already been appointed Thomas Story could not stay with him; but, although he said that he was "pretty easy and not very ill," his friend took leave of him with a heavily-burdened spirit, remembering how fervently he had prayed during the Yearly Meeting—"That the Lord would be pleased to accept of his life as a sacrifice for his people, that a stop might be put to the contagion." "I had thought," adds Thomas Story, "he would be taken at his word, though no such sacrifices are required; only therein appeared his great love and concern for Friends whom he had come so far to see." Therefore, although he knew that the sufferer was well taken care of, and that he could be of little use to him, Thomas Story most keenly felt the parting, weeping so exceedingly that his tears ran down to the floor; and Roger Gill, desiring that the Lord might be with him, said, "Thou breaks my heart, I cannot bear it any longer."

Deep was Thomas Story's mourning when the tidings of his friend's death, at the age of thirty-four, followed him, though he was convinced that he had not only obtained a crown of everlasting peace, but also that "his living testimony should not fall in those American parts." Many long years have passed away since the loving heart of this faithful follower of His Lord ceased to beat, when the wide waters of the Atlantic lay between it and all that it held most dear on earth, yet surely Roger Gill's memory is blessed still. It is probably that whilst at Philadelphia Story met for the first time with the daughter of Edward Shippen,* who seven years later, in 1706, became his wife; this happy union was a short one, being terminated by the death of Anne Story in 1711-12.

Thomas Story thus describes the conclusion of a Yearly Meeting at Choptank, which he attended, not long after the death of Roger Gill:—"Our meeting ended in the pure holy love of our Lord Jesus Christ, our holy Head, Life, and Comforter; who is ever near to the end of the world, to strengthen and support His own in the needful season, and to bind up His holy body, the Church, with the joints and sinews of Divine love that cannot be broken, against which the gates of hell can never prevail."

---

* Edward Shippen left England for Boston in 1675, and in that city received a public whipping for his religion as a Friend. Removing to Philadelphia, he had great success as a merchant, and was a Speaker in the House of Assembly in 1695. He sent valuable aid to the poor amongst his fellow-professors in England, by the gift of 12¾ ounces of gold, which he believed would sell in London for about £50 sterling.

Soon Thomas Story had the great pleasure of meeting with William Penn in his own province, from which he had been absent many years. The Governor found affairs in a very unsettled state, and greatly desired that Thomas Story (who was now nearly ready to return to England) should settle for some years in Pennsylvania, to aid him in framing regulations for the new city of Philadelphia, as well as in other responsible and difficult duties. To this proposal Story acceded, and afterwards filled many important posts in Philadelphia, whilst not confining himself so closely as to prevent visits to various meetings. In 1704 he undertook a religious journey to New England; at Bristol, on the Main, the meeting was held in the prison where two young men were confined in consequence of their refusal to bear arms. Having encouraged them to be faithful, Thomas Story went to the residence of the Judge of the Court, Colonel Byfield, in order to intercede for them. The reception he at first met with was a rough one; and even after the Judge had become calmer he remarked that he "thought it might be well if Friends were all settled in a place by themselves where they could not be troublesome to others by their contradictious ways!" Story answered, "If you should send us out of all countries where we reside into one by ourselves, that would not ease you, for more would spring up unavoidably in our places; for what would the world do if it should lose its salt and leaven?" The Colonel seemed surprised at this reply, yet kindly shook hands with Thomas Story before they parted. When at Boston Story spoke and wrote to the Governor on behalf of these young men, and they were set at liberty under certain conditions.

Shortly afterwards he held meetings in the neighbourhood of Salem, where great distress prevailed on account of the hostilities of the Indians, who—in revenge for the wrongs which they had too good ground for saying they had received from the professors of Christianity in New England—stealthily and cruelly attacked the white people, without regard to age or sex. Many houses in towns and in the country were turned into garrisons; but Thomas Story, not thinking it right to avail himself of military protection, went to the home of a Friend named Henry Dow, within pistol-shot of a swamp and thicket, and there rested "with consolation."

Dangerous as was the situation of this defenceless dwelling, its young mistress had been kept from fear by God, in whom she put her trust until, yielding to the entreaties of her mother, the family removed to the neighbourhood of a garrison. Here Henry Dow's wife was constantly distressed by terror of the Indians, and her poor mother, venturing to go in the early morning to fetch a few things from the house, was murdered by some of the enemy who were in ambush. The daughter, when these dreadful tidings reached her, instead of going into the garrison, led her little children to a thicket, and there her tormenting fears were taken from her, and her stricken heart was greatly comforted by the Lord whom she sought to make her fortress; for as soon as the interment had taken place Henry Dow and his family returned to their home.

Whilst still in this dangerous district Thomas Story was deeply perplexed with respect to the appointment of meetings, from the fear that in making such arrangements he might risk the lives of others; but these doubts all vanished as this thought was presented to his mind, He that walketh in darkness knoweth not whither he goeth, but to him who walketh in light there is no occasion of stumbling.

When he visited the island of Nantucket he spent a sleepless night, from the anxiety which he felt that a Friends' meeting should be established there. He thought it his duty to lay this matter before a family of the name of Starbuck. "I advised them," he writes, "to wait sincerely upon the Lord in such meetings, for they had no instrumental teachers, and assured them that I had a firm confidence in the Lord that He would visit them by His Holy Spirit in them, in His own time—if they were faithful, held on, and did not faint nor look back. Accordingly they did meet, and the Lord did visit them, and gathered many there unto Himself; and they became a large and living meeting in Him, and several living and able ministers were raised by the Lord in that family, and of others, to the honour of His own arm, who is worthy for ever!"

In 1709 Story visited the Barbadoes, etc., where for some years he had believed that there was a work for him to do. On his homeward voyage the vessel was captured by a French privateer, and taken into Hispaniola. Those on board were deprived of their goods, but were otherwise treated with kindness. After a while they obtained a passage to Guadaloupe, and thence under a flag of truce to Antigua. On the first of these voyages they were becalmed, and in that tropical clime the sufferings of Thomas Story, who was then violently ill, must have been extreme; indeed it would be no easy task to form a clear conception of them—lying, as he did, in an almost unventilated hold, crowded with a repulsive and blaspheming company, unable to quench his thirst with a limited supply of stagnant water, and unprovided with suitable food. Perhaps he fared better when he exchanged these quarters for the deck, though there unsheltered from rain, dew, and spray. It would have been far too hard for all his own strength, he says; but "through the grace of God I was fully resigned to His blessed will in death or life; and in His blessed visitations my soul rejoiced in remembrance of some of my nearest and dearest friends." Five years later Thomas Story again went to Barbadoes, and in the same year returned to his native land. Whilst on his way to the north, to see his aged father, who was now blind and ill, and greatly longed for his son's companionship, he spent a night at Burton; "where," he writes, "I had a secret opened to me by my dear Saviour, which my soul humbly desires of Him may be recorded in me for evermore."

In 1715 Story visited Holland and Germany, and, after returning from the Continent, laboured in Ireland, and subsequently in Scotland. After alluding to the large congregation at Aberdeen, he writes:—"I had travelled far in the goodwill and love of God to see them: and a little after my coming into the place, I was much broken in that love which reaches over sea and land, and engages in the greatest fatigues for the good of souls, for whom Christ died through a never-fading love." He greatly enjoyed his intercourse with Robert Barclay, which both would have gladly prolonged, though their friendship was of the kind which can well bear *any* strain of separation, and Thomas

Story characteristically remarks:—" We were made easier to part by the same that first made us acquainted in the time of our youth."

Four years later Story had several large and satisfactory meetings at Bath; one, especially, he describes as a great and glorious meeting, crowned with the presence of the King of Kings. Many of the nobility were present, some of them standing the whole time, though the meeting lasted for three hours, Story speaking for about two hours and a-half. Once, at Shrewsbury, on the last day of a Yearly Meeting, which had been eagerly attended by people of all ranks, whilst Thomas Story was speaking of the crucifixion of Christ, and of His being wounded to the heart for the sins of men, he was so completely overcome that he could not go on, until, as he says, his "spirit was a little unburdened by an efflux of many tears, and the whole auditory was bowed and generally broken; and many confessed the truth." Whilst spending some weeks at Bristol, he became interested in the young people belonging to that meeting, with whom he quaintly says he used "all decent plainness, but, as it was in the love of truth, they received it in the same ground." He greatly regretted the conduct of some ministers there, who had "unwarrantably and falsely applied to them all the judgments against old Israel in their most degenerate state; of whose sins these young people and others, knowing themselves not to be guilty, though perhaps in some things they want amendment, are greatly offended and hurt."

In 1721 an Act of Parliament was passed for accepting the affirmation of Friends in its present form; the one which had been previously used was very unsatisfactory, as it almost amounted to an oath. Thomas Story had undergone confinement for a year and a-half in the Fleet prison, in consequence of declining to take it, in which suffering he says that he had great peace and acceptance with the Lord. On his release he shared largely in the efforts which were made by Friends to obtain a new Act; he had interviews in reference to this subject with the Archbishops of Canterbury and York, the Bishop of Carlisle, the Duke of Somerset, and the Earls of Sunderland and Carlisle. The Archbishop of York, after a long conversation, expressed a wish to see some of the writings of Friends, and at parting took Thomas Story's hand in his own, and said: " I desire your prayers for me, as I also pray for you; we ought all to pray one for another."

On one occasion, when at Lowther Hall on business, a conversation which Thomas Story had with Lord Lonsdale on religious topics, introduced by the latter, was prolonged until 1 a.m. Thomas Story told his courteous listener that, " We must love God, love His judgments and reproofs, which are all in love, in order to the manifestation of Himself;" and referring to his own experience, remarked: " Whilst I was in an unconverted state I believed the being of God and all His attributes; but I did not actually know God to be holy till He reproved unholiness in me. . . . Nor had I known Him as a consuming fire, unless by the refining operation of His Spirit He had consumed my corruptions, or begun that work; or that He is love, Divine, unspeakable love, unless by His own power He had fitted me in some measure to enjoy the influences of His grace in a state of holiness; *in which He rules as a monarch in the soul* ... which through grace I know infinitely transcends, *even in this life,* all that can be named besides!"

In 1730 we find Thomas Story pausing in his travels and settling for nearly a year at Justicetown (an estate near Carlisle, inherited from his father), where he enjoyed spending a portion of his time in planting and improving his land, and in intercourse with his friends; his great interest in a large nursery ground of British and American forest trees being increased from the fact that there was an inconvenient lack of timber in that neighbourhood. During his long residence in Philadelphia he had formed an intimate friendship with James Logan (Penn's invaluable coadjutor), with whom he afterwards corresponded, manifesting an affectionate interest in his children, although he did not know them personally. In 1734 he writes, from London, to one of James Logan's little girls, who was probably much gratified at being addressed as: "Respected Friend, Sarah Logan, jun." His object in writing is to thank her for "a very acceptable present of her early ingenuity," which had been "greatly admired as the work of a person so young." From her answer we learn that he had not only remembered to thank her for what she styles "a small piece of my childish performance," but also "to retaliate it to a great excess with a valuable present." Reference is also made to another gift of a knife, fork, and spoon, in a shagreen case, which her kind friend had sent her when her father was last in England. In his next note Thomas Story expresses his hope "that heaven may preserve her by the sweet Divine dew from above, daily descending upon her tender heart."

Some portions of his letters to James Logan show how deep were his researches in certain branches of natural science, for his learning was extensive.

When he was attending the Quarterly Meeting at York, in 1738, a person who was present took down some of his sermons in shorthand. Thomas Story was unaware of this at the time, but consented to their publication, whilst remarking in his Journal, "No words can represent the Divine virtue, power, and energy in which the doctrines of the truth are delivered by those who are sent of God."

In one of these sermons he observes: "If we do indeed believe in the Lord Jesus Christ, He reconcileth us unto God, reforms our nature, and destroys the works of sin in us, according to the saying of John the Baptist: Behold the Lamb of God, which taketh away the sin of the world.'" Then, after quoting Mal. iii. 1, 2, 3, and Matt. iii. 12, he continues: "Now these things were not predicted concerning the outward coming of Christ in the flesh only, but rather of His inward coming or revelation in Spirit; for where sin is, there is the defilement, and where that is, there must the Refiner and Purifier be. . . . And there never can be any true reformation wrought in us until we come thus to believe and receive the Son of God; and by believing and receiving Him we are, and shall be, redeemed from all our sins, and the deadly effects of them in our souls. . . . He will fill us with His Holy Spirit, the new wine of His kingdom, which consists not of meat and drink, but righteousness, Divine peace, and joy unspeakable in the Holy Ghost—*an enjoyment, even in this life, transcending all the imagination and thought of man in his natural state."* In another sermon, after remarking that he was glad that there had been so long a silence in the meeting, he added: "The lust of hearing the voice of man remains until the voice of God be heard in the soul, and then cometh that satisfaction which no other voice can give." Not long afterwards he attended a General Meeting at Preston, during which many of the young, he writes, "were baptised of the Lord in the purifying flame of Divine love, to their great consolation, entering thereby into a covenant of light and life with Him, according to His sure promise of old."

Thomas Story was seized with paralysis in 1741 whilst in London, rendering what assistance he could to the deeply sorrowing widow of his friend Joseph Green (whose eldest son had died within a few hours of his father). Although his memory was much impaired by this attack, his amiability and cheerfulness were unchanged. During the summer his health much improved, and he returned to Justicetown; but in the spring of the following year a second paralytic seizure terminated his life. The funeral, which took place at the Friends' Cemetery, Carlisle, was largely attended by respectful mourners from the neighbourhood, as well as by a great number of Friends from a distance.

Such a life as Thomas Story's may well stimulate sincere Christians to press forward; for it serves to exemplify the truth, which was so dear to himself, that He, whose Divine strength is made perfect in human weakness, "is able to carry on His work in the soul, *when*, and *how*, and *to what degree* it pleaseth Him."

GILBERT LATEY AND HIS FRIENDS.

"As I read your letter, and heard that you desired for me, as your salutation, *the Crucified Saviour*, my heart and soul sprang up within for gladness. . . . . I have such joy and gladness in His promises that I cannot even think on these torments. . . . Yea, such joy and gladness as I cannot speak or write, or had thought could be experienced in a prison, for scarce can I sleep night or day for rejoicing." — LETTER FROM THE MARTYR JEROMYMOUS SEGERSON TO HIS IMPRISONED WIFE, ALSO A MARTYR; 1551.

GILBERT LATEY AND HIS FRIENDS.

> "How was it, lovers of your kind,
>   Though ye were mocked and hatred,
> That ye, with clear and patient mind
>   Truth's holy doctrine stated?
> In GOD, as in an ark, ye kept;
> Around,—and not above you,—swept
>   The flood till it abated."
>
> T. T. LYNCH.

"LET me talk with you ever so long, and you will tell me of the Spirit of God, and the grace of God, and the operation thereof, and the love of God you are made witnesses of through Jesus Christ, which I believe may, in a measure, be true; but do you not think it is well to have something to represent that which you so much love?" Such was the question not unnaturally asked by Lord D'Aubigny—a priest in orders of the Church of Rome, and Lord-Almoner of the Queen Dowager Henrietta Maria, whom he had accompanied to England—at the conclusion of a conversation with Gilbert Latey, the son of a Cornish yeoman, who had some six years earlier been convinced of the views of Friends. "*The substance of all things*," was Gilbert Latey's reply, "*is come, Christ in us, the hope of glory*, and all the outward types and representations must come to an end and be swallowed up in our blessed Lord.... He being so near men and women is the saint's daily Remembrancer."

When one day Lord D'Aubigny took him through the kneeling company in the Queen's Chapel to an apartment in which was another of her priests, we learn that " the word of the Lord " came to him to " preach Truth unto them," which he did. In consequence of an expression he made use of, this priest asked him of what altar he spoke, and he answered it was of that on which the saints daily offer up their prayers. " Friend," was the priest's reply, " there is no greater state attainable than that you speak of ! "

Gilbert Latey was born in the year 1626 in the parish of St. Issey, which lies near the bold, rugged and scantily-populated north coast of Cornwall. He wished to be bound to some trade, and chose that of tailor, and, whilst still young, exchanged his native place, with its bracing breezes, for Plymouth. His situation at Plymouth was a very promising one; but his master, although making a great profession of religion, did not carry it out in practice, and, therefore, notwithstanding the offer of the best wages given to any man in the town, Gilbert Latey, who had " breathings in his heart after the Lord," thought that it would not be right to remain with him.

He removed to London, where he became a successful tradesman in the Strand, and was patronised by gentlemen of high rank. But no outward prosperity could satisfy the cravings of his soul: neither could the four sermons he often heard in the course of a day, nor even his frequent private prayers; though doubtless, being offered in sincerity, they came up for a memorial before God. " To be a seeker," as his contemporary Oliver Cromwell said, " is to be of the best sect next to being a finder," and yet his heart must have often sunk as he went from one to another of the most eminent preachers of the day, without finding the enlightenment he longed for. Perhaps it was but with a faint hope of better success that he went one day, when about the age of twenty-eight, to the house of a certain widow in Whitecross Street, where he had been told that a meeting would be held by two Friends from the North. One of these was Edward Burrough, and the fervent ministry of the young dales-man, then only eighteen, was the means of showing him that what he had so long sought without, he might find within; and once finding his Lord, and experiencing that He had redeemed him to God by His blood, not for one moment does he seem to have hesitated on the right course to be pursued, though with his wonted keenness of perception he must have foreseen that a rough road lay before him. Nor did he enter on it with faltering steps, but rather with rejoicing alacrity; for the Pearl of Great Price was within his grasp, and he could only feel that it was worth selling all for. His Saviour had revealed Himself to him, and his soul was satisfied.

At this time Friends were scarcely known in London, and Gilbert Latey was one of the first-fruits of their labours; but twenty-four years later, in 1678—so richly did the blessing of the Lord crown their zeal—their number had swelled to 10,000 in that city alone. Gilbert Latey's good sense and sound judgment, dedicated as they were to the Lord's service, were of great use in settling the numerous meetings which soon sprang up in and around the metropolis. Amongst the latter was one at Hammersmith, where he was, we find, during forty-nine years a "frequent attender, and in measure supporter thereof, being as a nursing father thereto, and the Lord blessed his unwearied love."

This meeting was opened about 1658 after Hammersmith had been visited by a Friend named Sarah Blackbury, whose ministry so affected a woman named Hester Mason that she entertained her at her house, and obtained permission from her husband for the appointment of a meeting there; this, however, he withdrew after only one meeting had been held, in consequence of the many calumnies about Friends which reached his ears through his fellow-servants at a Westminster brewhouse. For a while it was removed to Chiswick, but was afterwards brought back to Hammersmith, where a regular meeting-house was built in 1677.

The first Friends' meeting established at Kingston was held in the house of two faithful followers of Christ, John and Ann Fielder, whose only daughter Mary became the wife of Gilbert Latey. The Lord Protector often resided at Hampton Court at the time of the settlement of Kingston Meeting, and amongst the many there "turned to the Lord" were—as Latey's nephew and biographer says—"several that then belonged to Oliver," and whom it is interesting to find, continued faithful. But for thirty years it was only at the cost of fines, imprisonments of long duration, kicks, blows, and violent beatings with clubs and carbines, that this meeting was kept up. In 1663 the Kingston Friends purchased a burying-ground in Norbiton Street, where Gilbert Latey was interred in 1705.

Allusion has already been made to his flourishing business as a master-tailor in the Strand. Not long after becoming a Friend conscientious motives made him decline taking orders for the gay, heavily-trimmed costume, with which the fashionable gentlemen of that day attired themselves. This was no slight test of principle, and some of his acquaintance called him mad for throwing away his opportunity for making a fortune. His numerous genteel customers left him, and he had to dismiss a large staff of workmen, not knowing but that he might be obliged to work as a journeyman himself. But, after awhile, a moderate yet regular custom returned to him; and we may be sure that he had no cause to regret this "world's ungathered prize."* In the very midst of this trial, sorely blamed by his kinsfolk as well as by others, he realised that "it is a blessed thing to be immediately under the guidance of God's hand, cost what it may," for his inward peace appears to have abounded, and he soon, felt that the Lord had work for him as a public minister of the Gospel;—"to call," as one of his converts writes, " me and many more out of the ways of the world, and the traditions of man, to make God's truth known."

Many of his former customers retained a high esteem for him, at which he must have rejoiced, as it frequently enabled him to obtain their aid on behalf of his persecuted brethren lying in loathsome dungeons. Gilbert Latey was himself once committed to the Gate-house prison in Westminster, with fifteen or sixteen others, who had met together to worship God. They were thrust into a perfectly dark cell, of ten feet by eleven, with wet walls, on the cold ground of which they in turn shared the privilege of lying, standing being the

---

* To one who asks his advice when, probably, perfect uprightness and worldly profit were in the balance—Thomas Scott writes—"'But seek ye first the kingdom of God and His righteousness, and all other things shall be added unto you.' Dare you believe this promise or not? *I dare:* and will act accordingly, by God's assistance."

only other alternative; but they knew their Lord was with them, and their faith did not fail. It could not have been long after their liberation that Latey and other Friends pleaded for permission to be imprisoned in the stead of some among the many hundreds of their brethren who were undergoing severe suffering from close confinement.

. Although not allowed to make good this noble offer, Gilbert Latey was successful in interceding with Lord Baltimore on behalf of the persecuted Friends in Maryland; and signally so in his oft-repeated appeals to Lord D'Aubigny with respect to the release of Katherine Evans and Sarah Cheevers from the Inquisition. It was when waiting on that nobleman in reference to this subject that Latey had the conversation which has been already related. Lord D'Aubigny had power and interest in Malta, and most readily listened to Latey's tale of the sufferings endured by the two Friends immured in the Inquisition there. "Some of our people think your friends are mad," he one day remarked, " but I entertain a very different opinion."

It was in the year 1658 that Katherine Evans and Sarah Cheevers sailed from London to Leghorn, on the perilous mission of propagating the views of Friends in some of the darker regions of the world. At Leghorn they distributed various books, and had daily conversations with people of all ranks, who perhaps thought that what two women had ventured so far to say must be worth the hearing. Thence they took passage for Alexandria, but the captain of the vessel put in at Malta, and as they were approaching the island Katherine Evans, exclaimed, "O, we have a dreadful cup to drink at that place!" But as they sailed into the harbour the fear of man was taken from her, and, whilst looking at the people who were standing on the walls, she said in her heart, "Shall ye destroy us! If we give up to the Lord He is sufficient to deliver us out of your hands." When the English Consul had seen some of their books, he told them of the Inquisition, probably wishing to warn them of the danger of their position; at the same time he invited them to his house, where they remained for three months. Here they received many callers, several of whom were affected as they listened to the solemn words of exhortation. At the request of the Governor's sister, they visited her in her convent, conversing with the nuns and giving them books. Once, when in a Roman Catholic chapel whilst the service was being conducted, Katherine Evans knelt in the midst of the congregation, and, with her back towards the high altar, lifted her voice in prayer. The priest seemed to be conscious of the heavenly influence pervading her petitions, for, instead of seeming shocked at such an unusual act, he laid aside his surplice and fell on his knees by her.

During their stay at the Consul's they were frequently examined by the Inquisitors, who, not daring to take them from his house without his leave, succeeded in obtaining it by the combined effect of flattery, bribery, and threats. We cannot wonder that his guests reminded him that Pilate would willingly do the Jews a pleasure—yet wash his hands in innocency. When the Chief Inquisitor told them they must retract the views which they had avowed, or take the consequences of a refusal to do so, they declined any recantation, adding, "Then God's will be done!" They were confined in a stiflingly hot room, which had only two small apertures for the admission of light and air.

In the course of a further examination, Katherine Evans was asked whether she owned that Christ had died at Jerusalem; she answered, "We own the same Christ and no other;" and to the inquiry what she would have done had she reached Alexandria, she replied, "The will of God: if the Lord had opened my mouth, I should call people to repentance, and declare to them the day of the Lord." They were told that they should be set free if they would take the Holy Sacrament, otherwise the Pope would not release them for millions of gold, and they would lose soul and body too. "The Lord," they answered, "hath provided for our souls, and our bodies are freely given up to serve Him." When a friar said, "If we do not eat the flesh and drink the blood of the Son of God we have no life in us,"—they replied, "The flesh and blood of Christ is spiritual, and *we feed upon it daily*, for that which is begotten of God in us can no more live without spiritual food than our temporal bodies can live without temporal food." To the remark that the Pope, being Christ's vicar, acted for the good of their souls, they responded with a holy confidence, "The Lord hath not committed the charge of our souls to the Pope nor to you; for He hath taken them into His own possession. Glory be to His name for ever!"

They were next removed to a room where the heat was so intense that it was thought they could not long survive it, for it parched their skin, caused their hair to fall off, and made them faint away; whilst the closeness of the apartment frequently compelled them to rise from their bed and lie down on the floor, in the hope of inhaling any breath of air that might find entrance under the door. In addition to these sufferings they were so violently stung by gnats that their faces became swollen as with small-pox. Even the friars—one would think—might have deemed it superfluous to offer them the use of a scourge of small cord with which they said they were in the habit of whipping themselves until the blood came. But the prisoners wisely and naïvely answered that their scourge could not reach the devil that sat upon the heart.

As the Inquisition-house was being altered it was often visited by citizens of the higher class, whom, strange to say, Katherine Evans and Sarah Cheevers were allowed to address on religious subjects; and the magistrates and chief Inquisitor, instead of being indignant at this, gave orders that they should be supplied with writing materials in order to communicate with their friends; indeed had it not been for the strong opposition of the monks they would probably have been released. At one time, when in daily expectation of being burnt, Katherine Evans dreamt that she saw a beautiful child sitting above a fire, playing, whilst the flames ascended around it. She was about to withdraw it from its apparent peril, when One who had been sitting near, and whom she took to be the Son of God, bade her let it alone; and then she saw that a guardian angel was present, and that the child was wholly unhurt. On awaking, she told her companion not to fear, for they also were surrounded by the heavenly host.

2 F

Soon the solace of mutual companionship was denied them, a parting which they felt as a greater trial than death. For nearly a year they were kept in separate rooms; but

> "Though evil hearts together leaguing
> May do the righteous wrong;
> And cruel craft, with force intriguing
> Feel confidently strong;
> We know, if but the Saviour's story,
> With heart of faith we read,
> That God through sufferings unto glory,
> Salvation's sons will lead."

Although they could not—as they write—"expect a drop of mercy, favour, or refreshment, but what the Lord did distil from His living presence," they were permitted not only to "behold the brightness of His glory," but also to see their distant brethren and sisters in the light of Jesus, and feel the benefit of their prayers, whilst they "were refreshed in all the faithful-hearted, and felt the issues of love and life which did stream from the hearts of those that were wholly joined to the Fountain." Thus were they borne up by God, and who can assert that their mission was a vain one? "The whole mystery of iniquity," they add, "is at its height, and is upheld by a law that, upon pain of death, none must speak against it, nor walk contrary to it. But, praises be to our God, He carried us forth to declare against it daily!" The prison in which Katherine Evans was confined being near the street, she often addressed the passers-by, particularly when going and returning to their chapel.

In one of her letters she writes as follows:—

"For the hands of John Evans, my right dear and precious husband, with my tender-hearted children, who are more dear and precious to me than the apple of my eye. Most dear and faithful husband, friend, and brother, begotten of my eternal Father, of the immortal seed of the covenant of light, life, and blessedness, I have unity and fellowship with thee day and night, to my great refreshment and continual comfort. Praises, praises be given to our God for evermore, who hath joined us together in that which neither sea nor land can separate ! . . . Oh, the endless love of God, who is an everlasting fountain of all-living refreshment, whose crystal streams never cease running to every thirsty soul that breatheth after the springs of life and salvation ! . . . Oh, the raptures the glorious, bright, shining countenance of our Lord God, who is our fulness in emptiness, our health in sickness, our life in death, our joy in sorrow, our peace in disquietness, our praise in heaviness, our power in all necessities. He is a full God unto us, *and to all that can trust Him*. He hath emptied us of ourselves, and hath wholly built us upon the sure foundation—the Rock of Ages, Jesus Christ. . . . I do believe we shall see your faces again with joy.—K. E."

One more testimony is this to the all-sufficiency of the grace of God—to those who take hold of His Covenant—and a testimony given at a time when we might naturally imagine that extreme physical pain and oppression would have forbidden fulness of joy, however powerless they might be to shake the confidence of faith. But as the sufferings of the prisoners abounded, so—it is manifest—their consolations abounded also. " Oh, the love of the Lord to my soul ! " writes Sarah Cheevers, " My tongue cannot express, neither hath it entered into the heart of man to conceive of the things that God hath laid up for them that fear Him. I cannot by pen or paper set forth the large love of God in fulfilling His gracious promises to me in the wilderness." In the same letter she urges her husband and children to " embrace God's love in making His truth so clearly manifest among you, by the messengers of Christ, who preached to you the word of God in season and out of season, directing you where you may find your Saviour to purge and cleanse you from your sins and to reconcile you to His Father." To her friends in Ireland she writes :—"My life is given up to the service of the Lord. Bonds, chains, bolts, irons, double-doors, death itself, are too little for the testimony of Jesus."

When one of the friars told Katherine Evans that he would load her with heavy chains, she answered that whatever he did to her he could not separate her from the love of God in Christ Jesus; and when he thereupon added that he would give her to the devil, she replied, "I do not fear all the devils in hell; the Lord is my Keeper." When told they had not the true faith, she answered, "By *faith* we stand. Dost thou think it is by *our* power and holiness we are kept from sin?" and in response to the accusation of pride she added, "We can glory in the Lord; we were children of wrath, but the Lord has quickened us by the living word of His grace, and hath washed, cleansed, and sanctified us in soul and spirit, in part, according to our measures; and we do press forwards towards that which is perfect." So entire was the resignation granted her that when she one day felt the spirit of prayer in an unusual degree, whilst the language applied to her soul was, "Ask what thou wilt, and I will grant it thee," she could only crave that which would be for the glory of God, whether bondage or liberty, life or death.

After their imprisonment had lasted about three years, earnest efforts for their liberation were made by a Friend named Daniel Baker, who spent more than three weeks on the island, visited them repeatedly at the risk of his life, supplied some of their wants, and took charge of several letters to their English Friends. In vain he pleaded with the Inquisitor on their behalf, although he offered, first his liberty, and then his life, in exchange for their release. When allowed to have an interview with them, through the prison-grates, he thus addressed them: "The whole body of God's elect, right dearly beloved, own your testimony, and ye are a sweet savour unto the Lord and His people." And these were seasonable words of cheer, for one of the sufferers answered that it was a sorrow to them that they could not be "more serviceable." Yet surely, to them might Milton's grand line be applied—

"They also serve who only stand and wait."

Their loyalty to their Lord in the midst of sore and solitary suffering must, in its steadfast strength, have been as "a spectacle unto the world, and to angels, and to men." Even their persecutors were constrained to admit that, although they had not the true faith, *they had all virtues*, so manifestly were they preserved by Him for whom they had suffered the loss of all things. "The time is too little," writes Katherine Evans, "for me to disclose the twentieth part of these terrible trials; but whenever we were brought upon any trial the Lord did take away all fear from us, and gave us power and boldness to plead for the truth of the Lord Jesus." Liberty was offered them if they would kiss the cross, but they of course declined it on such conditions.

Before his departure, Daniel Baker was told that they should be released if any one would engage to pay three or four thousand dollars should they ever return to

Malta; otherwise, the Pope's orders were that they should die in prison. But about six months later, after a captivity of nearly four years, their liberation was procured by the mediation of Lord D'Aubigny, to whom, in addition to the urgent and frequent solicitations of Gilbert Latey, George Fox had applied on their behalf. Before they left the Inquisition, when courteous leave was taken of them by the Inquisitor and magistrates, they knelt down and prayed that God would not lay to the charge of these officers what they had done to them. On their arrival in London they visited Gilbert Latey, who accompanied them to the residence of Lord D'Aubigny. During the interview they addressed him on the subjects which lay nearest to their hearts, and at its close added that, " were it in their power, they should be as ready in all love to serve him." " Good women," he answered, " for what kindness I have done you, all that I shall desire of you is that when you pray to God you will remember me in your prayers."

Gilbert Latey was about this time a constant attender at a meeting which had been established, chiefly in consequence of his efforts, in a house at Pall Mall, the home of a Friend named Elizabeth Trott. For a while the company who assembled there were unmolested—a rare circumstance in those days—but at length a justice of the peace, with whom Latey was acquainted, and to whose protection he had appealed, told him that he had been much blamed for his leniency in allowing a meeting to be held so near St. James's Palace, the residence of the Duke of York, and had now received positive orders to disperse it. These orders were soon executed, and Gilbert Latey and another Friend were taken away as prisoners; but, though imprisonment was often his lot, Latey patiently persevered in attending the meeting which after the death of Elizabeth Trott was removed to the Little Almonry, where for more than a hundred years a Friends' Meeting was kept up. One of the two tenants on the premises being the master of a *boys' school*, the Monthly Meeting, with prudent foresight, stipulated that *he* should keep the *windows* in repair.*

In 1665, the year of the Great Plague, although Gilbert Latey had engaged lodgings in the country, he abandoned the idea of leaving the city whilst so many of his brethren were in close confinement, and continued to minister to their necessities. He likewise visited in their own homes many Friends who had been stricken with the terrible pestilence, and for a long while escaped infection; but one day, after sitting in a cold, damp room, he took a severe chill, and was soon afterwards seized with the disease, at his recovery from which many grateful hearts must have rejoiced.

In 1670, after holding several meetings in his native county and during his journey thither, Gilbert Latey went to Kingsbridge, where the Friends were undergoing severe persecution, particularly two young ladies who had lately joined the Society and had been committed to prison by a fiery-tempered magistrate, Justice Bare, for non-attendance at church. As Latey was acquainted with some influential gentlemen of Devon, he determined to make an appeal on their behalf. One of these gentlemen, "a great knight," who, with his

---

* *London Friends' Meetings.*

wife and daughters, gave him a kind and courteous reception, said that he "would do more for Gilbert than for all his friends of his persuasion in the kingdom." Latey entreated him to attend the sessions which were soon to be held, to require that the young prisoners should be brought before the Bench, and to urge the justices to release them. When the sessions took place, this gentleman succeeded in appeasing Justice Bare's indignation, and whilst dining with him and the other magistrates, told them that he had been importuned to use his interest with them for "two fine young women Quakers," imprisoned for not going to church, and begged them to favour him by setting them at liberty. From his position there was little danger of such a request being refused, but he knew there was still a difficulty to be overcome: the Friends would probably feel a conscientious objection to paying the prison fees of an unjust confinement, and might therefore be detained on that ground. So he laid down some money on the table, and said, "We must among ourselves collect as much to give the gaoler as will answer their fees; and, here, I will begin." An account of the liberation of the Friends being sent to Latey, he did not forget to return "his humble acknowledgment to the knight."

Before leaving Cornwall Gilbert Latey had learnt, by letters from his London friends, that steps had been taken towards pulling down Horselydown Meetinghouse, and that Sir John Robinson, the Governor of the Tower, had given similar orders for that at Ratcliff; and finally he was informed that Wheeler Street Meeting-house, the title of which he owned, was doomed to like destruction. Sir John Robinson, a bitter persecutor of Friends, was a very formidable enemy, and had been in the habit of sending scores of the quiet Wheeler Street worshippers to the "New Prison," the gaoler of which fully carried out the Governor's wishes by his cruel treatment of the captives; not content with severely beating and half-starving them, he induced the felons under his care to rob them of the food which their friends brought them.

Latey made up his mind that this meeting-house should not share the fate of the others from any timidity with respect to defending the title of it. On his return to London he bade his attorney make a formal lease of the premises, and let them to a poor Friend. This being accomplished, he felt himself quite ready to face the Governor, who asked him how he dared own any meeting-house contrary to the King's laws. To this he answered that he had owned it before such a law was in existence. "I find you are a pretty fellow," said Sir John—" pray who lives in the meeting-house?" "My tenant," said Latey. "Your tenant! What is your tenant?" exclaimed the astonished Governor. "One that I have thought good to grant a lease to," was the quiet answer. The Governor finding himself fairly matched, turned to a Friend, who had previously had an interview with him, and said, "I think you have now fitted me. You have brought a fellow to the purpose; had your friends been all as wise as this fellow, you might have had your other meeting-houses!" This hint, given on the impulse of the moment, was taken full advantage of.

In company with George Whitehead, Gilbert Latey made many appeals, and often with success, to Charles

II., James II., and William III., for the persecuted Friends; a service in which they were frequently cheered by their consciousness of the Lord's help. In 1683 they went to Hampton Court, in order to lay before King Charles the case of sixty-three Friends of Norwich, who were suffering a cruel imprisonment for the offence of assembling for Divine worship. They met the King in the park and, at their entreaty, he stood still and readily gave heed to their complaint. He then entered into conversation with them, and, amongst other remarks, said, "You will not pull off your hats, and what have you to say for that?" "If to any mortal," was Gilbert Latey's answer, "then to the King in the first place; but it is a matter of conscience, and we only do it when we approach the Lord in prayer."* "I admire to see such wise men Quakers," observed Charles, who was in a gracious mood. The unusual clemency granted the Friends at the next assizes at Norwich, when they were released and not charged with prison fees, was, with good ground, supposed to be the result of this appeal.

Whilst deeply interesting himself in thus publicly aiding his distressed brethren, Gilbert Latey did not overlook more private cases of sorrow; to the poor, the

---

* "In the reign of Charles II., writes Hepworth Dixon, " men wore their hats in house and church as well as in the street and park. Men sat at meals in felt, and listened to a play in felt. ' I got a strange cold in my head,' wrote Pepys, ' by flinging off my hat at dinner.' Every one ate covered. . . . A preacher mounted to the pulpit in his hat: the audience wore their hats, and only doffed them at the name of God. . . . Hat lifting therefore was a sign of a depraved and foreign fashion recently brought into England from abroad. All sober men put on their hats, while wits and foplings carried them in their hands."

bereaved, and the sick, he was ever a friend in need. One day when he was receiving a business order from Lady Sawkell at her residence, her husband, who was accustomed to treat him with kindness and familiarity, entered the room, and asked him what meeting he usually attended. He replied that he sometimes went to one and sometimes to another. Sir William Sawkell, who had a command in a regiment of horse, then said, "The reason I ask is because I have had orders to break up a meeting of your people at Hammersmith next Sunday from so high a hand that I dare not omit executing them, and therefore I speak in kindness to you, that if at any time you go thither, you may refrain coming that day." On hearing this Latey at once felt that it would be right for him to go to Hammersmith, notwithstanding this warning, and so he told Sir William as he left his house. Commissioned by his Lord, and upheld by His protecting presence, he was powerfully engaged in ministry when the troopers entered Hammersmith Meeting. For some time they stood still, silently listening to his earnest words; but after a while one of them exclaimed, whilst suiting the action to the word—"This man will never have done, let us pull him down." "Let your officer know that I am here, and my name is Gilbert Latey," he said. The hale and jovial commander entered trembling, and did not speak at once; but, when somewhat less agitated, said, "Latey, did I not tell you that I was commanded to be here to-day?" "And did not I also tell thee I was commanded by a greater than thou, that I must be here also?" "Go, get thee gone about thy business," answered Sir William; "I will take care concerning the rest here met." "If thou hast any respect for me," was Latey's response, "then discharge all the rest, and let me be thy prisoner." This request was acceded to, and resulted in his being fined, whilst some who had been present were distrained upon. But Latey's repeated entreaties that others might not suffer in consequence of anything he had said or done were given heed to, and the goods were ultimately returned to their lawful owners. So ready was he to take on himself the penalties intended for his friends, that at one time there were warrants out against him for several hundred pounds.

His ministry, which was much blessed, was chiefly confined to London and its vicinity, where it was his wont to go to various meetings as his mind was attracted to them.* When at Exeter, in 1679, he solicited an interview with Bishop Lamplugh, whom he wished to thank for the frequent favours he had freely bestowed on the Friends residing in his diocese, sometimes in consequence of representations made him by Gilbert Latey. A warm welcome awaited him at the palace, where the Bishop took him in his arms and blessed him, and then, leading him into a private room, said, "All must not know how well you and I love one another. What wine shall I give you?" To this Latey replied that he had given his love, which was better than wine,—and then at his host's request, took a seat by his side. In a letter to Latey Dr. Lamplugh

---

* He would have united in the sentiment lately expressed by an American minister, on the great desirability of Friends attending different meetings in their own neighbourhood, " without waiting for any appointment but the appointment of the Holy Spirit."

remarks: "I never was nor will be for persecution, but shall endeavour that by any amicable way such as have erred may be brought into the way of truth, and that we may all enjoy one another in heaven. . . . God Almighty bless you: I am your true loving friend, Thomas *Exon*."

When James II. ascended the throne fourteen hundred and sixty Friends were confined in the prisons of England and Wales, in the damp and noisome dungeons of which many had already died. Husbands had been parted from wives, parents from children, and whole families deprived of the means of support. Gilbert Latey shared in George Whitehead's unwearied efforts and prayers for their relief; and the health of both was injured by the mental strain and physical fatigue incurred in obtaining warrants and getting them executed. At length the former, though scarcely able to get into a carriage, left his wife and children, with the hope of gaining some invigoration from country air; but, after only a week's rest, a letter from George Whitehead reached him stating that he was himself too ill to leave the house, and urging him to return to town if possible. He lifted his heart to the Lord for strength for the service which lay before him, went back to London, and attended at the "Pipe Office" until the matter was satisfactorily settled, resulting in the liberation of a great number of Friends. It was also at the solicitation of Whitehead and Latey that the meeting-houses at the Park, Southwark, and at the Savoy, in the Strand, were restored to Friends by the King, after being used as guard-houses; the former had been greatly damaged by the soldiers, who had carried off wainscotting, benches, doors, and casements; and then cut down and burnt the surrounding trees.

Latey's own dwelling was on the same premises as the Savoy Meeting-house, which stood in a paved yard, and was accessible through a passage which lay underneath his house, and terminated in a stone staircase. Mary Latey writes of how " her dear and well-beloved husband was given up in perilous times of sufferings, a constant testimony-bearer to the way of the Lord and His power, which was felt to attend His people in their meetings, even when they were kept without doors in the wet and cold, where he often stood, bearing witness to the truth and way of the Lord. In all which," she adds, " I never did persuade, or dared desire him either to go to this meeting or not to go to that, but always left him his freedom to go where his Lord did order him, in which I had, and still have, great peace."

One day Gilbert Latey met with George Whitehead and William Penn at Whitehall, and was asked to go with them to wait on the King. He did not at once fall in with the proposal, but presently felt it would be right to say a few words to King James, with whom they had an almost private interview. After his friends had addressed him, Gilbert Latey said that they wished to " humbly acknowledge " the kindness which he had manifested to them as a people in their time of great affliction. " I truly desire," he added, " that God may show the King mercy and favour in the time of his trouble and sore distress." James merely replied, " I thank you ; " but a considerable time afterwards, when in Ireland, he requested a Friend to give the following message to Latey, " Tell him, the words he spake to me

I shall never forget; the one part of them is come, and I pray God the other may also come to pass." When Latey uttered them he was wholly unaware that a political crisis was at hand.

In 1694, encouraged by the Meeting for Sufferings, Gilbert Latey and some other Friends laid before William III. the severity of suffering incurred by their brethren or themselves in consequence of their scruple with reference to oaths. They reminded him of how leniently some of his family had dealt with the Mennonites under similar circumstances, and begged that the English Friends " might partake of his royal favour." Cheered by his answer, they also applied to some of the Ministers of State, and leading members of the House of Commons; and even eminent Peers and Commoners suggested that they should present a petition on the subject. At every reading the House divided on the Bill, and a large number, who were usually inclined to be very hard upon Dissenters, gave it their support.

Great surprise was awakened by this, which one nobleman expressed to Latey. At the same time there were other members who violently opposed the measure, and one of these, a very influential man, when the Bill was about to be read for the last time, went out to gather together as many members as might be, from the Court of Requests and elsewhere, in order to induce them to accompany him to the House, and vote against it. But, when on the point of re-entering with his recruits, he found that all his pains would be unavailing, for he was just too late to take part in the division; the door was shut, and the order that the lobby should be cleared had been given. The Friends, whose fervent prayers had that day ascended for the aid of the Almighty, could but recognise His hand in this circumstance; nor did their faith fail during the long months that elapsed from the time of their first application to the King, to the day when the Bill finally passed the House of Lords. The extreme importance attached by Friends to this measure, the prayerfulness and intense earnestness with which they carried it to a successful issue, are ample proof of the vast amount of suffering they had endured in consequence of their steadfast adherence to a religious conviction.

In his old age, Gilbert Latey also occasionally applied to Queen Anne on behalf of his oppressed brethren. It was said of him by a contemporary—well able from his own position to make the estimate—that " of all the men among Friends he ever knew or heard of, he never followed a man that had a sweeter character than Gilbert Latey at Court." In addition to his interviews with royalty, he had many of a similar kind with dukes, marquises, earls, barons, and bishops. At such seasons it was his wont to give himself up to God's guidance; and he advised any who might be called to a like service " to feel the love of God in their hearts, and in that, and in great humility, to make their approaches, keeping to the anointing spoken of in 1 John ii. 27.

As his strength declined he spent much time in the country. His spiritual vigour was undiminished, and was especially conspicuous when, a few months before his death, he one day preached in Hammersmith Meeting what proved to be his last sermon. It would seem that no other minister was present, and a large company had assembled, whom he was enabled to address for nearly an hour with remarkable power and unction, inviting all to come to God "in and through the Lord Jesus Christ, the way and only means to restore man into the image and favour of God."

The night before his death he earnestly spoke to those around him—as if he had been in a meeting—of love and tenderness, and of how God would bless such as were found therein. The following day he did not leave his chamber, but was able to speak freely to his friends. "There is no condemnation to them that are in Christ Jesus," he said; "He is the lifter-up of my head, He is my strength and great salvation." He died in 1705, in his seventy-ninth year. He had been very solicitous for the best welfare of his children—eleven in number—only two of whom outlived an early youth. "I believe," writes his widow, "no woman ever parted with a better husband, nor children with a more tender father or more sincere man. It is the Lord's will to remove him, and in that I endeavour and desire to be content."

The same spirit that animated Gilbert Latey and upheld Katherine Evans and Sarah Cheevers may be manifested in very quiet lives, when placed at the Divine disposal. By the man of business who, strictly upright and unselfish, scorns to substitute any merely conventional standard of trade morality for the law of Christ, and who uses his leisure with conscientious care; by the earnest student who dedicates his cultivated intellect to the service of its Almighty Giver; by the patient mother ever striving to train her children for heaven, and consequently for good lives on earth; by the young and joyous freely yielding the fresh

2 G

fragrance of their lives to the Lord who died for them; by the chronic invalid animated to many small services by love and loyalty to Him who once said, "She hath done what she could;" by unmurmuring sufferers, bearing a secret cross, who live the life they now live by faith in the Son of God, with an absolutely unwavering trust in His love, and a calm certainty that what they know not now of the needs-be for His dealings with them, they shall know hereafter; by all and any who, having an intense and practical conviction that "the things which are seen are temporal, but the things which are not seen are eternal," and that

> " The world we cannot see, with that we view
> Is alway blending "—

can say, in the words of George Herbert, "*I am but finite, yet Thine infinitely.*"

GEORGE WHITEHEAD.

"... a vast, all-mastering, all-possessing faith answering all the ends of righteousness, nay, it is righteousness. ... The faith itself sweeps to the outermost skirts of conduct, and infuses its devotion into every act and feeling."—MUNGER.

GEORGE WHITEHEAD.

> "No mortal doth know
> What He can bestow,
> What light, strength and comfort do after Him go;
> So onward I'll move,
> And but Christ above,
> None guesses how wondrous the journey will prove."
> OLD HYMN.

"SIXTY blessed years of active service for his Lord." Thus spoke a minister of the Society of Friends in reference to George Whitehead. Addressing himself especially to his younger hearers, he queried, "Who were the chief workers in Apostolic times, and in the early days of our Society? Not the old, but the young. And why should it not be so now?"

George Whitehead was one of the ministers, more than sixty in number, to whom George Fox thus alludes under date of 1654:—"About this time did the Lord move upon the spirits of many whom He had raised up, to travel in the service of the Gospel." Upheld "not by might nor by power," but by the Spirit of the Lord, they went forth, and did His bidding, and the natural consequences of such heaven-commissioned labours ensued. Of many of their number it might be said—as Francis Howgill did say of Edward Burrough—"*his very strength was bended after God;*" men who could thank Him for having bestowed on them not only loyal hearts and willing hands, but also the good gifts of youthful vigour and manly strength, wherewith steadfastly to uphold and display the banner of the Captain of their salvation. Surely in this our day there is no less need of such standard-bearers for the army of the Lord of Hosts, who—

> "Saved by a Divine alliance
> From terror of defeat,"

would with unfaltering step and undaunted spirit follow Him who is going forth *now*, "conquering and to conquer," and "of the increase of whose government and peace there shall be no end."

George Whitehead was born in the parish of Orton, Westmoreland, about the year 1636, and his heart had in early life been drawn to seek after God, though such longings were too often quenched whilst he indulged himself in unsatisfying worldly pleasures. In reference to his state at the age of fourteen, after writing of his dissatisfaction with the teaching of the Presbyterians, he says:—"Being at a loss in my spirit for what I sometimes secretly desired, I was as one bewildered, and wandered, further, seeking among other people who had some higher and more refined notions concerning Spiritual gifts." Soon he hears of a people called Quakers, towards whom he feels so much attracted as even "to contend for them and their principles," before being present at any of their meetings. After a while, however, he attended one, which was held at the house of a Captain Ward, of Sunny-Bank, near Kendal. Here, although interested in the ministry of a Friend named Thomas Arcy, he was chiefly impressed by what he terms "the great work of the power of the Lord in the meeting, breaking the heart of divers into great sorrow."

One young girl in the bitterness of her grief left the meeting, and was followed by George Whitehead, who found her sitting on the ground, with her face towards it, so regardless of everything but her own overwhelming sense of sinfulness that she was crying out, "Lord, make me clean!" This circumstance reached his heart more effectually than any sermon he had ever heard; for he believed that the distress he had seen that morning was effected by the Spirit of God, and that it was the forerunner of pardon, regeneration and sanctification through Christ—as in many cases it proved to be.

His belief that the Lord was about to raise up a people to worship Him in spirit and in truth grew stronger; and as it did so, notwithstanding the bitter speeches of his kindred, he regularly attended the meetings at Sedbergh and Grayrigg, and soon identified himself with Friends, whose conversation and fellowship were very congenial to him. Meanwhile he was learning, from no human teacher, that "without being converted as well as convinced," he could not enter into the Kingdom of God. Fervent also were his yearnings to be "truly renewed in the spirit of his mind, and therein joined to the Lord;" and whilst willingly enduring His Fatherly chastening, his heart was melted by the realisation of His mercy through Christ.

In the meetings which George Whitehead attended from his sixteenth to his eighteenth year there was but little preaching, indeed they were often held in silence; but it must have been a "*living* silence," for he writes of "many blessed and comfortable seasons of refreshment from the presence of our Heavenly Father;" and it was in these and similar meetings in the North, that the Lord was raising up a noble band, whose influence should soon be felt throughout the length and breadth of the land. "Waiting in true silence upon Him," writes George Whitehead, "and eyeing His inward appearance in spirit, and the work of His power in us, we came truly to feel our strength renewed in living faith, true love, and holy zeal for His name. O! thus keeping silence before the Lord, and thus drawing near to Him, is the way for renewing our strength, and to be His ministers to speak to others only what He first speaks to us." Already, to the comfort of his friends, he occasionally expressed a few words in these meetings. At the same time, having yielded himself to the control and teaching of Christ, he was led on, surely if slowly, towards "the victory over Satan." With the firm belief that God will reveal to the seeking soul — in His own good time — the mystery of "Christ in us the hope of glory," he was constrained to wait in faith for this revelation, by which he might experience more and more of "the power and coming of Christ in Spirit, as his Sanctifier, Teacher, and Guide."

After striving to influence for good those amongst whom he dwelt, when in his eighteenth year a weighty concern, he says, came on him to travel Southwards. A young friend of his offered to bear him company, and they set out on foot in the direction of York. In the course of this journey his heart was cheered by meeting with George Fox, Alexander Parker, John Whitehead, and also Richard Hubberthorn, whom he visited in Norwich Castle, where he was confined in a cell on a cross-wall. At Diss, George Whitehead met with

William Barber, a man of influential position and a captain in the army, who was deeply affected during a religious interview which Whitehead had with himself and some others. "Truth was near in him," writes George Whitehead, "and I felt him near it, and my heart was open and tender towards him in the love of Christ." Both his wife and himself became Friends, and patiently bore the long trial of his twenty years' imprisonment in Norwich Castle, the result chiefly of the malice borne him by an elderly clergyman in consequence of his scruples with respect to the payment of tithes. On his return to Norwich, George Whitehead soon found himself an inmate of the city gaol, where he suffered much from cold during a confinement of eight weeks. Whilst he was riding out of the town of Repham, after holding a meeting there, he thought it right to address the people in the streets; as they violently stoned him, he could not at first keep his horse sufficiently still for his purpose, but when they grew calmer, he "cleared his conscience" to them, and felt that the presence of the Lord kept him from bodily injury.

George Whitehead held several meetings in a private house at Wymondham, one of which was attended by a Captain John Lawrence, who was so much impressed as to ask Whitehead to hold a meeting at Wramplingham, an invitation which the latter gladly accepted. Three clergymen, who greatly despised his youth, were present in order to oppose him; but they found that the boyish preacher, though answering them in the spirit of meekness, was invested with an authority which they could not withstand; for ere this he had learnt that "the more low he was in himself, the more God would manifest His power, and bless his service." After this meeting, the wife of one of the clergymen said to a sister-in-law of John Lawrence, in allusion to a playful remark which that lady had previously made, "Now Mrs. Bedwell, I know you will be of the Quaker's side, for you said you would be for the strongest." This surmise was a correct one, and from Whitehead we learn that Elizabeth Bedwell "continued a faithful innocent Friend until death;" and also that Captain Lawrence, and many members of his family, as well as several others, were "convinced of the Truth." Notwithstanding the persecution which befell him Captain Lawrence steadfastly stood his ground, and there were many who were led by the example of his family and himself to seek for Christ as their Saviour, their Teacher and their High Priest. He had been a member of an Independent congregation, the pastor and elders of which now desired to excommunicate him; and when in the following year they summoned him to a meeting held in a church at Norwich, he was accompanied thither by George Whitehead.

After John Lawrence had explained his reasons for separating from them, George Whitehead arose to address the large company who had assembled, but soon found himself on the ground, held down in a pew, whence he was dragged out of the church and consigned to the mercies of the clamorous mob, who were waiting to lay violent hands on the young preacher, whom they pulled through the Market-place and streets, and sometimes threw down on the stones. Soon they reached one of the city gates, near which was the residence of a certain

Lady Hubbard; just at that moment, although still pursued by the rabble, he could choose whether to go towards her house, or to leave the city by the road which lead to Wramplingham—a choice which filled him with perplexity, for he was well aware that his life was in imminent peril. But in the midst of the bewildering tumult he lifted his heart to the Lord, asking Him to grant him His guidance;—a prayer which was answered by the idea which at once arose in his mind that, if he must needs lose his life, his death would be more likely to tend to the glory of God within the city. To whatever might be His will he abandoned himself; and then turned to ascend the hill on the summit of which the mansion stood. The shouting of the infuriated crowd made Lady Hubbard's chaplain and most of the family come out to discover the cause of so great an uproar. One would hardly think it an appropriate time for a theological discussion, yet the chaplain engaged George Whitehead in one of half-an-hour's duration, while his persecutors formed a circle around them. When this conversation was ended a soldier came up to Whitehead and offered to accompany him to his lodgings, whither he safely guarded him, whilst with his hand laid on his sword he ordered the crowd to make way. Twenty-five years later, when a prisoner in Norwich Castle, George Whitehead met with a friend from Lynn, named Robert Turner, whom, it would seem, he had previously known by report, and, to his astonishment, found in him his magnanimous rescuer from the rabble. Notwithstanding the cruelties imposed on imprisoned Friends, often with flagrant criminals for their companions, it is not strange that George Whitehead should say that in those days prisons were as sanctuaries to them from the fury of the mob. Ignorant and undisciplined as the latter were, with passions, if suppressed, ready to burst into flames at any moment, we may well believe that less guilt rested upon them than upon the cultivated clergy and magistrates who, well knowing what consequences would ensue, deliberately laid the match to such materials.

Much blessing rested on these early labours of George Whitehead, and in his old age he writes that it was still a very memorable matter to him that by "preaching livingly *the New Covenant, the Word nigh to people in their hearts, yea, the Gospel of the free grace and love of God to mankind*, many were effectually convinced and persuaded of the blessed ever-living truth as it is in Christ Jesus. And how diligent," he continues, "were many in those days, in going many miles to Friends' meetings, both ancient and young, men and women, maidens and children! What love, what brokenness and tenderness would be in meetings in those days of their first love and espousals unto Christ Jesus in His light, life, and spirit."

After the release of Richard Hubberthorn, George Whitehead and he held some meetings in Norfolk. One of those who cast in his lot with Friends from that part of England was William Bennet, who afterwards advocated his Redeemer's cause by his holy life and conversation, his ministry, and his patient endurance of much and severe persecution. Tribulation had taught him, like many others, how to comfort the sorrowful. In an Epistle to Friends, dated from Bury Common Gaol, he writes:—
"And the Lord comfort the mourning ones among you,

that *those who have lain mourning in the pits of distrust, fears, doubtings, carnal reasonings, may mount over all upon the wings of Faith,* and flow to the goodness of the Lord, and eat of His house, and drink of the river of His pleasures, and be satisfied; and *bless, praise, and magnify the Lord in the land of the living."* Gough writes :—" He was carried forth in meetings in more than ordinary manner, and was a blessed instrument to many, in turning them to God."

At Charfield, near Woodbridge, George Whitehead had a remarkable meeting in an orchard, with a slippery stool for his pulpit; a very large and varied crowd had surrounded him, amongst whom, he believed, were not a few true seekers after God. Whilst the people were eagerly waiting for His words, he was waiting upon the Lord, " for His power to arise ;" nor did he wait in vain. Wonderful ability was given him "to preach the everlasting Gospel, in the Name and Power of our Lord Jesus Christ," for the space of nearly five hours. And the truths declared found an entrance into many hearts as an effectual message from the Lord. Whilst George Whitehead was speaking a Baptist preacher expressed disapproval of the views held by Friends with respect to the ordinances. " I gave answer to him in the spirit of meekness," says George Whitehead, "being called into a spiritual ministry in order to bring people out of shadows to the substance; .... nor to rest only in a literal knowledge of Christ, but that they might *know Him livingly and inwardly after the Spirit."* The Baptist soon ceased to argue, and so deep was the impression made on his mind that, after a while, he exchanged his position as the leader of a Baptist congregation for that of a learner of the Lord in a Friends' meeting: joining the Society, he became in later years an earnest minister, striving to bring his hearers to a true knowledge of Christ and His spiritual baptism. In both Norfolk and Suffolk many meetings were before long established.

Whilst at Colchester, George Whitehead visited James Parnel, who was imprisoned in the castle, and who, although younger than his friend, had preached the Gospel to thousands in that town, fearlessly shaking the sandy foundation on which too many were standing. "Profession and talk of religion and Church," writes George Whitehead, "did greatly abound in those days; . . . summer shows of religion which would not endure a stormy winter." James Parnel was comforted by his visit, and then the two young men, both under twenty years of age, parted probably not to meet again on earth; the one soon to obtain a martyr's crown; the other to labour on for nearly seventy years more, glorifying God alike in willing service and patient suffering; yet each led by a *right* way to a city of habitation,—that way in which, whether rough or smooth, the sons of God* would elect to walk, because, whether always realising the comfort of His presence or not, they know that He is ever with them there.

At Bures, George Whitehead and a Friend named Harwood, who was then travelling with him, were arrested and taken before a justice of the peace. Although quite unable to charge them with breaking the law, he

---

* "*Son* of God, applied to a Christian, signifies one born of God, in the deepest relation to Him, and hence a partaker of His nature."—*Alford.*

committed them to the gaol at Bury St. Edmund's, there for a period of two or three months to await the sessions, at which they were tried as common disturbers of the peace. This judge was himself their accuser in spite of his position on the bench, and found it expedient to threaten the gaoler with a fine of forty shillings if he did not silence the prisoners should they speak in self-defence. An accommodating jury brought in a verdict of Guilty, and a fine of twenty nobles each was imposed on the Friends. This they refused to pay, on the ground that such payment would imply an acknowledgment of guilt; so they were sent back to prison, where, with some other Friends, they suffered cruelly during a year's captivity. They were released by an order from Oliver Cromwell, to whom application had been made, especially by a gentlewoman of his household. This lady had been convinced of the principles of Friends during Francis Howgill's visit to the Protector, and had afterwards joined the Society. "The place was sanctified to us," says George Whitehead, after stating that they were confined with felons in the common ward which bore a close resemblance to a noisome dungeon. Here they were kicked and wounded by one of their drunken companions, who took advantage of the fact that they would not retaliate, although so well fitted by youthful strength and spirit to do so. "But," Whitehead writes—"We esteemed it greater valour, and more Christian, patiently to suffer such injuries for Christ, than to fight for Him or avenge ourselves;" a triumph of grace greater than the taking of a city. So violently were they often struck by some of their fellow-prisoners, or by the gaoler, that the blood gushed from their mouths and noses; and once they were confined for nearly four hours in a dark and loathsome dungeon, where, as was often their wont, they sang praises to the Lord, " in the sweet enjoyment and living sense of His glorious presence." During this long imprisonment their health did not materially suffer. " The Lord by His power," writes George Whitehead, " so sanctified the confinement to me, that I had great peace, comfort, and sweet solace; and was sometimes transported and wrapt up in spirit as if in a pleasant field, having the fragrant scent and sweet smell of flowers and things growing therein: though I was not in an ecstasy or trance, my senses being affected therewith." The consolation freely and graciously granted in that time of great trial could never have been forgotten; and was perhaps given him not only for present aid, but also as an earnest of sufficient grace for every future need.

A sharp ordeal was near at hand. After " very good service" in London, Essex, etc., George Whitehead appointed a meeting at the house of a Friend who lived at Nayland, in Suffolk, and who, before the meeting began, came to him weeping with the news that some vicious men of that town threatened to kill him if he carried out his intention. They would have been greatly astonished had they seen the calmness with which he received this menace; for his was a courage which, bestowed by Christ, could only be understood by those who knew its source. " I pitied the man," he writes, " and told him I did not fear them, and would not disappoint the meeting." But, lest the house should be pulled down, the large congregation adjourned to a meadow, where they remained for nearly three hours, and George Whitehead "had a good and full opportunity to declare and demonstrate the living Truth with power and dominion given of God, whose power was over all."

When holding another meeting at Nayland, a few weeks later, George Whitehead was violently arrested and taken—as he says—to his "old adversary," the justice who had previously acted with extreme unfairness. Whilst waiting in his hall Whitehead silently prayed that, if it were in accordance with the will of God, he might not undergo another imprisonment in the gaol at Bury St. Edmunds; this prayer was answered, and the belief given him that it was not by loss of liberty, but by stripes, that he was now to suffer. His comment on this is an illustration of what has been called, "the marvellousness and utter unnaturalness of the new creature." "Whereupon I was greatly refreshed, strengthened, and given up in the will of the Lord patiently to endure that punishment, . . . it being for Christ's sake, and His gospel truth; wherein I had great peace and strong consolation in Him." A warrant was drawn up sentencing him to be whipped on the following day "till his body be bloody." That night, lodging at a public-house, he "rested quietly in much peace." He bore the punishment, "by the Lord's power," not only with patience, but with praise and rejoicing, although it was inflicted with such cruelty as to make some of the numerous bystanders weep, whilst others cried out to the constable to desist. As might be expected, the people of that district afterwards flocked together to hear him; the hearts of many were effectually reached, and the truths which he was commissioned to preach were more widely sown; so that, to quote his own words, "the dark wrath of man turned to the praise of God." He found himself especially called to labour in that part of the country which had been the scene of his persecution, and did so unmoved by threats of branding and hanging. His visits also to some of the Midland counties were attended with blessed effects; for he writes: "The Word of Life being plenteously in my heart and ministry, enabled me by His power largely to preach, and greatly assisted me in the defence of the Gospel of our blessed Lord Jesus Christ."

In the midst of these labours he was laid low by a dangerous fever; but one night when it was at its height, he was revived by the clear sense given him, that the Lord would raise him up to continue to labour for Him. When, after an absence of three years, he re-entered his father's house, he was received as one restored from death, for tidings of his hardships and sufferings had reached his distant home. The bitter prejudice against Friends with which his parents' hearts had been filled by the clergy had altogether passed away, and George Whitehead did not doubt that the Lord had secretly pleaded his cause. The storms he had encountered, were now exchanged for a restful season spent in visits to several northern meetings, where he was warmly welcomed by Friends in whom, he says: "The first love was fresh and lively, and was retained to the end of their days." But soon the eastern counties again attracted him, where, as it proved, an imprisonment of sixteen weeks in Ipswich Gaol was in store for him.

During the years 1658 and 1659, Whitehead was engaged in many public religious disputations, in consequence of the utterly erroneous ideas current concerning the views of Friends, and which were the more readily accepted from the fact that many of the clergy denounced the Quakers from their pulpits. A detailed account of these discussions might not be of general interest, but perhaps a few extracts from the voluminous writings of George Whitehead may be suitably substituted, many of these being of a controversial character:—

"He who was as a Lamb slain from the foundation of the world, and by the grace of God tasted death for every man, ever liveth to make intercession for man according to the will of God. . . . His being given as our Mediator between God and men, and His giving Himself a ransom for all men, a testimony in due time, and His tasting death for every man—did all proceed from the great love of God, and not to pay a strict or rigid satisfaction for vindictive justice or revenge on God's part. . . . Surely that righteousness and forbearance of God, declared by the propitiatory sacrifice of our Lord Jesus Christ for the remission or forgiveness of sins that are past, upon true repentance, cannot justly be deemed revenge or vindictive justice, as some have asserted against us. . . . Oh! Behold the Lamb of God which taketh away the sin of the world. 1st. As an universal and most excellent offering, and acceptable sacrifice for sin, in order to obtain redemption and forgiveness by His precious blood, etc. 2nd. Jesus Christ as the Lamb of God takes away the sin of the world, by purging the conscience and purifying the hearts of all them who truly receive Him and believe in Him, even in His Holy Name and Divine Power. . . . He never designed to leave men in sin and transgression all their days, but to afford all men grace to lead them to true repentance, that they might receive that remission, forgiveness, atonement and reconciliation, obtained for them. . . . The Holy Ghost takes and shows unto us the most excellent properties of our great and glorious Mediator — His great universal love, meekness, humility, and compassion, that we may by degrees partake thereof, as we truly obey and follow Him in the manifestation of the same Holy Spirit, whereby the mystery of Christ is revealed in and unto the truly spiritually-minded believers."

In one of these discussions he maintained that " the grace of God, in and through Jesus Christ, was sufficient for the blessed attainment of perfect sanctification, perseverance in grace, and abiding in Christ." * But although Whitehead and some of his brethren thought it good to engage in these arguments at times, it was more frequently their wont " to press upon men to look more to the genuine *fruits* of the Spirit, as the tests of their Christianity, than to any form of words, or *any explanation of Divine truth which human wisdom had been able to propose.*"

The issue of the proclamation against conventicles, soon after the accession of Charles II., caused a renewal of attacks on Friends with more tangible and formidable weapons than words from pulpit or platform. One day, when George Whitehead was travelling alone on the highway, he besought the Lord, with deep feeling and fervour, to plead the cause of His people; and an assurance was given him that the evil schemes of the persecutors should be finally frustrated, and that God would defend, and in due time deliver, His suffering

---

* " The question what attainments we have made, *lies wholly between our consciences and our God*. The question what are our revealed privileges is to be settled, not by an appeal to the conscious or visible attainments of any individual or class of individuals, but . . . by reference to the law and to the testimony. The Spirit of the Lord does know, and He alone can know, what ' things are possible with God' on the one hand, and what ' things are possible to him that believeth ' on the other."—" *Out of Darkness into Light;* " *by Dr. Asa Mahan*, p. 357.

children. "Yea, and much more of the same tendency," he writes, "has the Lord livingly signified and revealed to me by His Holy Spirit, even in times of deep suffering."

About this time (the winter of 1660-1) George Whitehead, and his friends William Barber and John Lawrence, who have been already mentioned, were arrested at a meeting at Pulham-Mary, in Norfolk; the quiet assembly was violently disturbed by a constable, who, although without a warrant, was attended by a company of horsemen and footmen, apparently of an irregular kind, for in addition to halberds, swords and pistols, they were armed with pitchforks, hedgestakes, and clubs. They dragged several Friends out of the meeting, who were on the following day committed to Norwich Castle, which, like many other prisons throughout the land, now contained a large number of Friends. The lodging-place of George Whitehead and his companions was a narrow cell roofed by an old stone arch, through which the rain freely penetrated; and when, in order to warm themselves during the cold winter evenings, they burnt a little charcoal, the absence of a chimney caused it to be—as George Whitehead patiently puts it—"somewhat injurious and suffocating." On his part, he was struck with the manner in which his two associates, who had formerly been captains in the army, now passively and patiently suffered for the cause of Christ. The Friends held many "comfortable meetings" in the prison, which were sometimes attended by several persons from without.

After a while, George Whitehead became so ill of ague and fever that his friends thought he would die in prison; but, as the time for holding the spring assizes at Thetford approached, he believed that he should be strengthened to ride the twenty miles which separate that place from Norwich. Soon after his arrival at Thetford, an elderly Friend told him with tears of the terrible threats to Dissenters which the judge had made use of in his charge; but, with his unfailing faith, George Whitehead tried to raise her spirits, by saying, that the Lord would stand by them, and that he hoped no Friends would be cast down, but that they would be faithful to God and valiant for the Truth. This was no mere precept, but what he was enabled to practise fully himself; and according to his faith was it unto him, for he writes of feeling the Lord's power over all, and of how his fellow-prisoners and himself were kept in great peace throughout the trial; and when, as he had anticipated, he was sent back to Norwich Castle with several others who were thought to be "the most eminent among the Quakers," he cheerfully resumed his bonds, and felt deep gratitude for the restoration of his health, which the purer air and change of scene had probably been the means of effecting.

As might be expected, the strong faith granted to himself enabled him to sympathise with those in whom it was less fully developed; and whilst in Thetford prison during the assizes his heart was drawn out in loving interest towards an elderly Friend who was also confined there. This gentleman, who had been the mayor of that town and a justice of the peace, when walking one day with George Whitehead in the prison yard, told him of how he was harassed by the urgency with which his relatives pressed him to take the Oath of Allegiance, in order to save his family and himself from ruin; he also confessed that his own faltering faith had made this trial harder to bear. Yet he added, "I have considered Christ's words, 'No man having put his hand to the plough, and looking back, is fit for the kingdom of God.'" Choosing inward peace rather than outward ease, he was, although in direct violation of Magna Charta, removed from his own corporation to Norwich, to share the imprisonment of the Friends confined in the county gaol. But all the pains taken by his prosecutors to bring him under the penalty of a præmunire were unavailing, for at the termination of sixteen weeks the prisoners were released, in consequence of the king's "Proclamation of Grace."

About this time more than 4,200 Friends of both sexes were imprisoned in the various parts of England for attendance at their meetings or for refusal to take any oath. Often cruelly beaten, sometimes confined in detestable dungeons, or so closely crowded together that all could not sit down at one time; exposed to severe cold, and, in many cases, deprived of some of their clothing; kept without food for several successive days, and obliged for lack of straw, to lie on the cold ground —it would have been strange if many had not died. The meetings in London were frequently dispersed with violence; and on one such occasion, George Whitehead and his "beloved brethren," Richard Hubberthorn, and Edward Burrough, were taken to Newgate, where the two former shared a small pallet-bed, in a stiflingly close cell. They might have had somewhat better accommodation, notwithstanding the crowded state of the prison, but chose this lodging-place out of consideration for the poorer Friends who slept in the same part of the gaol. A violent fever, the natural result of over-crowding in warm summer weather, soon ended the sufferings of some of the prisoners; and Richard Hubberthorn and Edward Burrough were amongst the number. George Whitehead was twice imprisoned in 1664 for the offence of worshipping in "other manner than is allowed by the Liturgy of the Church of England;" although even this was perhaps scarcely proved against him; for at a trial of some similar case we find one of the jurymen saying: "My lord, I have that venerable respect for the Liturgy of the Church of England as to believe it is according to the Scriptures, which allow of the worship of God in spirit; and therefore I conclude to worship God in spirit is not contrary to the Liturgy: if it be, I shall abate of my respect for it."

During the Plague, although George Whitehead was, as can be easily imagined, borne up "in living faith, and true and fervent love, above the fear of death," his heart—the more keenly susceptible of sanctified human affection because of its abiding in Divine love—was deeply moved, even to "great suffering and travail of spirit, with earnest prayer," on behalf of his stricken brethren; and he visited them alike in their own houses and in the prisons where their persecutors still detained them. Although he had been previously engaged in visiting meetings in the country, he felt that the Lord had work for him in London in this season of sore distress, and accordingly took up his abode at the house of a tobacconist in Watling Street. With sympathy for those who did not altogether share his own vigorous faith, he addressed two epistles to Friends, in which the following remarks occur:—

"Retire to Him who is a sure Hiding Place to the upright in the day of calamity, and the hour of temptation; in Him you will witness plenteous redemption, and the refreshments of His life over all the troubles and sufferings of the present time, and over all the fears and doubtings which thereupon would beset any of you either inwardly or outwardly. . . . And live in the immortal seed and spiritual communion where life and peace is daily received, and your mutual refreshment and consolation stands, and wherein the spirits of the just are seen and felt; even in *this spiritual communion which reaches beyond all visibles, and is above all mortal and fading things.*"

And these are the words of no dreamy mystic, but the testimony of a man who was spending his youthful vigour in active service for his Lord.

The meetings held at the Meeting-house built at White Hart Court, after the great fire, were often broken up with violence, and many of those who attended them taken before the mayor. On such occasions George Whitehead usually chose imprisonment rather than the alternative of freedom on condition not only of a promise to appear at the next sessions, but also "in the meantime to be of the good behaviour;" for he knew that the public worship of God with his brethren would be held as a breach of this, and had far greater fear of a shackled soul than of a fettered body.

The general cause of religious liberty was zealously advocated by George Whitehead, in the reigns of Charles II., James II., William and Mary, Anne, George I., and George II.; and, in a preface to Whitehead's Autobiography, Samuel Tuke expresses the belief that he was in a "considerable degree instrumental in obtaining those civil and religious privileges now enjoyed by the

Society of Friends." In 1672 he succeeded in procuring from the king, the liberation of more than 400 Friends, some of whom had spent ten or eleven years in prison. The King's Letters Patent under the Great Seal, containing the names of the 400 prisoners eleven times repeated, was a very bulky document on eleven skins of vellum;* and in these days of steam and electricity we can hardly enter into the difficulties which Whitehead and his friends encountered in promptly conveying this mandate to numerous prisons in England and Wales. With strength already worn down by his lengthened labours in obtaining this "pardon," Whitehead now went on horseback, with two other Friends, into Essex, Suffolk, Norfolk, Huntingdon, Cambridge, and Hertford, and in a fortnight's time the "Patent" they carried with them—an unwieldy bundle in a leathern case and tin box—had accomplished its work in those counties. Two duplicates which George Whitehead had obtained of the original document were sent by messengers to five other counties. His greatest perplexity was, however, with regard to the speedy release of the Friends confined in "prisons so remote" as those in Wales, and in the north and west of England; and which the approach of winter made him very solicitous to effect, as longer confinement might well cause the death of some of the captives. Sir Matthew Hale, to whom, as Lord Chief Justice, he appealed for aid, gave full and kind attention to the

---

* John Bunyan who, from his misapprehension of their views, had bitterly decried Friends, was now released from his twelve years' imprisonment in Bedford Gaol, in consequence of the inclusion of his name with that of a few other Dissenters in the royal patent.

subject, saying that if the prisoners would remove themselves by Habeas Corpus and come before him, he would liberate them on the king's pardon. But their health was too seriously impaired for them to undertake the long journey to London without hazarding their lives, even had they not been too much impoverished to do so. The plan finally adopted by George Whitehead and Ellis Hooks, was that of showing the king's patent to the under sheriffs from the counties in question, when they came to town at the Michaelmas term, and thus obtaining "*liberates*" from them to be sent to the various gaols.

In 1680, George Whitehead and Thomas Burr, a fellow-minister, were arrested whilst the former was preaching in the Friends' meeting at Norwich, and confined in the gaol. Their defence at the next quarter-sessions was a very spirited one. The Recorder had said, "There is a law, and the Church of England will never be quiet till some of you be hanged by that law;" and we find George Whitehead afterwards winding up a remonstrance with the words, "Let us have a fair hearing and trial; let us be tried before we are hanged!" And again:—"I beg of the Court, for God's sake, and the king's sake, to be heard fairly without being thus run upon. It is preposterous to run us upon the Oath in the first place, we not being committed for that, but for other causes." When sent back to prison George Whitehead and his companions wrote to the mayor and aldermen; but, although their trial was voted out of place by the common council, and the Earl of Yarmouth and other gentlemen exerted themselves on their behalf, they were not liberated until the time of the ensuing regular sessions.

In the winter of 1680-1, George Whitehead, with several other Friends, attended the Committee on the Bill for exempting Dissenters from the penalties of certain laws. He was particularly struck by the comments made by Sir Charles Musgrove, who, although a zealous supporter of the Church, openly spoke of "the shame and scandal" which rested on it in connection with the cruel persecution of Friends. In the two following years Whitehead was four times convicted under the Conventicle Act; on one of these occasions he was fined £40, without being given the opportunity of vindicating himself. The distraint was made by a constable and two assistants, who seized every bed in the house, and a variety of other valuable furniture, as well as shop wares, and when two of his friends begged that the goods might be appraised before being carried away, the constable arrested them, stating on oath that they were guilty of riot; in consequence of this they were committed to Newgate for ten weeks. Whitehead obtained a reversal of the magistrate's sentence, yet only £11 was returned to him, although the articles distrained were worth three times that amount.

During the severe persecution in 1683, George Whitehead and his friend Gilbert Latey perseveringly and successfully exerted themselves on behalf of a large number of Friends imprisoned at Norwich, and who—as Whitehead told King Charles—were "like to be buried alive in holes and dungeons." In this year, notwithstanding a three months' frost of such severity that the Thames was used as a street, the Friends, still shut out from their own meeting-houses, held their meetings in the intense cold of the open air; displaying that unshaken firmness which can, perhaps, be only manifested in a good or an evil cause, by those who are aided by God in the one case, or stimulated by Satan in the other. Comfort came to them in their silent waiting on the Lord, and they gladly made use of any opening for street preaching, though often as soon as a sentence or two had been spoken the minister would be forcibly dragged away.

Truly it was a season for glorifying God by strong faith in Him, and George Whitehead did not fail to use it as such. "In those days I clearly saw," he writes, "that the testimony required of us to bear, was not so much in words, declaration, or ministry, as to stand our ground in faith and patience, and to travail in spirit with secret breathing and earnest supplication unto God. It was often then before me that the Lamb and His faithful followers should have the victory, which was matter of secret comfort to me many times: glory be to His name for ever!" And he was right. Those downtrodden Quakers, a scorn and a bye-word, were winning a conquest little dreamt of by their mocking persecutors, and wholly beyond their ken. What could they conceive of a spirit which "takes its kingdom with entreaty, and not with contention?" for as in the natural, so in the spiritual world, vision avails nothing without light; and evil-doers hate and shun that light, in the ever-increasing brightness of which the pure in heart press forwards, on the new and living way, seeing more and more of God, and of those things which He has prepared for them that love Him, and will reveal to them by His Spirit.

On the accession of James II., George Whitehead,

Gilbert Latey, and Alexander Parker,* presented him with a petition on behalf of the 1,460 Friends then lying in prison, " only for tender conscience towards Almighty God." The petitioners stated that *some hundreds* had died in consequence of long captivity, and alluded to " the woful spoil made by merciless informers, etc., all tending to the ruin of trade, husbandry, and industrious families; to some not a bed left; to others, no cattle to till their ground or give them milk, nor corn for bread and seed, nor tools to work withal." Three or four months later, after a renewed appeal, James gave a general warrant for the release of the prisoners, some of whom had been in bonds for periods of ten, twelve, or fifteen years.

A wonderful relief it must also have been to the Friends of those days when " Informers " were suppressed, in consequence of George Whitehead's application for a commission to inquire into their fraudulent practices—for he likens them to " beasts of prey, lurking, creeping, and skulking about in most parts of the nation " where meetings were held. His friends, hearing of the informers' furious threats concerning him, were afraid lest they should carry them into execution: but for himself he told the informers that he feared them not: that he was bound in conscience to acquaint the Government with their barbarities, and that no menaces of theirs would hinder him from so doing. One of their leaders,

---

* Gough writes of Alexander Parker as "being one in the number of the worthies of this age, who were given up to the service of their Maker, and the promoting of pure religion, and the practice of piety in the nation—as the principal purpose of their lives;"—and also states that he was "well-educated, and had a gentleman-like carriage and deportment as well as person."

who had caused Whitehead severe suffering, showed his faith in the reality of the religion which it had been his trade to assault, by applying to him for assistance with regard to clothing, before entering the establishment of a gentleman who had engaged him as his servant. This was, of course, a too favourable opportunity of returning good for evil for Whitehead to lose.

George Whitehead was twice married, and each union was a happy one; his second marriage—with a widow named Ann Greenwell—took place in 1688. Her maiden name was Downer, and Sewel writes of her, when she was about the age of thirty, as "the first among women in this Society that preached at London publicly." In 1656, when George Fox and two other Friends were confined in Launceston Gaol, they asked her to come to them, to buy and dress their meat, and to write for them in shorthand.* She peformed this journey of two hundred miles on foot, and both in going and returning her ministerial labours were much blessed. Gough describes her as being "an extraordinary woman helpful to many, tender to all, ready to communicate, laying out herself for the good of others." The evening before she died she said to her husband: "The Lord is with me, I bless His name. I am well. It may be you

---

* It was during this imprisonment that George Fox was placed in a fearfully loathsome dungeon where many he was told had died, and also that it was haunted by spirits. But George Fox had too long made use of the believer's privilege of trusting in "the exceeding greatness of God's power," to be daunted now. "If all the spirits and devils in hell are there"—was his reply—" I am over them *in the power of God*, and fear no such thing. For Christ, our Priest, will sanctify the walls and the house to us. He who bruised the head of the devil, . . . Who sanctifies—both inwardly and outwardly—the walls of the house, the walls of the heart, and all things to His people."

are afraid I shall be taken away, and if it be, the will of the Lord be done. Do not trouble yourselves nor make any great ado about me. But, my dear, go to bed, go to rest; and if I should speak no more words to thee, thou knowest the everlasting love of God!"

In the early part of the reign of William III. George Whitehead's heart was gladdened by the discovery that many high in office had at last opened their eyes wide enough to see that the granting of liberty of conscience was not only an imperative Christian duty, but also an essential element of the well-being of the Government and nation. He was struck by the remark of a conspicuous member of the Church of England: "Neither we nor you are safe without toleration." George Whitehead took an active part in the earnest exertions to which Friends were incited by their great anxiety that the Act of Toleration should be made an effectual measure. And in a satisfactory interview with the king we learn that he spoke to him on "divers weighty matters," finding an attentive and serious listener. George Whitehead told him that it was true that Friends had "of late been aspersed and misrepresented with such nicknames as *Meadites* and *Pennites*, as if we set up sect-masters; yet we own no such thing; but Christ Jesus to be our only Master as we are a Christian society and people."

In concluding "Christian Progress" (his autobiography), George Whitehead remarks, "Manifold exercises, trials, and tribulations, hath the Lord my God supported me under, and carried me through, in my pilgrimage for His name and Truth's sake, more than could possibly be related in this history; having spent a long time, even the greatest part of my life from my youth upward, in the testimony, service, and vindication of the living unchangeable truth as it is in Christ Jesus my Lord." A lively address to his friends, written in his eighty-sixth year, was printed and circulated amongst them. He is described as being a tender father in the Church, and, as such, of great compassion, sympathising with Friends under affliction, whether in body or mind. In his last illness he patiently awaited the summons, "Come up higher," to the unveiled glory of that presence which, by faith, had been for so long a time the strength and joy of his soul. He died at the beginning of the year 1722, at the age of eighty-seven, and was interred in the Friends' Burial-ground, at Bunhill Fields.

"One of the finest sayings in the language"—writes Charles Buxton—"is John Foster's '*Live mightily.*'" And George Whitehead had learnt the secret of doing this; a secret revealed not alone to those who, in "obeying the ideal of life" set before them,* conspicuously glorify God, but also to the humblest followers of Christ, in obscurest corners of the world, who cleave to their Lord with that living *faith* which of necessity bears the fruit of *faith*-fulness:—"*Not by might, nor by power, but by my Spirit, saith the Lord.*"

---

* Of Edward Denison, Canon Liddon writes:—"He, too, had passed through a momentary indecision, whether he would or would not 'obey the ideal of life which had come before him.'" How many besides the young man who went away sorrowful from his loving Lord lose inconceivably for lack of willingness to accept Christ's proffered vocation! Doubtless it might lead them in a narrower path than their self-chosen one; yet, even when roughest and steepest, it could not lie far away from "the still waters" of His peace, and "the green pastures" of His love.

www.ingramcontent.com/pod-product-compliance
Lightning Source LLC
Chambersburg PA
CBHW021424300426
44114CB00010B/628